GMRS

Beginner's Guide

Complete Navigation Guide on Enhanced Communication
with GMRS Radio for Adventures and Teams

Quentin Fox

Disclaimer and Terms of Use

The author and publisher of this book and the accompanying materials have used their best efforts in preparing this book. The author and publisher make no representation or warranties with respect to the accuracy, applicability, fitness, or completeness of the contents of this book. The information contained in this book is strictly for informational purposes. Therefore, if you wish to apply the ideas contained in this book, you are taking full responsibility for your actions.

Printed in the United States of America

TABLE OF CONTENTS

TABLE OF CONTENTS..III

INTRODUCTION 1

CHAPTER ONE 2

UNDERSTANDING GMRS RADIOS.. 2

OVERVIEW 2
ABOUT GMRS RADIO... 2
HISTORY AND FUTURE OF GMRS 2
GMRS KEY FEATURES... 3
    The Evolution of GMRS.. 3
    Regulatory Changes and Modernization... 3
    Looking ahead to the future of GMRS... 4
ADVANTAGES AND APPLICATIONS OF GMRS 4
    Extra Features 5
    Applications of GMRS.. 5
COMPARING GMRS TO OTHER RADIO SERVICES (E.G., FRS, CB, HAM RADIO) 6
    GMRS Licensing Requirements... 7
    Family Radio Service (FRS) 7
    Citizens Band Radio (CB Radio) 7
    Amateur Radio (Ham Radio) 8
EXAMINING GMRS IN COMPARISON TO OTHER RADIO SERVICES 8
GMRS CHANNELS... 9
    Exploring the GMRS Channel Spectrum 9
LICENSING AND REGULATIONS 10
    Applications of GMRS Channels 11

CHAPTER TWO 12

GMRS RADIO BASICS 12

OVERVIEW 12
HOW TO GO ABOUT GMRS RADIO PROGRAMMING 12
    Obtaining a GMRS License 12
DECIDING ON THE PERFECT GMRS RADIO 13
PROGRAMMING YOUR GMRS RADIO 14
    Manual Programming... 14
    Programming with Software.. 14
TIPS FOR OPTIMIZING GMRS RADIO PROGRAMMING 15
TYPES OF GMRS RADIOS... 16
    Handheld GMRS Radios 16
    Base/Mobile GMRS Radios... 17
OTHER FEATURES AND FACTORS TO CONSIDER... 18

DECIDING ON THE PERFECT GMRS RADIO 19

GMRS RADIO: FEATURES AND COMPONENTS 19

FEATURES OF BASE STATION GMRS RADIO 21

FEATURES OF HANDHELD GMRS RADIO 23

    Technical Specifications 23

    Common Uses of Handheld GMRS Radios 24

    Advantages of Handheld GMRS Radios 24

CHAPTER THREE **26**

LICENSING AND LEGAL CONSIDERATIONS **26**

OVERVIEW 26

WHO NEEDS A GMRS LICENSE? 26

HOW TO GET A GMRS LICENSE 26

    The Application Process 27

    Using Your GMRS License 28

    Ensuring Regulatory Adherence 28

FCC REGULATIONS AND COMPLIANCE 29

    Frequency Allocation 29

    Licensing Requirements 29

    Technical Regulations 29

    Operational Regulations 30

    Enforcement and Penalties 30

    Guidelines for Ensuring GMRS Compliance 31

COMMON LEGAL ISSUES AND PITFALLS TO AVOID 31

    Common Traps to Avoid When Licensing 31

    Operating within the boundaries of the law 32

    Misuse of GMRS Frequencies 32

    Consequences of Breaking GMRS Regulations 33

LICENSING FEES AND RENEWAL.. 33

    The Licensing Process 33

    Licensing Fees 34

GMRS LICENSE RENEWAL 34

    When to Renew 34

    The Renewal Process 34

    Maintaining Compliance 34

CHAPTER FOUR **35**

ADVANCED GMRS FEATURES **35**

OVERVIEW 35

PRIVACY CODES AND TONES (CTCSS/DCS) 35

    What is CTCSS? 35

    What is DCS? 35

THE SIGNIFICANCE OF PRIVACY CODES AND TONES IN GMRS 36

How to Use CTCSS and DCS in GMRS Radios *36*

Tips for Using Privacy Codes and Tones Effectively *37*

SCANNING AND MONITORING 37

Advantages of Scanning and Monitoring in GMRS *38*

How Scanning Works *38*

Enhanced Scanning Capabilities *38*

APPLICATIONS OF SCANNING AND MONITORING IN GMRS 39

INTEGRATION WITH OTHER RADIO SERVICES 39

Integration with FRS *40*

AMATEUR RADIO INTEGRATION 40

Advantages of Integrating GMRS and Amateur Radio *40*

Challenges and Limitations *40*

INTEGRATION WITH MURS 41

Advantages of Integrating GMRS-MURS *41*

Challenges and Limitations *41*

GPS AND DATA TRANSMISSION CAPABILITIES 42

CHAPTER FIVE **43**

SETTING UP GMRS RADIOS **43**

OVERVIEW 43

HOW TO OPERATE FREQUENCIES AND CHANNELS 43

OPERATING GMRS RADIOS: KEY CONSIDERATIONS 43

How to set up a GMRS Repeater *44*

Equipment Required for a GMRS Repeater *44*

Choosing the Perfect Spot for Your Repeater *46*

Setting up the Repeater *46*

TESTING AND TROUBLESHOOTING 47

GMRS REPEATER MAINTENANCE 48

Creating a Communication Plan *48*

WHY IS IT COMPULSORY TO USE A GMRS REPEATER 50

Understanding the Significance of Range and Coverage *50*

Benefits of Using a GMRS Repeater *51*

Applications of GMRS Repeaters *52*

REGULATORY CONSIDERATIONS 52

Advanced modulation schemes *52*

Advanced Modulation Schemes *53*

Advantages of Advanced Modulation Schemes in GMRS *53*

Challenges and Considerations *54*

ABOUT RADIO WAVE BEHAVIOR AND INTERFERENCE 54

Several factors influence the behavior of radio waves *55*

Issues with GMRS Communication Interference *55*

Addressing Interference in GMRS Communication *56*

MASTERING THE ART OF PROPER CHANNEL ETIQUETTE AND PROTOCOLS 57

Getting a GMRS License 57

Proper Etiquette for GMRS Channels 57

GMRS PROTOCOLS FOR EFFICIENT COMMUNICATION 58

CHAPTER SIX **60**

GMRS RADIO WORKSPACE SETUP **60**

OVERVIEW 60

SETTING UP GMRS WORKSPACE RADIO 60

Step 1: Getting a GMRS License 60

Step 2: Choosing the Appropriate Equipment 61

Step 3: Setting up Communication Protocols 61

Step 4: GMRS Radio Setup 62

Step 5: Consistent Maintenance and Updates 62

POWER SOURCE AND BATTERY MANAGEMENT 62

Disposable Batteries 63

Rechargeable batteries 63

Nickel-Cadmium (NiCd) Batteries 63

Nickel-Metal Hydride (NiMH) Batteries 63

Lithium-Ion (Li-ion) Batteries 64

BEST PRACTICES FOR MANAGING BATTERIES 64

HOW TO INTEGRATE GPS AND LOCATION SERVICES 65

Exploring the Potential of GMRS with GPS 65

Integrating GPS with GMRS 66

TIPS FOR SEAMLESSLY COMBINING GPS AND GMRS 66

HOW TO PROPERLY TUNE A GMRS ANTENNA 67

Tools and Equipment 67

Tuning a GMRS Antenna 67

UNDERSTANDING WHAT SWR IS ABOUT AND HOW TO SET GMRS RADIO SWR 70

What is the Significance of SWR? 70

Reasons for High SWR 70

Measuring SWR 71

Reducing SWR 71

HOW TO BOOST GMRS RADIO POWER 72

Deciding on the Perfect GMRS Radio 72

Upgrading the Antenna 73

Using a Repeater System 73

Reducing Interference 74

HOW TO MAINTAIN YOUR GMRS RADIO 74

Legal Compliance 75

ENHANCING GMRS RADIO RANGE 75

Upgrade to High-Gain Antennas 75

Use Repeaters 76

Maximize Radio Settings 76

Minimize Interference *76*

Environmental Plan *77*

Enhance Your Radio Communication Practices *77*

CHAPTER SEVEN **78**

GMRS ADVANCED FUNCTIONS **78**

OVERVIEW 78

CTCSS AND DCS CODES 78

Understanding CTCSS *78*

Understanding DCS *79*

APPLICATIONS OF CTCSS AND DCS IN GMRS 79

ADJUSTING CTCSS AND DCS CODES ON GMRS RADIOS 80

Configuring CTCSS Codes *80*

Configuring DCS Codes *80*

FACTORS TO KEEP IN MIND 81

Scanning Modes and Features *81*

Advanced Features *82*

Applications and Use Cases *82*

GROUP CALLS FEATURES 83

Group Call Features in GMRS *83*

PRACTICAL APPLICATIONS OF GMRS GROUP CALL FEATURES 85

MULTI-USER AND GROUP COMMUNICATION IN GMRS 85

Group Communication in GMRS *86*

Advanced Functions for Enhanced GMRS Communication *87*

GMRS IN PRACTICAL SCENARIOS: USING MULTI-USER AND GROUP COMMUNICATION 87

CHAPTER EIGHT **89**

GMRS FOR EMERGENCIES AND PREPAREDNESS **89**

OVERVIEW 89

GMRS IN DISASTER PREPAREDNESS AND EMERGENCY RESPONSE 89

GMRS IN EMERGENCY RESPONSE 90

Challenges and Considerations *91*

GMRS FOR NEIGHBORHOOD WATCH AND COMMUNITY SAFETY 91

Benefits of GMRS for Neighborhood Watch *91*

Ease of Use *91*

Dependable Communication *92*

Group Communication *92*

Emergency Preparedness *92*

BEST PRACTICES FOR GMRS IN NEIGHBORHOOD WATCH AND COMMUNITY SAFETY 92

CONNECTING GMRS TO OTHER EMERGENCY SERVICES 93

GMRS in Emergency Situations *93*

Integrating GMRS with Other Emergency Services *94*

CHAPTER NINE 96

GMRS ACCESSORIES AND PROGRAMMING 96

OVERVIEW 96
LIST OF GMRS ACCESSORIES 96
LIST OF GMRS ANTENNAS 98
    Types of GMRS Antennas 99
FACTORS TO CONSIDER WHEN CHOOSING A GMRS ANTENNA 102
RECOMMENDED GMRS EQUIPMENT 103
GMRS EQUIPMENT ACCESSORIES 104
DECIDING ON THE APPROPRIATE GMRS EQUIPMENT 105
UNDERSTANDING WHY RADIO PROGRAMMING CABLE DOES NOT WORK 105
    Diverse Equipment Standards 105
    Regulatory Compliance 106
    Limitations of Software and Firmware 106
    Challenges Arising from Human Error and Technical Issues 106
    Effective Solutions and Recommended Practices 107
TROUBLESHOOTING COMMON PROGRAMMING ISSUES 107
TROUBLESHOOTING INTERFERENCE AND SIGNAL RANGE ISSUES 108
ADDRESSING HARDWARE AND FIRMWARE ISSUES 109
PROGRAMMING TECHNIQUES FOR GMRS RADIOS 109
    Tools and Software for Programming GMRS Radios 110
ADVANCED PROGRAMMING TECHNIQUES 110

CHAPTER TEN 112

GMRS RADIO COMMUNICATION WAYS 112

OVERVIEW 112
HOW TO UNDERSTAND GMRS ENCRYPTION 112
    What are the Benefits of Encryption in GMRS? 112
TYPES OF ENCRYPTION IN GMRS 112
HOW TO IMPLEMENT GMRS ENCRYPTION 113
BEST PRACTICES FOR GMRS ENCRYPTION 114
UNDERSTANDING THE BENEFITS OF GMRS ENCRYPTION 114
HOW GMRS ENCRYPTION WORKS 115
BENEFITS OF GMRS ENCRYPTION 115
IMPLEMENTING GMRS ENCRYPTION 116
    Challenges and Considerations 116
    How to become an expert in GMRS Encryption 116
    Optimizing GMRS Range and Clarity 117
    Proper Licensing and Regulations 117
    Effective Strategies for GMRS Communication 118
DECODING THE MYSTERIES OF GMRS ENCRYPTION 118
    GMRS and Data Encryption 119

Legal and Ethical Considerations *119*

Alternatives to GMRS Encryption *119*

CHAPTER ELEVEN **120**

GMRS RADIO SETTINGS **120**

OVERVIEW 120

HOW TO ADJUST SQUELCH AND VOLUME LEVELS.. 120

How Squelch Works *120*

What does Volume Control mean? *120*

The Significance of Volume Control *120*

ADJUSTING SQUELCH ON GMRS RADIOS.. 121

HOW TO ADJUST VOLUME ON GMRS RADIOS.. 121

Troubleshooting Common Issues *121*

Tips for Optimal Squelch and Volume Adjustment *122*

HOW TO INTEGRATE AND INTERFACE A RADIO SYSTEM.. 122

Step 1: Determine the Purpose and Scope *123*

Step 2: Acquire a GMRS License *123*

Step 3: Choose GMRS Radios and Equipment *124*

Step 4: Setting Up and Customizing Your GMRS System.. *124*

Step 5: Connect with Other Communication Systems *124*

Step 6: Set Up Communication Protocols... *125*

Step 7: Keep it up to date Your GMRS System *125*

TIPS AND TRICKS ON USING GMRS RADIO EFFECTIVELY 125

Establishing a Communication Protocol *126*

Using GMRS Radios in Different Environments.. *126*

GMRS Radios for Emergency Preparedness *126*

CHAPTER TWELVE **128**

CARING FOR YOUR GMRS RADIO **128**

OVERVIEW 128

HOW TO REGULARLY CHECK AND INSPECT YOUR GMRS RADIO 128

Regular Inspection *128*

TESTING RADIO FUNCTIONALITY.. 129

GMRS RADIO MAINTENANCE 130

TROUBLESHOOTING COMMON GMRS RADIO ISSUES 130

HOW TO KNOW BASIC SPECTRUM ANALYZER OPERATION 133

Spectrum Analyzers with Swept-Tuning.. *133*

FFT Spectrum Analyzers *133*

Important Features of Spectrum Analyzers *133*

Sweep Time and Span *134*

Reference Level *134*

Using Spectrum Analyzers for GMRS *134*

USING SPECTRUM ANALYZER IN GMRS.. 135

TIPS TO MAINTAIN YOUR GMRS RADIO..136

   Maintaining Your Battery 136

   Antenna Care 137

MICROPHONE AND SPEAKER MAINTENANCE 137

   Regular Maintenance and Testing..137

   Properly Storing Your GMRS Radio 138

TROUBLESHOOTING COMMON ISSUES 138

CHAPTER THIRTEEN 139

GMRS RADIO INTEGRATION WITH ADDITIONAL RADIO SYSTEMS..139

OVERVIEW 139

WHAT IS THE COMPATIBILITY WITH FRS RADIOS? 139

COMPATIBILITY BETWEEN GMRS AND FRS RADIOS 139

   Shared Channels..139

   Comparing FRS and GMRS 139

   Licensing Requirements 140

   GMRS-Specific Features 140

PRACTICAL APPLICATIONS 140

COMPLIANCE AND BEST PRACTICES..141

HOW TO USE FRS AND GMRS RADIOS FOR LOCAL DISASTER 141

   Why choose FRS and GMRS for Local Disaster Communication?..142

GETTING READY FOR EMERGENCIES WITH FRS AND GMRS RADIOS 142

   Using FRS and GMRS Radios When faced with a disaster 143

   Working in collaboration with Emergency Response Teams 144

HOW TO CONNECT TO GMRS REPEATERS IN YOUR VICINITY 145

   Locating GMRS Repeaters in Your Area 145

   Connecting to the GMRS Repeater..146

RESOLVING CONNECTION PROBLEMS 147

CHAPTER FOURTEEN 148

GMRS RADIO SAFETY GUIDELINES 148

OVERVIEW 148

WHAT IS THE LIST OF SAFETY GUIDELINES FOR GMRS USERS 148

ENVIRONMENTAL CONSIDERATIONS FOR GMRS 150

   Regulatory Framework and Environmental Impact..150

   Energy Consumption and Environmental Impact..150

   Electromagnetic Interference and Wildlife 151

   Sustainable Practices in GMRS..151

FUTURE TRENDS AND ENVIRONMENTAL CONSIDERATIONS 151

CHAPTER FIFTEEN 152

RESOURCES AND GLOSSARY TERMS 152

OVERVIEW 152

GMRS ORGANIZATIONS AND COMMUNITIES 152

   The Role of GMRS Organizations 152

   Building Communities through GMRS 152

GMRS AND EMERGENCY RESPONSE 153

   The Future of GMRS Organizations and Communities 153

KEY TERMS AND DEFINITIONS IN GMRS RADIO 154

ACRONYMS AND ABBREVIATIONS USED IN GMRS RADIO 155

CHAPTER SIXTEEN 158

FREQUENTLY ASKED QUESTIONS AND THE FUTURE OF GMRS 158

OVERVIEW 158

COMMON QUESTIONS ABOUT GMRS RADIOS 158

   What is GMRS? 158

   Is a License Required for GMRS? 158

   What are the frequencies used by GMRS? 158

   What is the Range of GMRS Radios? 158

   What is a GMRS Repeater? 159

   Can GMRS Radios be used for Emergency Communication? 159

   What is the necessary equipment for GMRS? 159

   Do GMRS Radios Work with FRS Radios? 159

   What advantages does GMRS offer compared to other radio services? 159

   Is it possible to use GMRS radios internationally? 160

   How can I properly maintain my GMRS radios? 160

   Are GMRS Radios Secured? 160

   What factors should you take into account when purchasing GMRS radios? ... 160

CONCLUSION 161

INDEX 162

INTRODUCTION

Amidst the ever-changing landscape of communication technology, the General Mobile Radio Service (GMRS) emerges as a dependable and easily accessible choice for those in search of efficient communication. GMRS radio is a versatile and easy-to-use platform that can be used for outdoor adventures, emergency preparedness, or coordination during events. GMRS, short for **"General Mobile Radio Service,"** is a radio service in the United States that enables convenient two-way communication over short to medium distances. GMRS radios generally operate on UHF frequencies and provide greater power and extended range in comparison to Family Radio Service (FRS) radios. Operating GMRS radios legally requires obtaining a license from the Federal Communications Commission (FCC). This service is commonly used for both personal and recreational communication, as well as for business and professional purposes. GMRS radio is a licensed radio service in the United States that operates on specific frequencies within the Ultra High Frequency (UHF) band. It is specifically created for convenient and efficient voice communication over short distances, allowing individuals and groups to easily connect. GMRS is highly favored by a wide range of individuals and groups, including families, outdoor enthusiasts, emergency response teams, and event organizers. This is because of its straightforward nature and its ability to deliver reliable results. The GMRS frequency range spans from 462 to 467 MHz, offering a total of 22 channels for communication. GMRS stands out from other unlicensed services like Family Radio Service (FRS) due to its higher power output, which significantly extends the communication range. GMRS offers a wide range of applications thanks to its additional power and the option to use repeaters for extended coverage.

CHAPTER ONE
UNDERSTANDING GMRS RADIOS

Overview

Chapter one introduces us to GMRS Radios as a whole. In this chapter, you will learn what GMRS Radio is, its history and future, its advantages, its applications, and its comparison with other radios.

About GMRS Radio

The General Mobile Radio Service (GMRS) is a land-mobile FM UHF radio service in the United States that is regulated by the Federal Communications Commission (FCC). GMRS is commonly used by families, businesses, and communities for a range of applications, as it is specifically designed for short-distance, two-way communication.

GMRS radio is a highly versatile communication tool that can be used in a wide variety of applications. This product provides a higher power output, repeater capability, and multiple channels, making it a versatile option for personal, family, business, and emergency use. It is important to take into account the licensing requirement and the possibility of interference when selecting GMRS radios.

History and Future of GMRS

GMRS, also known as General Mobile Radio Service, was developed in the United States as a licensed radio service specifically for personal and business communication. It became popular in the 1960s as a solution to the demand for a communication system that was easier to use and more adaptable for individuals, families, and businesses. GMRS stands out from other radio services by providing users with the ability to communicate privately, while still enjoying the advantages of wider coverage when compared to regular walkie-talkies. GMRS operates within the ultra-high frequency (UHF) band, specifically within the 462-467 MHz range. This frequency range is highly effective at penetrating obstacles, making it ideal for use in urban and suburban environments. GMRS is known for its ability to deliver reliable communication over short to moderate distances, which has made it a popular option among recreational users, emergency services, and businesses in need of dependable communication.

GMRS Key Features

GMRS stands out due to its licensing requirement. In contrast to the Family Radio Service (FRS), which operates in the same frequency range without the need for a license, GMRS users in the United States must obtain a license from the Federal Communications Commission (FCC). The licensing system enables the FCC to effectively regulate the utilization of GMRS frequencies and uphold order on the airwaves. GMRS provides a variety of communication options, such as voice communication and data transmission. GMRS radios can be used in two modes: simplex and repeater. In simplex mode, communication takes place directly between radios. On the other hand, repeaters can be utilized to extend the range of communication. Repeaters are commonly used in emergencies to expand the coverage area and ensure reliable communication in hard-to-reach areas.

The Evolution of GMRS

GMRS has adapted over time to keep up with the evolving needs of users and advancements in technology. GMRS radios in their early days were simple devices with few features, mainly used for verbal communication. As technology progressed, GMRS radios evolved to include new features like digital data transmission, integrated GPS functionality, and compatibility with other radio services. GMRS has become increasingly popular due to its enhanced versatility, attracting a diverse group of users. GMRS radios are essential for outdoor enthusiasts like hikers and campers who need reliable communication in remote areas without cell phone signals. In addition, GMRS is commonly utilized by emergency response teams, search and rescue organizations, and businesses that rely on dependable communication across moderate distances.

Regulatory Changes and Modernization

Over the years, there have been changes in the regulatory landscape surrounding GMRS. The FCC in the United States has made changes to licensing requirements and operating rules to better accommodate the increasing popularity of GMRS. The licensing process for GMRS users was simplified by the FCC in 2017, with a reduction in fees and a more streamlined application procedure. This modification has made GMRS more easily accessible to a wider range of people.

Interoperability with other radio services has been a key focus of modernization efforts. Certain GMRS radios can operate in both GMRS and FRS modes, enabling users to establish communication with a broader selection of devices. GMRS has become a popular choice for families, groups, and businesses due to its flexibility and versatility, thanks to its interoperability.

Looking ahead to the future of GMRS

GMRS is constantly evolving, with various trends and developments indicating the future direction of the service. The future of GMRS is heavily influenced by technological advancements. **Here are a few important trends to keep an eye on:**

1. GMRS radios are now incorporating digital features, including digital voice transmission and data exchange, to enhance integration with digital technologies. These enhancements greatly enhance the quality and reliability of communication. With the help of digital capabilities, GMRS can now offer exciting new features such as text messaging and GPS tracking, opening up a whole new world of possibilities.
2. With the ongoing expansion of repeater networks, GMRS users can look forward to enjoying wider coverage and enhanced reliability. This expansion has the potential to attract more emergency response teams and businesses in need of long-range communication.
3. The integration of GMRS with other radio services, such as FRS and amateur radio, has the potential to enhance interoperability and foster collaboration. This development has the potential to enhance communication networks and expand coverage for GMRS users.
4. GMRS has already demonstrated its value in disaster response scenarios, and its role is expected to expand. As more organizations begin to understand the advantages of GMRS in emergency communication, it has the potential to play a crucial role in disaster response and recovery efforts.
5. GMRS has seen a significant increase in adoption within the business and industrial sectors, going beyond its original use for personal purposes. GMRS is being used by industries like construction, logistics, and agriculture to enhance communication and coordination within teams. It is anticipated that this trend will persist as companies increasingly acknowledge the advantages of GMRS for streamlining their operations.
6. GMRS has gained popularity worldwide, sparking interest in various countries. Other regions' regulatory bodies are considering the adoption of GMRS-like services, potentially leading to the global expansion of GMRS.

Advantages and applications of GMRS

GMRS offers several key advantages that can be grouped into a few main areas: coverage and range, power output, licensing, and additional features. Each of these factors contributes to the distinct advantages that GMRS provides to users.

- **Coverage and Range**

GMRS offers a notable advantage over FRS with its impressive range. GMRS radios are known for their ability to transmit signals over longer distances due to their higher power output. GMRS radios have a decent range that can cover several miles, depending on the terrain and obstructions. This makes them a great choice for outdoor activities and situations that require longer-range communication.

- **Increased Power Output**

GMRS radios have the advantage of operating at higher power levels compared to FRS radios. FRS radios have a power limit of 0.5 watts, while GMRS radios can reach up to 50 watts on specific channels. The enhanced power output of this device not only increases its range but also ensures more reliable communication, even in difficult conditions. Users can easily communicate across hills, through dense forests, or even between buildings in urban settings.

- **Licensing**

GMRS has an additional benefit in the form of its licensing system. GMRS, unlike FRS, necessitates users to acquire a license from the Federal Communications Commission (FCC) in the United States. The licensing system in place provides a strong level of oversight and control, effectively minimizing the risk of interference from unauthorized users. The license can be obtained quite easily with just a fee and some basic user information. It's convenient for families as it covers everyone in the household, allowing multiple users to operate under a single license.

Extra Features

GMRS radios frequently include a range of features that enhance their usefulness. These features may include support for repeater systems, which greatly enhance communication range, weather alert functions, and compatibility with FRS channels. The repeater functionality is especially valuable for community-based networks or large-scale events, as it allows for the expansion of coverage across a broad area. In addition, the compatibility with FRS channels provides more flexibility for communication with users who may not have GMRS radios.

Applications of GMRS

GMRS has a wide range of applications, from recreational use to professional settings, thanks to its numerous advantages. Its versatility makes it a popular choice for a wide range of communication needs.

- **Recreational Activities**

GMRS is a popular choice for various recreational activities like hiking, camping, and off-roading. Its extended range and higher power output make it perfect for groups that may become spread out over large areas. GMRS radios are known for their durability and ability to withstand outdoor conditions, making them a reliable choice for use in these environments. Using repeater systems can be extremely advantageous in areas with challenging terrain or limited connectivity, ensuring dependable communication even in the absence of cell phone coverage.

- **Emergency Preparedness**

GMRS plays a vital role in emergency preparedness and response. When faced with situations where conventional communication networks are unreliable, like during natural disasters or power outages, GMRS offers a dependable method of communication. GMRS is widely utilized by emergency response teams and community groups to effectively coordinate activities and exchange crucial information in times of emergencies. The licensing system ensures that only authorized users are operating on GMRS frequencies, which helps to minimize the risk of interference during critical situations.

- **Family and Neighborhood Communication**

GMRS is often used for communication among families and neighbors. GMRS radios are a great way for families to stay connected during outings, vacations, or other events when cell phone coverage may be limited. GMRS is commonly utilized by neighborhood watch groups to effectively coordinate activities and bolster security within their communities. GMRS is a valuable tool for maintaining contact in settings where communication over longer distances and through obstacles like buildings is necessary.

- **Business and Professional Use**

GMRS is commonly used in a range of business and professional environments. Construction sites, event management companies, and agricultural operations frequently depend on GMRS for effective communication within their teams. With its impressive power output and extensive range, this device enables seamless coordination of activities across vast sites or properties. In addition, the repeater capability enables businesses to establish larger communication networks as required.

- **Community-Based Networks**

GMRS is a great tool for creating communication networks within communities. These networks are commonly established in rural or remote areas where traditional communication infrastructure is limited. Repeater technology enables communities to establish a robust communication network that spans vast geographical regions. This is especially beneficial for facilitating coordination among farmers, ranchers, or other groups that operate in rural settings.

- **Disaster Response and Public Safety**

GMRS is commonly used in disaster response and public safety applications. When emergencies strike, effective communication becomes crucial. In these situations, GMRS offers a dependable and trustworthy alternative to conventional communication systems. Emergency responders search and rescue teams and volunteer groups rely on GMRS for efficient coordination and seamless information sharing. GMRS is well-suited for critical applications due to its higher power output and extended range.

Comparing GMRS to Other Radio Services (e.g., FRS, CB, Ham Radio)

GMRS, also known as General Mobile Radio Service, is a licensed radio service available in the United States for personal and business communication purposes. The device operates in the UHF band, specifically between 462 MHz and 467 MHz, providing a total of 30 channels. GMRS is specifically designed for short-distance communication, making it ideal for families, businesses, or community use. One notable aspect of GMRS is its capability to use higher power output, reaching up to 50 watts, as well as the availability of repeater systems to extend its range.

GMRS Licensing Requirements

GMRS stands out due to its licensing requirement. Unlike FRS or CB, which can be used without a license, GMRS users are required to obtain an FCC (Federal Communications Commission) license. This license provides coverage for the entire family, allowing multiple users to be included under a single license. Although it may appear as an obstacle, it serves the purpose of informing users about regulations and promoting responsible usage. The licensing process is straightforward and requires filling out an online form and submitting the necessary fee.

Family Radio Service (FRS)

FRS is a widely used radio service that is specifically designed for personal and family communication. It operates in a similar frequency range as GMRS, but there are notable distinctions. FRS radios have a maximum power output of 2 watts, resulting in a shorter communication range compared to GMRS. In addition, the use of repeaters is not permitted with FRS, which further restricts its range. FRS is available to a wider range of people because it is license-free. This feature makes it a compelling choice for casual users who require fundamental communication capabilities. Although FRS has its limitations in terms of power and range, it may not be the most ideal choice for long-distance communication or complex applications.

Citizens Band Radio (CB Radio)

CB radio has a long-standing history, dating back to the mid-20th century. CB radio operates in the 27 MHz band and provides 40 channels, making it a popular choice for truckers, off-road enthusiasts, and hobbyists. CB radio is readily available to the public without the need for a license, unlike GMRS. There is a notable distinction between CB and GMRS in terms of the frequency band and communication range. CB operates in the HF (high frequency) band, enabling longer-distance communication, particularly in favorable atmospheric conditions. Although CB radios have a power output limit of 4 watts, their range may be restricted in certain conditions. CB radios are commonly used in vehicles, making them perfect for road trips and outdoor adventures due to their convenient portability. Nevertheless, the absence of repeaters and potential interference from other users can occasionally pose a challenge. Communication on CB is less private compared to GMRS, as anyone on the same channel can listen in.

Amateur Radio (Ham Radio)

Amateur Radio, also known as Ham Radio, is a highly flexible and extensive radio service that enables licensed operators to communicate across a broad spectrum of frequencies, spanning from HF to VHF and UHF. Ham Radio stands out due to its versatility, allowing operators to freely explore different frequencies and modes of communication without any restrictions. Obtaining a license from the FCC is a requirement for Ham Radio operators. This involves passing an exam that tests their knowledge of radio theory, regulations, and operating practices. This licensing requirement ensures that Ham operators possess the necessary knowledge and exhibit responsible behavior when using the radio spectrum. Ham Radio offers a wide range of advantages due to its versatility and flexibility. Operators can communicate at different levels, ranging from local to global, depending on factors such as frequency and conditions. Ham Radio offers a wide range of communication options, including repeaters, satellite communication, and digital modes, which enhance the communication experience. Nevertheless, the licensing requirement and technical knowledge necessary for Ham Radio can be intimidating for certain users. In addition, it's worth noting that Ham Radio is primarily designed for non-commercial purposes, which means it may not be the best choice for business or commercial applications.

Examining GMRS in Comparison to Other Radio Services

When considering GMRS concerning other radio services, there are several factors to take into account:

1. **Licensing Requirements**: It is important to note that licenses are required for GMRS and Ham Radio, whereas FRS and CB do not have such requirements. GMRS licensing is more straightforward and applies to the entire family, whereas Ham Radio necessitates passing

an examination. FRS and CB are perfect for casual users who prefer not to go through the process of obtaining a license.

2. **Power Output and Range**: GMRS has the advantage of higher power output (up to 50 watts), which translates to a greater range. FRS has a power limit of 2 watts, whereas CB has a power limit of 4 watts. Ham Radio is capable of operating at higher power levels, which enables communication over longer distances.

3. **Use of Repeaters**: Repeaters are supported by GMRS and Ham Radio, allowing for a substantial increase in communication range. FRS and CB have restrictions on repeaters, which can limit their overall range.

4. **Applications**: GMRS is commonly used for personal and business communication, while Ham Radio is primarily intended for non-commercial use. CB radios are commonly used for road trips and outdoor activities, while FRS radios are great for family and casual communication.

5. **Privacy and Security**: GMRS provides enhanced privacy features when compared to CB radios. By using repeaters and sub-audible tones, interference can be minimized, ensuring a more secure communication experience. Ham Radio communication is typically open, enabling individuals with a license to tune in.

GMRS Channels

GMRS falls under the umbrella of **"personal radio services,"** which encompasses other services like Family Radio Service (FRS), Citizens Band (CB), and Multi-Use Radio Service (MURS). One notable aspect of GMRS is its licensing requirement and the option to utilize more powerful transmitters, resulting in extended communication ranges when compared to other personal radio services. GMRS enables communication on 22 designated channels, along with extra sub-channels referred to as repeater channels. While FRS does not require a license, operating GMRS requires an FCC-issued license. The license is usually given to individuals or families, allowing them to use GMRS equipment within a specific framework.

Exploring the GMRS Channel Spectrum

GMRS Simplex Channels and Frequencies			
Channel	Frequency	Max Power	Bandwidth
1	462.5625	5W	25kHz*
2	462.5875	5W	25kHz*
3	462.6125	5W	25kHz*
4	462.6375	5W	25kHz*
5	462.6625	5W	25kHz*
6	462.6875	5W	25kHz*
7	462.7125	5W	25kHz*
8	467.5625	0.5W	12.5kHz
9	467.5875	0.5W	12.5kHz
10	467.6125	0.5W	12.5kHz
11	467.6375	0.5W	12.5kHz
12	467.6625	0.5W	12.5kHz
13	467.6875	0.5W	12.5kHz
14	467.7125	0.5W	12.5kHz
15	462.5500	50W	25kHz*
16	462.5750	50W	25kHz*
17	462.6000	50W	25kHz*
18	462.6250	50W	25kHz*
19	462.6500	50W	25kHz*
20	462.6750	50W	25kHz*

GMRS operates within the UHF (Ultra High Frequency) band, specifically ranging from 462 MHz to 467 MHz. The 22 main channels are categorized into two groups: primary channels and interstitial channels. The primary channels are commonly utilized for general communication and are available to both GMRS and FRS users, whereas the interstitial channels are usually designated for more specific purposes.

Here's a comprehensive overview of the GMRS channel spectrum:

- **Channels 1-7:** These channels operate in the 462 MHz range and are shared with FRS. They are ideal for direct communication between radios.
- **Channels 8-14:** They are designated for FRS use and fall within the 467 MHz range.
- **Channels 15-22:** They operate in the 462 MHz range and are designated as GMRS channels. These channels have higher power limits and can utilize repeaters.

In addition, GMRS also offers repeater channels which enable users to expand their communication range by using repeaters. These devices receive signals and transmit them at higher power levels. The repeater channels are located within the 467 MHz range and are linked to specific primary channels.

Licensing and Regulations

Obtaining a license from the FCC is necessary for operating GMRS radios. The application process is simple and convenient, requiring an online form and a fee. The license, once granted, remains valid for ten years. It also extends its coverage to the immediate family members of the licensee, enabling them to operate GMRS radios without the need for individual licenses.

The GMRS regulations outline specific rules for operation, including:

- **Power Limits:** GMRS radios can transmit at higher power levels than FRS radios, which results in an increased range of coverage. Typically, simplex channels have a maximum power of 5 watts, while repeater output can reach up to 50 watts.
- **Channel Use:** Users need to adhere to the designated channel assignments and ensure that they do not cause any interference with other radio services. Additional coordination is necessary to prevent conflicts with repeater channels.
- **Call Signs and Identification**: It is required for GMRS operators to use their FCC-assigned call signs for identification purposes during transmissions. This ensures accountability and traceability.
- **Repeater Operations**: GMRS permits the use of repeaters, although it is necessary to register them with the FCC. This process guarantees that repeaters do not disrupt other licensed services.

Applications of GMRS Channels

GMRS channels have a diverse range of applications, catering to personal use, business needs, and emergency communication.

Below are some typical situations where GMRS is used:

- **Family Communication**: GMRS radios are commonly used by families during outdoor activities like camping, hiking, or road trips. GMRS is perfect for maintaining communication over long distances due to its extended range and clear reception.
- **Emergency Preparedness:** GMRS radios are an essential tool for effective emergency communication. During times of crisis when cell phone networks may be unreliable, GMRS offers a dependable method of communication. GMRS is widely used by preppers and emergency response organizations for this very purpose.
- **Business and Commercial Use**: GMRS is commonly used by small businesses, event organizers, and construction teams for internal communication. Operating repeaters and using higher power levels makes GMRS a highly practical solution for effectively coordinating large teams.
- **Community and Recreational Activities:** GMRS channels are used by various community groups, recreational clubs, and off-road enthusiasts. They offer a way for groups to communicate without depending on cellular networks.

CHAPTER TWO
GMRS RADIO BASICS

Overview

In this chapter, you will about GMRS Radio basics including how to go about GMRS Radio programming, how to obtain a license, how to decide on the perfect GMRS Radio, the types of GMRS Radios, and so son much more.

How to go about GMRS Radio programming

Before delving into the programming process, it is crucial to have a solid grasp of the fundamentals of GMRS radios and their distinctions from other radio services. GMRS radios are specifically designed for personal and family communication, providing users with the ability to communicate over a broader range in comparison to the Family Radio Service (FRS). GMRS radios have the advantage of higher power outputs, allowing for extended communication range. Additionally, they can operate on the same 22 primary channels as FRS radios. GMRS users must obtain a license from the Federal Communications Commission (FCC), unlike FRS.

Obtaining a GMRS License

Obtaining a license from the FCC is the first step in using a GMRS radio. Compliance with regulations and adherence to permitted frequency bands and power limits are ensured through licensing.

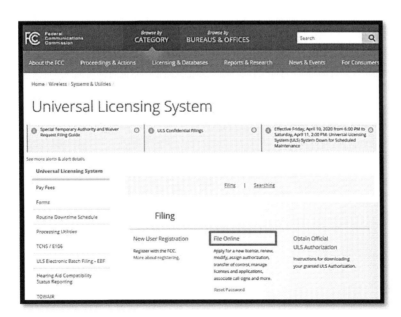

Here are the steps to obtain a GMRS license:

1. **Check out the FCC Website**: Head over to the FCC's Universal Licensing System (ULS) website to get started on the application process.
2. **Sign up for an FCC Account**: If you haven't done so yet, create an account to easily manage your license applications.
3. **Fill Out Form 605**: Fill out Form 605 to ensure all necessary information is provided for the selected radio service (GMRS).
4. **Submit the Application and Fee:** Once you've finished filling out the form, it's time to submit your application and take care of the licensing fee. The fee typically amounts to around $70.
5. **Receive your License**: Upon successful processing and approval of your application, you will be issued a GMRS license that remains valid for 10 years.

It's worth mentioning that a single license can be used by your entire family, enabling all members of your household to utilize GMRS radios without requiring separate licenses.

Deciding on the Perfect GMRS Radio

Once you have obtained your license, the next step is to choose a GMRS radio that meets your requirements. There are different types of GMRS radios available, including handheld, mobile, and base station units.

Take these factors into account when selecting a GMRS radio:

1. **Range and Power:** The power output plays a crucial role in determining the range of your GMRS radio. Handheld radios usually have a power range of 2 to 5 watts, while mobile and base station units can provide a higher power output of up to 50 watts. Select a radio that has sufficient power for your specific needs.
2. **Channels and Frequency Compatibility:** Make sure the radio can access all 22 GMRS channels and is compatible with shared FRS/GMRS channels in terms of frequency.
3. **Durability and Design**: When choosing a radio, it's important to think about durability and design. If you plan on using it outdoors, look for radios with sturdy, weather-resistant designs.

Programming Your GMRS Radio

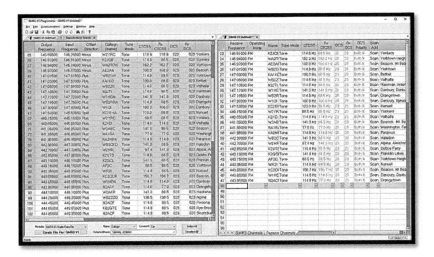

After selecting your GMRS radio, the next step is to program it with the frequencies, tones, and settings you want. Programming can be accomplished either manually or with the help of software, depending on the capabilities of the radio.

Here is a detailed guide on how to program a GMRS radio:

Manual Programming

1. **Identify your Channels:** Consider the channels you want to program, including both the primary GMRS channels and the shared FRS channels.
2. **Set Tones (CTCSS/DCS):** The use of the Continuous Tone-Coded Squelch System (CTCSS) and Digital-Coded Squelch (DCS) helps to minimize interference and maintain clear communication. Ensure that the tone of each channel aligns with the communication group.
3. **Input Repeater Frequencies**: Make sure to program the correct frequencies and offset settings if you intend to use repeaters. Having a good grasp of the local repeater information, such as frequency and tone, is essential for this step.
4. **Set Power Output:** Select the suitable power output for each channel according to your communication requirements and FCC regulations.
5. **Save your Settings**: Once you've programmed your channels, tones, and power output, make sure to save them so they'll be preserved even when the radio is turned off.

Programming with Software

GMRS radios often include programming software, which enables users to customize settings and manage them more efficiently.

Here is a step-by-step guide on programming your GMRS radio using software:

1. **Software Installation**: Set up the radio's programming software on your computer. Make sure it works with your operating system.
2. **Connect the Radio**: Use a programming cable to establish a connection between your GMRS radio and your computer.
3. **Launch the Software**: Begin by opening the programming software and choosing your radio model from the available options.
4. **Set up the Channels**: Enter the preferred frequencies, tones, and other configurations into the software. This step is frequently more efficient than manual programming, enabling you to easily replicate settings across multiple channels.
5. **Upload the Settings:** After programming the channels and other configurations, transfer the setup to your GMRS radio.
6. **Test Your Radio**: Once you have finished programming, it is important to test your GMRS radio to make sure that all settings are functioning correctly.

Tips for Optimizing GMRS Radio Programming

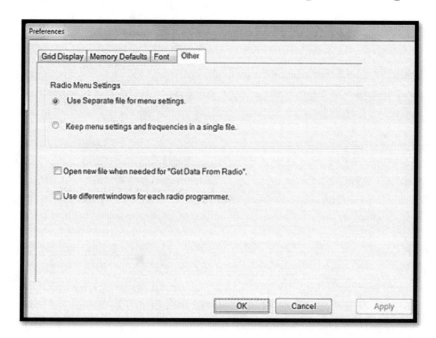

For a smooth GMRS radio programming experience, keep these tips in mind:

1. **Record Your Settings**: It's important to keep track of your programmed channels, tones, and other settings for future reference. This documentation is a valuable resource for anyone who needs to reprogram the radio or troubleshoot any issues that may arise.

2. **Test with Others**: Connect with fellow GMRS users to verify that your settings align and that you can establish effective communication.
3. **Stay Informed:** It is important to regularly update your programming software and firmware to maintain compatibility with the latest radios and features.
4. **Adhere to FCC Regulations:** It is important to ensure that you are in full compliance with all FCC regulations about power output, frequency use, and licensing requirements.
5. **Connect with GMRS Communities**: Engage with experienced users and seek advice on programming and other radio-related topics from knowledgeable individuals in GMRS user communities.

Types of GMRS Radios

GMRS radios are specifically designed to facilitate communication over short to medium distances, which can vary from a few miles to more than 20 miles. The range is influenced by factors such as the terrain, antenna type, and power output. Operating in the UHF (Ultra High Frequency) band, their frequency range falls between 462 MHz and 467 MHz. GMRS radios are perfect for a wide range of uses, from family communication during outings to emergency preparedness, thanks to their excellent balance of range and clarity in this frequency range. There are two primary types of GMRS radios available: handheld devices and base/mobile units. Now, we can explore each type to gain a better understanding of their distinct characteristics and practical uses.

Handheld GMRS Radios

Handheld GMRS radios are compact devices that are perfect for people who are always on the move. Compact, battery-operated, and often equipped with a built-in antenna.

These are the main features of handheld GMRS radios:

- **Portability**: Handheld GMRS radios are highly portable, making them perfect for outdoor activities like hiking, camping, and off-roading. With their lightweight design and compact size, these devices can easily be attached to a belt or backpack, providing users with convenient access.
- **Battery-Powered**: Handheld GMRS radios typically come with rechargeable batteries, allowing for several hours of uninterrupted use. Additionally, certain models can use standard AA or AAA batteries, providing users with the convenience of choosing their preferred power source.
- **Durability**: Handheld GMRS radios are built to endure tough conditions. Several models come with durable casings that can withstand water exposure, making them ideal for outdoor use.
- **Range**: Handheld GMRS radios typically have shorter ranges than base/mobile units, but they can still cover several miles under ideal conditions. Various factors, including terrain, obstructions, and weather conditions, can affect the range.

Handheld GMRS radios are highly sought after by families, hikers, and outdoor enthusiasts because of their convenient size and user-friendly nature. They are commonly utilized in team-based activities and events where effective communication between participants is essential.

Base/Mobile GMRS Radios

Base/mobile GMRS radios are larger units intended for stationary or vehicle-mounted use. They provide a significant boost in power and an extended range when compared to handheld radios.

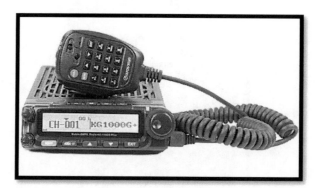

These are the main features of base/mobile GMRS radios:

- **Increased Power Output**: Base/mobile GMRS radios have a higher power output, typically up to 50 watts, in contrast to handheld models. The enhanced power enables extended communication range and improved signal penetration even in challenging environments.

- **Fixed Antennas**: These radios often use larger antennas that are more efficient and can be easily mounted on vehicles or buildings. The increased size of the antenna enhances the range and signal quality.
- **Versatility**: Base/mobile GMRS radios are incredibly versatile and can be used in a wide range of settings, such as vehicles, homes, or emergency response centers. They are great for facilitating communication across a wider region.
- **Power Supply**: Base/mobile units are typically powered by a vehicle's electrical system or an AC power source, unlike handheld radios. This allows for extended operational hours without the hassle of constantly replacing or recharging batteries.

Base/mobile GMRS radios are commonly utilized by emergency responders, off-road enthusiasts, and individuals in need of dependable communication across long distances. They are also useful for organizing activities during outdoor events or large gatherings.

Other Features and Factors to Consider

In addition to the basic differences between handheld and base/mobile GMRS radios, there are other features and factors to consider.

Consider these factors when choosing a GMRS radio:

- **Channels and Privacy Codes:** GMRS radios usually provide a variety of channels for communication. Additionally, certain models offer privacy codes that provide an extra level of security. These codes enable users to communicate on a shared channel without any disruptions from external sources.
- **Repeater Capability**: Some GMRS radios can access repeaters, which are radio stations that rebroadcast signals to increase the range of communication. This feature is particularly beneficial for covering extended distances and navigating through difficult landscapes.
- **Emergency Features**: Numerous GMRS radios are equipped with essential emergency features, including NOAA weather alerts and emergency call buttons. These features are extremely useful in emergencies or when exploring remote areas.
- **Audio Quality and Clarity:** The audio quality of GMRS radios can differ. Higher-end models typically feature superior speaker quality and advanced noise reduction technology, which guarantees crystal-clear communication even in loud surroundings.
- **Licensing Requirements**: As previously stated, GMRS radios must be licensed by the Federal Communications Commission (FCC) to operate legally in the United States. Adhering to regulations and maintaining the integrity of the GMRS frequency band is crucial, and licensing plays a vital role in ensuring this.

Deciding on the Perfect GMRS Radio

The selection of the appropriate GMRS radio is contingent upon your requirements and intended application. If you're interested in having reliable communication while enjoying outdoor activities, a handheld GMRS radio is an excellent option. Alternatively, if you need a greater range and more power for communication in vehicles or stationary setups, a base/mobile GMRS radio could be a more suitable choice. Take into account factors like range requirements, power sources, antenna options, and additional features when deciding which option is best for you. It's crucial to become acquainted with the FCC's licensing process to guarantee adherence to regulations.

GMRS Radio: Features and Components

GMRS is a licensed radio service in the United States that enables personal or business communication on designated radio frequencies. GMRS radios are widely utilized for a variety of purposes, including recreational activities, family communication, outdoor events, and even business operations. They provide a straightforward and efficient communication system. Let's take a closer look at the features and components of GMRS radios to understand why these devices are highly regarded and widely used by various user groups.

- **Frequency Range**

GMRS operates within the UHF (Ultra High Frequency) band, specifically ranging from 462 MHz to 467 MHz. This range is perfect for ensuring consistent communication over short to moderate distances, making it ideal for use in urban, suburban, and rural areas. GMRS has designated channels within this band that serve specific purposes, offering users flexibility in communication.

- **Channels and Privacy Codes**

GMRS radios provide users with a variety of channels, usually 22 in total, which are divided into simplex and duplex channels. The use of simplex channels allows for direct radio-to-radio communication, while duplex channels utilize repeaters to extend range and improve signal strength. GMRS radios often come equipped with privacy codes, such as Continuous Tone-Coded Squelch System (CTCSS) or Digital-Coded Squelch (DCS), in addition to channels. The codes effectively minimize interference by filtering out unwanted transmissions, enabling users to communicate with specific groups.

- **Requirements for Licensing**

GMRS, unlike FRS, requires a license from the Federal Communications Commission (FCC) in the United States. Obtaining a GMRS license is a breeze, thanks to its straightforward application process and a one-time fee that covers a 10-year term. The purpose of this licensing requirement is to promote responsible use of the GMRS frequencies and avoid any potential interference with other communication services.

- **Transmission Power**

GMRS radios typically provide a higher transmission power compared to FRS radios, with a maximum output of 50 watts. With the enhanced power, you can achieve an extended range, especially when utilizing repeaters. Nevertheless, the majority of handheld GMRS radios function at lower power levels, usually ranging from 1 to 5 watts. This allows for a well-balanced combination of range and battery life. Base stations and mobile units can operate at higher power levels, which allow for an extended communication range for individuals who possess GMRS licenses.

- **Antenna Options**

GMRS radios usually include built-in antennas for handheld devices and removable antennas for base stations and mobile units. Users can easily customize their setup with detachable antennas to meet their specific needs. For instance, they can opt for a longer antenna to enhance the range or a directional antenna for more focused communication. The adaptability of GMRS is a crucial aspect, allowing users to customize their communication systems to suit their surroundings and specific needs.

- **Repeater Capability**

GMRS radios have the advantage of being compatible with repeaters, which is a standout feature. Repeaters are devices that receive and retransmit signals at a higher power, greatly expanding the communication range. GMRS repeaters are commonly utilized in larger areas like campgrounds, neighborhoods, or business complexes, where having a wider communication range prove advantageous. Using repeaters greatly enhances the versatility of GMRS, allowing it to be used in a variety of applications.

- **NOAA Weather Alerts**

Several GMRS radios come with NOAA weather alert features. Users can conveniently access real-time weather information, including severe weather alerts, through their radios. This is incredibly helpful for outdoor activities such as camping, hiking, or emergency preparedness, as it adds an extra level of safety and awareness.

- **Reliability and Construction**

GMRS radios are built to endure tough conditions, making them perfect for outdoor adventures and challenging surroundings. These devices are typically constructed using sturdy materials that can withstand water, dust, and shock. GMRS radios are designed to withstand a wide range of conditions, ensuring their performance remains uncompromised. This makes them a dependable option for both outdoor enthusiasts and professionals.

- **Intuitive and easy-to-use interface**

GMRS radios greatly benefit from being user-friendly. The interfaces of these devices are designed to be user-friendly, with clear displays, intuitive controls, and easy-to-use channel selectors. The simplicity of GMRS radios allows users of all experience levels to easily understand and operate them, without the need for extensive training. Additionally, numerous models are equipped with voice activation (VOX) capabilities, enabling convenient hands-free operation and improving overall usability.

- **Applications and Use Cases**

GMRS radios have a diverse range of applications, catering to both recreational and business needs. GMRS radios are commonly used by families for communication during outdoor activities, camping trips, or road trips. They offer a reliable way to stay in touch without depending on cell service. GMRS radios are commonly used by businesses and event organizers to facilitate on-site communication, coordinate activities, and prioritize safety during events or operations. GMRS radios are incredibly versatile and can be used in a wide range of situations.

- **Seamless integration with various communication systems**

Some models of GMRS radios also can integrate with other communication systems. For instance, some GMRS radios can connect to computer systems or smartphones, which greatly expands their communication capabilities. This integration is highly valuable for effectively managing large-scale events or facilitating crucial communication during disaster response scenarios. GMRS radios are incredibly versatile tools that can bridge different communication platforms, making them ideal for a wide range of communication needs.

- **Battery Life and Power Options**

GMRS radios require a significant battery life, particularly when used outdoors. Handheld GMRS radios often come equipped with rechargeable batteries, ensuring a reliable power source that lasts for extended periods. Additionally, certain models offer compatibility with regular alkaline batteries, allowing for greater versatility in terms of power options. In addition, GMRS radios designed for mobile or base station use often come with convenient power options like DC car adapters or AC power supplies. These options ensure a reliable power source for uninterrupted operation.

- **Ensuring Regulatory Compliance and Prioritizing Safety Features**

Compliance with regulatory standards is essential for ensuring the safe and responsible use of GMRS radios. The FCC oversees GMRS in the United States, establishing guidelines for transmission power, frequency use, and licensing requirements. In addition, numerous GMRS radios come equipped with safety features such as emergency alert buttons, lockable controls, and automatic power-saving modes. The safety features in place ensure a secure and reliable communication experience for users.

Features of base station GMRS Radio

The GMRS base station is a crucial communication hub, offering dependable long-range communication for a wide range of situations, such as emergency response, recreational activities, and business coordination. GMRS radios operate within the 462-467 MHz frequency range, which requires a Federal Communications Commission (FCC) license in the United States. This allows for effective communication over significant distances. Here is a detailed examination of the features of GMRS base stations.

- **Frequency Bands**

GMRS radios usually function on 22 channels that fall within the 462-467 MHz frequency range. The proper allocation of frequencies is essential to ensure effective communication with minimal disruptions. The initial 7 channels coincide with Family Radio Service (FRS) frequencies, which do not necessitate a license. However, GMRS provides greater power outputs, enabling an extended range. Base stations can use the complete range of GMRS frequencies for seamless communication with other GMRS radios, repeaters, or mobile units.

- **Power Output**

Power output is a significant distinguishing factor for GMRS base stations. Handheld GMRS radios typically have a limited output ranging from 0.5 to 5 watts, whereas base stations can operate at higher power levels, reaching up to 50 watts. The increased power greatly improves the range and reliability of communication, enabling broader coverage in urban and rural areas.

- **Antenna Design and Height**

The effectiveness of a GMRS base station can be greatly influenced by the type of antenna used and its placement. An antenna with high gain, usually installed on a mast or tower, can enhance signal strength and expand the coverage area. The height of the antenna plays a critical role in ensuring optimal signal quality. By positioning the antenna at a higher elevation, it becomes possible to overcome obstacles such as buildings and trees, leading to reduced signal attenuation and interference. The majority of base stations use omnidirectional antennas to transmit and receive signals in all directions. However, it is also possible to employ directional antennas to concentrate communication in a particular area.

- **Repeaters and Duplex Operations**

GMRS base stations commonly include repeater functionality, enabling them to expand the communication range. The function of repeaters is to receive signals on a specific frequency and then transmit them on a different frequency, thereby extending the range of the signal. In hilly or mountainous regions, this becomes particularly useful as it overcomes the limitations of direct line-of-sight communication. Base stations with duplex operations enable the transmission and reception of signals on separate frequencies, allowing for smooth communication via repeaters.

- **Channel Scanning and Privacy Codes**

A GMRS base station typically comes equipped with channel scanning capabilities, enabling users to monitor multiple frequencies for incoming communication. This feature is incredibly valuable for efficiently coordinating activities across various channels or swiftly locating an active channel for seamless communication. In addition, GMRS radios often include Continuous Tone-Coded Squelch System (CTCSS) or Digital Coded Squelch (DCS) codes, which are commonly referred to as privacy codes. These codes effectively minimize interference by filtering out transmissions from other users on the same frequency. Users can ensure they only hear communications intended for them by setting a specific code.

- **Enhancing Voice Modulation and Clarity**

The quality of voice communication is a crucial factor to consider when evaluating GMRS base stations. Numerous models provide cutting-edge voice modulation technologies to guarantee clear and precise communication. With the help of noise-canceling microphones and advanced audio processing, background noise can be effectively eliminated, resulting in a significant improvement in the quality of communication. This is particularly advantageous in loud settings, like construction sites or bustling urban areas.

- **Seamless compatibility with mobile and handheld devices**

GMRS base stations are specifically designed to seamlessly integrate with mobile and handheld units, providing users with versatile communication options. This feature is extremely valuable for organizations or groups that need to have both fixed and mobile communication capabilities. Ensuring seamless communication across different environments and scenarios is made possible by the ability to integrate with various GMRS devices.

- **External Connectivity and Accessories**

GMRS base stations often include external connectivity options, which enable users to connect extra accessories for added functionality. In noisy environments, it is possible to enhance communication by connecting external microphones, speakers, or headsets. Additionally, certain base stations provide data ports or interfaces that allow for seamless integration with other communication systems or computers. This enables the establishment of advanced communication setups and the ability to remotely control the station.

- **Emergency Features**

GMRS base stations must prioritize safety and emergency communication. Several models come equipped with emergency features like a built-in emergency button or alert function. Users can easily request assistance or send out emergency messages to all other users tuned in to a particular frequency. Certain base stations also offer support for NOAA Weather Radio channels, ensuring access to important weather alerts and information, which is essential for emergency preparedness and response.

- **Durability and Environmental Resistance**

GMRS base stations need to be highly durable, especially when used in challenging outdoor environments. The construction of base stations prioritizes durability and resilience against various environmental factors such as weather conditions, temperature changes, and physical impacts. The device is designed to withstand challenging conditions, making it reliable even in the presence of water and dust. The durability of these base stations is crucial for their use in remote locations, emergency response scenarios, or industrial settings.

- **Intuitive Interface and Easy-to-Use Controls**

An easy-to-use interface and intuitive controls are crucial for any communication system. GMRS base stations are designed with user-friendly features such as clear displays, intuitive buttons, and simple menu systems. The user-friendly features allow users to easily navigate channels, customize settings, and handle communication tasks without needing specialized training or technical knowledge.

Features of handheld GMRS Radio

Portable communication devices known as Handheld General Mobile Radio Service (GMRS) radios are designed for personal and family use in the United States. These radios operate on a specific set of frequencies designated by the Federal Communications Commission (FCC). These radios are highly regarded for their versatility, durability, and user-friendly design, providing dependable communication in a wide range of situations, from casual family outings to critical emergency preparedness scenarios.

Technical Specifications

- **Frequencies and Channels**

Handheld GMRS radios usually operate on 22 channels, with 8 channels exclusively for GMRS use and 14 shared with Family Radio Service (FRS). Shared channels enable communication with FRS radios, while GMRS radios can operate at higher power levels. GMRS radios are incredibly versatile, allowing for seamless communication with a wide array of devices.

- **Power and Range**

GMRS radios are renowned for their superior power output in comparison to FRS radios, typically ranging from 1 to 5 watts. Some models may offer higher power levels, reaching up to 50 watts, although these are typically base or mobile units. With a higher power output, handheld units can achieve impressive distances of 1 to 5 miles under ideal conditions, providing a greater range. Nevertheless, the range can be influenced by various factors such as terrain, weather, and obstructions.

- **Privacy Codes and Squelch**

GMRS radios often include privacy codes such as Continuous Tone-Coded Squelch System (CTCSS) and Digital-Coded Squelch (DCS). Users can easily filter out unwanted transmissions and exclusively communicate with others who are using the same privacy code. Although these codes do not offer actual encryption, they do serve to minimize interference and offer a sense of privacy in busy radio settings.

Common Uses of Handheld GMRS Radios

- **Family Communication**

GMRS radios are a common choice for family adventures like camping, hiking, and road trips. Family members can stay connected even in remote areas, where cellular networks may not be available. Families can communicate without any interruptions from other radio users thanks to the implementation of privacy codes.

- **Outdoor and Recreational Activities**

Handheld GMRS radios are commonly used in outdoor and recreational environments, in addition to being used by families. Hunters, fishermen, and off-road enthusiasts frequently rely on GMRS radios for effective coordination and to prioritize safety. With their impressive power output and extended range, these devices are perfect for a wide range of applications. They ensure reliable connectivity, even in the most demanding environments.

- **Emergency Communication**

GMRS radios are essential for emergency preparedness and disaster response. Due to their independence from cellular networks, they serve as a crucial backup communication tool in situations such as power outages or when other communication systems experience failures. GMRS radios are highly recommended by emergency response organizations and community groups due to their reliability and user-friendly nature.

Advantages of Handheld GMRS Radios

- **User-Friendly Design**

Handheld GMRS radios are designed to be easy to use, with controls that are easy to understand and interfaces that are straightforward. This allows users of all skill levels, from children to adults, to easily access them. The displays on most models are designed to be easy to read, while the channel selection process is straightforward. Additionally, the designs of these models are ergonomic, ensuring comfortable handling.

- **Durability and Portability**

These radios are designed to endure tough conditions, with numerous models equipped with weather-resistant or waterproof features. The durability of these radios is crucial for outdoor activities, as they may be subjected to harsh elements. Handheld GMRS radios are incredibly portable, allowing you to conveniently carry them in backpacks, pockets, or lanyards, so you'll always have them close by.

- **Licensing and Regulation**

The process of obtaining an FCC license for GMRS radios is quite straightforward. With a single license, GMRS radios can be used by all family members, providing a cost-effective solution for family communication. The licensing requirement also helps improve spectrum management, which in turn reduces interference among users and ensures reliable communication.

- **Understanding Licensing Requirements**

Before purchasing a GMRS radio, users need to familiarize themselves with the licensing requirements. Using GMRS radios without a license is against the law and may lead to financial penalties. Applying for a GMRS license online is possible through the FCC's Universal Licensing System (ULS). This license has a validity of 10 years and provides coverage for the entire family, making it a valuable investment for individuals who frequently use GMRS radios.

- **Compatibility with Other Radios**

Users need to take into account the compatibility of a GMRS radio with other radios in their communication network. GMRS radios provide a convenient solution for families and groups that use a combination of radio types, as they can communicate with FRS radios on shared channels. To use all GMRS channels and higher power levels, all radios in the network must be GMRS-compliant.

- **Battery Life and Charging Options**

Considering battery life is essential when choosing handheld GMRS radios. Rechargeable batteries are commonly used in many models, providing convenience and helping to minimize waste. Users need to have backup power sources, like spare batteries or portable chargers, particularly when engaging in outdoor activities or facing emergencies.

CHAPTER THREE
LICENSING AND LEGAL CONSIDERATIONS

Overview

Chapter three talks about the licensing and legal considerations relating to GMRS Radios including who needs a GMRS license and the issues to avoid when trying to obtain one.

Who Needs a GMRS License?

One of the main purposes of obtaining a GMRS license is to guarantee the efficient and interference-free use of the radio spectrum. The use of GMRS frequencies is regulated by the FCC to prevent overcrowding and ensure clear communication channels. The FCC can maintain a record of authorized users by requiring a license, which enables better management of the radio spectrum. Operating a GMRS radio, regardless of the purpose, necessitates obtaining a GMRS license.

Below is a breakdown of the various groups that may require a GMRS license:

- **Individuals and Families:** For individuals and families who rely on GMRS radios for communication during outdoor activities, travel, or emergencies, obtaining a license is necessary. The license includes coverage for the individual and their immediate family, enabling multiple users to be covered under a single license.
- **Businesses and Organizations**: Companies and organizations that use GMRS for internal communication are also required to obtain a license. This encompasses businesses that use radios for coordinating field operations, facilitating communication between various locations, or staying connected with mobile units.
- **Emergency Services and Preparedness Groups**: Organizations involved in emergency response, such as volunteer fire departments, search and rescue teams, and disaster preparedness groups, frequently rely on GMRS due to its reliability and user-friendly nature. These groups must obtain a GMRS license to ensure their communication is effective in times of emergencies.

How to Get a GMRS License

To obtain a GMRS license, certain criteria must be met:

- **Age Requirement:** Applicants must be at least 18 years old to apply for a GMRS license. Although, if you are under 18, you can still use GMRS radios with the permission of a licensed family member.

- **Citizenship Requirement:** Applicants for a GMRS license must be either a U.S. citizen or a legal resident.
- **No Examination:** Unlike amateur radio licenses, a GMRS license can be obtained without the need to pass an exam. The application process is clear and easy to follow.

The Application Process

The FCC has streamlined the licensing processes, allowing for more convenient application for a GMRS license.

Here are the steps you need to follow to obtain your license:

Step 1: Register with the FCC

To get started, you'll need to acquire an FCC Registration Number (FRN). This identifier is used to monitor your licensing and other engagements with the FCC.

Here are the steps to obtain a FRN:

- Visit the website of the FCC's Universal Licensing System (ULS).
- Click on the option for "**New User Registration**."

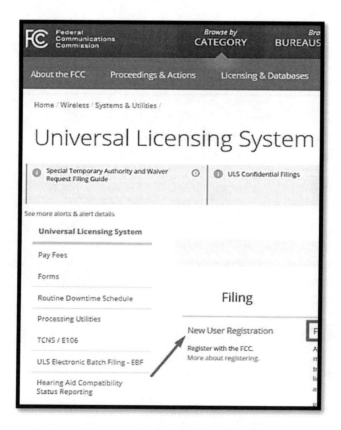

- Provide the necessary information, such as your name, address, and contact details.
- Submit the form to receive your FRN.

Step 2: Complete the application process for a GMRS License

Now that you have your FRN, you are eligible to apply for a GMRS license.

- Access the FCC's ULS by providing your FRN and password.
- Choose the option "**Apply for a New License**."
- Select "**ZA - General Mobile Radio Service**" from the list of services provided.
- Fill out the application form. As part of the process, you will need to provide your contact information, choose your payment method, and agree to the terms and conditions.
- Submit the application and make the necessary payment for the application fee (as of 2024, the fee is $35).

Step 3: Await Approval

Once your application is submitted, it will be reviewed by the FCC. The approval process can vary in duration, ranging from a few business days to a few weeks. The timeframe is influenced by factors such as the volume of applications and other variables. After your approval, an email confirmation will be sent to you, and you can access your license information on the ULS website.

Using Your GMRS License

After obtaining your GMRS license, you will be able to operate GMRS radios in compliance with the law. You will need to renew your license after 10 years to continue using GMRS frequencies.
Having a GMRS license enables you to:
- **Use GMRS Frequencies**: Voice communication is possible on any GMRS frequency, as long as the power limits set by the FCC are adhered to. GMRS radios provide a higher power output compared to FRS radios, enabling communication over greater distances.
- **Use Repeaters**: GMRS permits the use of repeaters, which can greatly enhance the communication range. This is particularly beneficial in rural or mountainous regions.
- **Stay Connected with Family Members**: Your GMRS license extends to your immediate family members, granting them the privilege to use GMRS radios without the need for additional licensing. GMRS is a convenient option for family communication during trips, emergencies, or other activities.

Ensuring Regulatory Adherence

Here are some guidelines to help you stay compliant with FCC regulations:

- **Power Limits**: GMRS radios have designated power limits for each frequency. Please make sure that your radios stay within these limits to prevent any interference with other users.
- **Antenna Restrictions:** GMRS permits the use of external antennas, but they must adhere to specific height limitations. Make sure to refer to the FCC guidelines to ensure that your antenna setup complies with the permitted parameters.

- **Operating within Authorized Frequencies**: Ensure that you are using GMRS frequencies that are authorized by the FCC. It is important to note that using frequencies without proper authorization can lead to penalties or even the revocation of your license.
- **License Renewal:** It is important to stay on top of your license's expiration date and make sure to renew it promptly to prevent any disruptions in your authorization.

FCC Regulations and Compliance

GMRS operates in the ultra-high frequency (UHF) band and has designated channels for public use. GMRS, unlike certain other radio services, does require an FCC license for operation. However, it's worth noting that this license does not necessitate a test, unlike the ones for amateur radio licenses. GMRS licenses are granted to individuals or families, enabling them to communicate with each other using a variety of frequencies.

Frequency Allocation

The GMRS frequencies can be found between the 462 MHz and 467 MHz range. The FCC has designated specific channels for GMRS use, some of which are available for simplex (direct communication between two radios) or repeater (communication through a relay station) operations. Users of GMRS have the freedom to select the communication method that best suits their requirements.

Licensing Requirements

To operate a GMRS radio within the bounds of the law, users are required to obtain a license from the FCC. This requirement distinguishes GMRS from other unlicensed radio services such as Family Radio Service (FRS), which is commonly utilized for comparable purposes. The validity of a GMRS license extends for ten years, providing coverage for the licensee, their immediate family members, and their spouse. All members of the household can freely use GMRS radios without the requirement of individual licenses. The process for obtaining a GMRS license is quite simple. Applicants are required to complete FCC Form 605 online, providing essential information such as their name, address, and contact details. After the application has been processed and approved, the license will be granted. The cost for a GMRS license is determined by the FCC and may vary over time.

Technical Regulations

GMRS radios must meet specific technical standards to ensure compliance with FCC regulations. The standards encompass power output limits, frequency stability, and modulation characteristics. GMRS radios usually have a maximum power output of 50 watts, although handheld units generally operate at lower power levels. Manufacturers must ensure that GMRS radios comply with FCC standards before being sold to consumers. Obtaining FCC certification involves demonstrating that the radios meet the prescribed technical requirements. People need to seek out radios that are labeled with an FCC ID. This label signifies that the product has undergone thorough testing and is in compliance with FCC rules.

Operational Regulations

GMRS users need to adhere to specific operational rules to remain in compliance with FCC regulations. The purpose of these rules is to ensure a smooth and uninterrupted use of the radio spectrum.

Important operational regulations for GMRS users are:

- **Designated Frequencies:** GMRS radios are only authorized for use on specific GMRS frequencies. Operating on frequencies or bands without proper authorization can result in interference with other radio services and potential penalties from the FCC.
- **Repeater Use:** GMRS repeaters enhance communication range by relaying signals. Nevertheless, repeaters must be licensed and used exclusively by authorized individuals as per the FCC regulations. It is important for GMRS users who operate repeaters to adhere to these regulations.
- **Call Signs**: GMRS licensees are given a distinct call sign that must be utilized during radio communications. This requirement is crucial for the FCC to effectively monitor radio traffic and maintain accountability among GMRS operators.
- **Interference**: GMRS users need to be mindful of potential interference with other radio services. When interference happens, users need to take the necessary steps to address the problem.
- **Public Safety and Emergency Communications:** GMRS radios are a reliable option for public safety or emergency communications during disasters or critical events. Nevertheless, using these channels for non-emergency purposes is not allowed.

Enforcement and Penalties

The FCC is responsible for ensuring that GMRS regulations are followed. We thoroughly investigate any reports of interference, unauthorized use, or other violations of the rules. Failure to comply with GMRS regulations can result in penalties imposed by the FCC. Penalties can range from fines to license revocation, or other enforcement measures. Understanding responsibilities and adhering to FCC rules is crucial for GMRS users to avoid potential penalties. It is essential to maintain compliance by keeping accurate records of communication activities, using proper call signs, and operating on authorized frequencies.

Guidelines for Ensuring GMRS Compliance

For GMRS users to comply with FCC regulations, it is important to adhere to the following best practices:

1. **Get a GMRS License**: Make sure you have obtained an FCC license before using a GMRS radio. The process is clear and easy to follow, and the license provides coverage for your entire family.
2. **Ensure Equipment Authorization**: When acquiring GMRS radios, it is crucial to select models from trustworthy manufacturers that have obtained proper FCC certification. It is important to refrain from using radios that have been altered or are not authorized.
3. **Adhere to Operational Rules**: Ensure the use of correct call signs, operate within assigned frequencies, and take care to prevent interference with other radio services. Make sure to follow the rules for using repeaters, if they apply to you.
4. **Maintain Records**: Keep accurate records of your GMRS communications, including dates, times, and frequencies used to maintain proper documentation. This can prove to be useful in case of an FCC investigation.
5. **Stay Informed**: Stay up to date with FCC regulations and any changes to GMRS rules. Consider joining GMRS user groups or forums to gain insights from fellow enthusiasts and stay up-to-date on the latest best practices.

Common Legal Issues and Pitfalls to Avoid

GMRS is highly favored by radio enthusiasts and families alike for its ability to facilitate short-distance communications. GMRS stands out from other radio services due to its requirement for a license to operate. However, it provides a wide range of frequencies and high-powered equipment, making it highly versatile for a multitude of applications. Nonetheless, users must have a clear understanding of the legal issues and potential pitfalls to comply with regulations and avoid severe consequences such as hefty fines or penalties.

Common Traps to Avoid When Licensing

1. **Failure to Obtain a License**: Operating without a license is the most common legal issue associated with GMRS. Many times, this issue arises from a lack of awareness or misunderstanding of the requirements. If caught, the FCC has the authority to impose fines, and individuals who repeatedly violate regulations may face more severe consequences. It is important to always have a valid license before using GMRS equipment to prevent any issues.
2. **Not Renewing the License**: The GMRS licenses have a validity period of 10 years, after which they need to be renewed. Failure to renew could result in an illegal operation. Remember to set reminders and renew your license before it expires.

3. **Inaccurate Licensing Information**: When applying for a GMRS license, it is essential to provide precise and correct information. Accurate information is crucial to avoid complications and potential invalidation of the license, such as incorrect addresses or misspelled names. Ensure that you review all information thoroughly before submitting your application.

Operating within the boundaries of the law

GMRS has rules that must be followed when it comes to power output, frequencies, and usage. **It is crucial to have a clear understanding of these limitations to prevent any potential legal complications.**

1. **Power Output Limits:** GMRS radios are subject to power output limits, which vary depending on the type of equipment and frequency. These limits typically range from 1 to 50 watts. It is important to note that surpassing these limits is against the law and can potentially disrupt other radio services. It is important to always verify the power output of your equipment and make sure it meets the regulations set by the FCC.
2. **Authorized Frequencies**: GMRS uses a designated range of frequencies for communication purposes. These radios are distinct from the ones utilized by other radio services such as FRS (Family Radio Service) or ham radio. It is important to avoid using unauthorized frequencies to prevent interference and potential penalties. Make sure you're using the correct designated GMRS frequencies by familiarizing yourself with them.
3. **Unauthorized Equipment**: Some radio equipment is not authorized for GMRS use. Certain devices, such as modified ham radios or unlicensed radios, can operate on GMRS frequencies, but their usage is considered illegal. It is important to always buy GMRS-certified equipment to prevent any potential legal complications.

Misuse of GMRS Frequencies

GMRS is designed for close-range communication, like within families or among small groups. **Using these frequencies incorrectly can result in legal consequences and cause interference for other users.**

1. **Commercial Use:** GMRS is not designed for commercial purposes. GMRS cannot be used for business operations, advertising, or any other commercial activity. If you require radio communication for your business, it may be worth exploring alternative services such as the Business Radio Service or the Industrial/Business Pool.
2. **Broadcasting or Transmission of Music**: GMRS regulations prohibit the broadcasting or transmission of music, advertisements, or any non-communication content. Using it for any purpose other than two-way voice communication would be a violation of FCC rules.
3. **Interference with Other Services**: Operating GMRS equipment in a manner that disrupts other radio services is against the law. This may happen if you use too much power, frequencies that are not authorized or equipment that is not certified. It is important to

be mindful of fellow radio users and make sure that your equipment does not create any interference.

Consequences of Breaking GMRS Regulations

The FCC considers violations of GMRS rules to be a matter of great importance. Penalties can vary, ranging from fines to the confiscation of equipment or, in severe cases, imprisonment.

These are a few possible outcomes if GMRS regulations are violated:

1. **Penalties**: The FCC has the authority to levy fines on individuals or organizations found to violate GMRS rules. The fines can be quite significant, particularly for individuals who have committed multiple offenses.
2. **Equipment Confiscation**: If unauthorized equipment is used or illegal frequencies are operated on, the FCC has the authority to seize radio equipment. GMRS radios can be quite expensive.
3. **License Revocation**: In case of repeated violations of GMRS rules, the FCC has the authority to revoke your license, which would prevent you from legally operating GMRS equipment.
4. **Criminal Charges**: In certain instances, such as deliberate disruption of emergency communications or other severe infractions, individuals may face criminal charges that could result in imprisonment.

Licensing fees and renewal

A license from the FCC is required to operate GMRS equipment. The GMRS license does not require an examination or specialized technical knowledge, unlike Amateur Radio (ham radio). Applicants are expected to complete an application form, pay a licensing fee, and follow the FCC's rules and regulations for GMRS operations.

The Licensing Process

Getting a GMRS license is a simple and easy process. To complete the application process, the applicant is required to submit Form 605 to the FCC. This form includes providing personal information, contact details, and payment of a licensing fee. Each license issued by the FCC is assigned a distinct call sign that operators are required to use when communicating to establish their identity. After the license application is approved, the license remains valid for 10 years starting from the date of issuance. During this period, the licensee needs to adhere to all GMRS regulations, such as power limits, frequency usage, and operating procedures. Failure to follow these rules may lead to fines or the revocation of your license.

Licensing Fees

There is a licensing fee for GMRS applications imposed by the FCC to cover administrative costs and spectrum management. The current licensing fee is $35, but it may be modified following the FCC's budgetary requirements and adjustments. The fee must be paid in full upon application submission and is non-refundable. The licensing fee plays a crucial role in the GMRS regulatory framework. The service's integrity is upheld and users are motivated to comply with FCC rules by having a financial stake in it. In addition, the fee helps support the funding of FCC operations, which are responsible for overseeing various radio services, such as GMRS.

GMRS License Renewal

Renewing a GMRS license involves carefully following the FCC's procedures and being mindful of the timing. Renewing licenses every 10 years is necessary to ensure the legal operation of GMRS equipment. The renewal process is comparable to the initial application, but there are a few notable distinctions.

When to Renew

GMRS license holders have the option to renew their license up to 90 days before its expiration date. Renewing within this timeframe is crucial to ensure uninterrupted service. If a license expires before renewal, the operator must stop using GMRS radios until a new license is obtained.

The Renewal Process

To renew a GMRS license, the licensee must fill out Form 605 and send it to the FCC along with the appropriate fee. The renewal process can be easily completed online through the FCC's Universal Licensing System (ULS), streamlining the procedure and minimizing processing time. Once the renewal application is submitted, the FCC carefully reviews it. If the application is deemed satisfactory, the license is then renewed for an additional 10-year period.

Maintaining Compliance

GMRS licensees must continue to adhere to FCC rules and regulations even after renewing their license. It is important to follow power limits, use authorized frequencies, and keep all communications within the scope of the GMRS service. Licensees should stay informed about any updates to FCC regulations that could impact their use of GMRS.

CHAPTER FOUR
ADVANCED GMRS FEATURES

Overview

Going further, this chapter talks about the advanced GMRS Features such as privacy codes and tones, how to use CTCSS and DCS in GMRS Radios, the advantages of scanning and monitoring in GMRS, and others.

Privacy Codes and Tones (CTCSS/DCS)

Privacy codes, also referred to as sub-channels or sub-tones, do not offer complete privacy. They effectively minimize unwanted noise and interference on shared channels by filtering out transmissions that do not use the same code. GMRS radios operate on shared frequencies, allowing multiple users to access the same channel simultaneously. The result is a cacophonous atmosphere filled with overlapping discussions and disruptions. Privacy codes are specifically created to address and reduce this issue.

What is CTCSS?

CTCSS, also known as Continuous Tone-Coded Squelch System, is a system that utilizes low-frequency tones to regulate the squelch on a radio. The squelch is a feature that automatically silences the radio's speaker when it doesn't detect any signal. With CTCSS, you can assign a particular tone to your transmissions, guaranteeing that your radio will only respond to signals that possess that specific tone. The CTCSS system operates within a frequency range of 67 Hz to 254.1 Hz and includes a standard set of 38 tones. When a radio is set to a specific CTCSS tone, it will only activate its squelch when it detects a signal transmitting that tone. This feature ensures that you only receive transmissions from users on the same channel who are using the same tone.

What is DCS?

DCS, also known as Digital-Coded Squelch, is a system that fulfills a similar purpose to CTCSS, but it operates using digital codes rather than analog tones. DCS utilizes a 3-bit binary pattern to generate distinct digital codes, providing a wider array of choices in comparison to CTCSS. There are 104 standard codes available in DCS, which provides greater flexibility in selecting a distinct code. The radio will only open its squelch when it detects a signal with the correct digital code in DCS. This offers similar noise-reduction advantages as CTCSS, along with extra coding choices.

The Significance of Privacy Codes and Tones in GMRS

Privacy codes and tones are essential for enhancing the user experience on GMRS radios. Here are some of the main advantages:

1. **Minimized Interference:** Given that GMRS radios function on frequencies that are shared, interference can pose a significant challenge. Privacy codes and tones are essential for ensuring uninterrupted communication by effectively blocking out unwanted transmissions.
2. **Improved Clarity:** Using CTCSS or DCS allows for selective signal reception, minimizing unwanted noise and static interference. This results in communications that are clearer and easier to understand.
3. **Enhanced Privacy**: Although these codes cannot ensure absolute privacy, they do provide an additional level of selectivity. The communication between users is restricted to those with matching codes, which greatly minimizes the risk of eavesdropping by casual listeners.
4. **Enhanced Coordination**: When it comes to group settings like camping trips, neighborhood watches, or event coordination, using a shared privacy code can greatly contribute to the organization and efficiency of communication. Group members can easily share the same frequency without any interruptions from other users.

How to Use CTCSS and DCS in GMRS Radios

GMRS radios make it easy to use privacy codes and tones. Here is a clear and concise guide to help you set up CTCSS or DCS on your radio:

1. **Choose a Channel:** Begin by selecting a GMRS channel for your communication. It's important to keep in mind that GMRS radios have different channels for different purposes, so make sure to select one that aligns with your specific needs.
2. **Choose a Privacy Code or Tone**: When it comes to choosing a Privacy Code or Tone, it's important to consider your radio model. You have the option to select either a CTCSS tone or a DCS code. Refer to your radio's manual for a comprehensive list of the codes and tones that are at your disposal. Choose an option that is less commonly utilized by others in your vicinity.
3. **Set up the Code or Tone**: After choosing your privacy code, adjust your radio settings to use it. Typically, you'll need to navigate the radio's menu system and choose the correct option for CTCSS or DCS. It is important to ensure that the code is set consistently on all radios within your group.
4. **Test the Setup**: Once you've configured the privacy code or tone, it's important to verify the setup by transmitting and receiving messages with another radio. Make sure the squelch only opens when the correct code is detected.

5. **Monitor for Interference**: Be aware of potential interference: Despite having privacy codes, other users may be using the same code. If you come across any interference, it might be worth trying out a different code or tone.

Tips for Using Privacy Codes and Tones Effectively

For optimal use of privacy codes and tones in GMRS radios, it is advisable to keep the following best practices in mind:

1. **Collaborate with Your Group**: When utilizing GMRS radios in a group setting, it's important to make sure that everyone is in sync when it comes to channels and codes. Clear and effective communication is crucial for preventing misunderstandings.
2. **Steer clear of popular codes**: Certain privacy codes tend to be more widely used than others. If you happen to come across any interference or unwanted transmissions, consider opting for a less commonly used code. This will help minimize the chances of your conversations overlapping with others.
3. **Ensure Proper Channel Usage:** GMRS radios are equipped with designated channels for various activities, such as travel or business purposes. Choosing the appropriate channel for your activity can significantly minimize the chances of interference.
4. **Ensure Your Group's Understanding**: It is important to educate everyone in your group on how to properly set up and use privacy codes and tones. This promotes clarity and facilitates effective communication.
5. **Consider Using DCS for Increased Options**: If you find yourself in a densely populated area with numerous GMRS users, DCS can provide you with greater flexibility thanks to its extensive range of codes. If you're experiencing interference from CTCSS tones, you might want to consider using DCS.

Scanning and Monitoring

In GMRS, scanning involves a radio's capability to quickly cycle through a predetermined set of channels in search of any ongoing transmissions. This feature is extremely beneficial for users who wish to keep track of various frequencies or who need to swiftly locate ongoing conversations in a specific region.

GMRS scanning typically involves two primary modes:

1. **Channel Scanning**: The radio conveniently cycles through a list of channels that you've set, pausing whenever it detects a signal so you can easily listen in. After the transmission is complete, the scanner continues to cycle through the channels.
2. **Continuous Monitoring**: Unlike channel scanning, continuous monitoring allows for uninterrupted listening to a specific channel, making it ideal for focused attention on a single frequency.

Advantages of Scanning and Monitoring in GMRS

The scanning and monitoring features provide a variety of advantages for GMRS users:

- **Discovering Active Conversations:** Scanning is extremely useful for users who want to locate active channels, particularly in busy areas or during events where multiple groups are utilizing GMRS. This feature enables users to effortlessly switch to ongoing conversations without the need for manual channel adjustments.
- **Emergency Situations**: In times of crisis, the ability to scan multiple frequencies can be of utmost importance. Users can easily identify emergency transmissions or calls for help, enhancing safety and communication.
- **Coordinated Operations:** Scanning allows teams to efficiently check multiple channels to ensure all team members are connected and in communication during coordinated operations, such as search and rescue missions or event management.
- **Monitoring Activity:** Consistently keeping an eye on a specific channel proves beneficial in situations where it is crucial to concentrate on a particular communication stream, such as during a group camping trip or outdoor activity where staying connected with a base station is vital.

How Scanning Works

Scanning-capable GMRS radios are specifically engineered to quickly search for any ongoing transmissions on various channels. The scanning speed of the radio plays a crucial role in determining its effectiveness. Radios that have faster scanning speeds can swiftly detect active channels, whereas radios with slower speeds might overlook brief transmissions. Users can customize their radio settings to target specific channels or a limited range of frequencies while scanning. You have the freedom to customize your scanning experience according to your preferences, whether they want to scan all GMRS channels or just a few selected ones. In addition, certain radios provide priority scanning functionality, allowing for more frequent checks on a specific channel to ensure that no important transmissions are overlooked.

Enhanced Scanning Capabilities

GMRS radios have seen significant advancements in their scanning features, which greatly enhance their overall utility.
Here are some of the features:
- **CTCSS/DCS Scanning:** Numerous GMRS radios offer the capability to scan for Continuous Tone-Coded Squelch System (CTCSS) or Digital-Coded Squelch (DCS) signals. This feature enables radios to scan for both active channels and specific tone-coded squelch signals. These signals can indicate group-specific transmissions or private channels, providing enhanced functionality.

- **Priority Channels**: You can designate certain channels as priority channels. The radio will consistently monitor these channels while scanning, even if it's currently paused on another frequency. This feature is particularly helpful for users who want to remain connected to a specific frequency while also scanning others.
- **Dual-Watch Scanning:** Certain radios provide a dual-watch feature that enables users to monitor two channels at the same time. This feature is particularly beneficial for efficiently managing operations across various channels or when users require seamless communication between two distinct groups.
- **Scan Lockouts:** This feature allows users to selectively exclude specific channels from the scan, minimizing the chances of receiving unwanted transmissions or interference. This is especially helpful when working in busy environments where certain channels may be constantly in use because of other users or background noise.

Applications of Scanning and Monitoring in GMRS

GMRS radios are incredibly versatile due to their advanced scanning and monitoring features, making them suitable for a wide variety of applications:
- **Family Trips and Camping**: Scanning enables families on road trips or camping to stay connected. By scanning a set of predefined channels, families can ensure they stay connected and informed without any important information slipping through the cracks.
- **Event Coordination**: Scanning can be particularly useful for events that involve multiple teams and require seamless communication. The platform enables event organizers to stay connected with different groups and keep track of the overall communication landscape.
- **Emergency Preparedness:** Scanning is an incredibly useful tool for emergency preparedness. During a disaster or emergency, scanning enables users to swiftly identify active channels broadcasting emergency updates, ensuring they receive the latest information.
- **Outdoor Adventures:** Continuous monitoring is essential for groups participating in outdoor activities like hiking, hunting, or fishing, as it provides a safety net. The platform enables team members to maintain communication while exploring, ensuring the safety and whereabouts of everyone.

Integration with Other Radio Services

GMRS is a great option for localized communication, but there may be times when broader communication is preferred.
They include the following:
- **Emergency Situations**: During emergencies, effective communication with various radio services becomes crucial for coordinating responses and exchanging critical information.

- **Community Events**: Integrating different radio services can greatly enhance communication among volunteers, security personnel, and event organizers when organizing events that span a wide area.
- **Business Operations:** Companies that have a wide range of communication requirements might discover that incorporating GMRS with other radio services can improve efficiency and provide more flexibility.

In light of these scenarios, the importance of integrating GMRS with other radio services is growing more and more apparent.

Integration with FRS

FRS is a widely used radio service in the U.S., commonly utilized by families and for recreational activities. Similar to GMRS, FRS operates on UHF frequencies and does not require a license. GMRS and FRS can be integrated to some extent, but there are certain limitations imposed by FCC regulations.

Amateur Radio Integration

Amateur radio (ham radio) is a versatile radio service that is widely embraced by hobbyists, experimenters, and emergency communication operators. There are significant benefits to be gained from integrating GMRS and amateur radio, but it's important to be aware of the regulatory and technical challenges that come along with it.

Advantages of Integrating GMRS and Amateur Radio

- **Extended Communication Range**: Amateur radio operators have the advantage of an extended communication range, thanks to their access to a wider range of frequencies and more powerful equipment. Integrating with GMRS can significantly expand the communication range for both services.
- **Emergency Communication**: Amateur radio plays a vital role in emergency communication networks. Integrating with GMRS enables enhanced coordination in disaster response scenarios.
- **Technical Flexibility**: Amateur radio provides a wide range of technical options, enabling the use of advanced communication methods such as digital modes. This flexibility can be harnessed by integrating with GMRS to meet specific communication requirements.

Challenges and Limitations

They include the following:
- **Regulatory Compliance:** FCC regulations clearly distinguish between GMRS and amateur radio. Integrating the two services necessitates adherence to specific regulations, often involving the acquisition of additional licenses and technical expertise.

- **Technical Complexity:** Amateur radio requires a higher level of expertise in handling intricate equipment and configurations. Integrating with GMRS may require a certain level of technical expertise to ensure effective communication and adherence to regulatory requirements.
- **Limited Direct Integration**: Direct integration between GMRS and amateur radio is limited due to regulatory restrictions. Nevertheless, there are alternative methods available to enable communication between the two services, such as cross-band repeaters and radio gateways.

Integration with MURS

MURS is an unlicensed radio service in the U.S. that operates on VHF frequencies. Although MURS is not as widely used as GMRS and FRS, it provides distinct advantages. Combining it with GMRS can greatly enhance communication options.

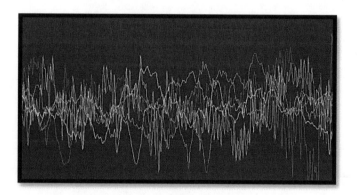

Advantages of Integrating GMRS-MURS

- **Different Frequency Bands**: MURS operates on the VHF frequency band, while GMRS operates on the UHF frequency band. The integration of the two services enables a wider range of communication across various frequency bands, offering enhanced redundancy and flexibility.
- **Unlicensed Accessibility:** Similar to FRS, MURS is unlicensed, allowing a wider range of users to access it. Integrating with GMRS can expand communication capabilities without the need for extra licensing.

Challenges and Limitations

They include:
- **Technical Differences**: Integrating MURS and GMRS can be a bit more complex due to the different frequency bands they operate on. This may require additional equipment such as cross-band repeaters or radio gateways.

- **Regulatory Compliance**: Users must ensure compliance with FCC rules, just like with other integrations. Respecting frequency allocations and power limits for each service is an essential part of compliance.
- **Limited Range**: MURS radios generally have a shorter coverage distance compared to GMRS radios. This is because MURS radios operate at lower power levels and use VHF frequencies, which have certain propagation limitations. It is important to take into account these limitations when planning communication networks.

GPS and Data Transmission Capabilities

In addition to GPS, advanced GMRS radios can transmit data, which greatly enhances their functionality beyond just voice communication. **Numerous new applications can be explored through data transmission.**

1. **Text Messaging**: GMRS radios equipped with data transmission capabilities allow for the exchange of text messages between devices. This feature is useful in situations where voice communication is not possible or when users require a discreet way to share information. Text messaging on GMRS radios can be used in situations where verbal communication may not be suitable or disruptive.
2. **Weather Alerts**: Stay informed about weather conditions with GMRS radios that have data transmission capabilities. These radios can receive weather alerts from external sources, giving you real-time updates. This feature is highly beneficial for individuals who enjoy outdoor activities, professionals who organize events, and those who work in emergency response. It enables them to stay well-informed and make informed decisions by taking into account the fluctuations in weather patterns.
3. **Telemetry Data:** Certain GMRS radios can transmit telemetry data, including battery levels, device status, or sensor readings. This capability can prove to be valuable in industrial or agricultural settings, where the need for remote monitoring of equipment or environmental conditions arises.
4. **Remote Control:** GMRS radios can be used for remote control applications through data transmission. You can operate drones, cameras, or other remote devices using their GMRS radios. This feature has proven to be extremely advantageous in the fields of photography, videography, and industrial inspections.

CHAPTER FIVE
SETTING UP GMRS RADIOS

Overview

This is the most important part of GMRS Radios, which is the process of setting it up. This chapter also emphasizes the need to set up a GMRS Repeater, how to operate frequencies and channels, GMRS Repeater maintenance, and others.

How to operate frequencies and channels

GMRS has a total of 22 standard channels, which are shared with FRS, along with some extra repeater channels. **Here's a comprehensive overview of the GMRS channels and frequencies:**

1. **Channels 1-7:** These channels are shared with FRS, but GMRS radios can operate with higher power on these frequencies (up to 5 watts), resulting in improved range and clarity.
2. **Channels 8-14:** They are dedicated to FRS use only and have limitations on power output. GMRS radios can be received on these channels, but transmitting is not possible.
3. **Channels 15-22:** They are designated specifically for GMRS use and have a higher power limit of up to 50 watts. These channels are perfect for long-distance communication and are frequently used for GMRS repeater operations.
4. **Repeater Channels:** GMRS repeater channels are used to enhance communication range by transmitting signals over longer distances. These channels operate within the 462 MHz to 467 MHz range and usually necessitate the use of extra hardware, such as a repeater setup.

Operating GMRS Radios: Key Considerations

When it comes to operating GMRS radios, there are several important factors to keep in mind:

1. **Licensing Requirements**: For GMRS users, it is necessary to obtain an FCC license that remains valid for ten years. This license provides coverage for an entire family, enabling multiple users to operate using just one license. The application process is easy to follow and can be done online through the FCC's Universal Licensing System (ULS).
2. **Power Limits**: GMRS radios have specific power restrictions depending on the channel in use. Channels 1-7 have a power limit of 5 watts, whereas channels 15-22 allow for a maximum of 50 watts. It's important to keep in mind that using higher power levels will decrease battery life. To ensure you're always prepared, it's a good idea to have spare batteries or a charging solution on hand.
3. **Repeater Operation:** GMRS repeaters can greatly enhance communication range, allowing for more effective communication. To utilize a repeater, it is essential to know

the repeater's frequency, tone, and offset. Accessing most GMRS repeaters typically involves the use of a CTCSS (Continuous Tone-Coded Squelch System) or DCS (Digital Coded Squelch) tone. Repeater offsets usually require transmitting on a frequency that differs from the receive frequency, ensuring the repeater operates correctly.

4. **Channel Selection**: It is important to carefully consider your communication needs and be mindful of not causing interference with other users when choosing a channel. It is advisable to check the channel for any ongoing transmissions before sending your message. Channels 15-22 are often less congested and can be a suitable option for communicating over longer distances.

How to set up a GMRS Repeater

You need to have a clear understanding of the regulatory landscape of GMRS in your country before you start. The Federal Communications Commission (FCC) regulates GMRS in the United States.

Here are a few important factors to keep in mind:

- **Licensing**: Operating a repeater requires a GMRS license. Currently, there is no test that you need to take, but you will need to apply for a license through the FCC. The license remains valid for ten years and provides coverage for your immediate family members.
- **Frequencies**: GMRS operates on specific frequencies in the UHF (Ultra High Frequency) band, typically ranging from 462 to 467 MHz. It is important to use the correct frequencies when setting up a repeater to prevent interference with other services.
- **Power Limits**: The FCC has established power limits for GMRS repeaters. A GMRS repeater has a maximum power output of 50 watts.

Make sure to thoroughly review all regulations before proceeding with the setup of a repeater.

Equipment Required for a GMRS Repeater

To set up a GMRS repeater, certain equipment is required. Presented below is a comprehensive list of the vital components:

1. **Repeater Station**: The repeater station serves as the central component of your setup.

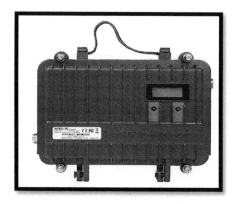

The device usually consists of a transceiver that can receive signals on one frequency and transmit them on a different frequency.

2. **Antenna System**: An antenna system is essential for optimal repeater operation, requiring a high-gain antenna. It would be best to install it at a high point to maximize coverage.

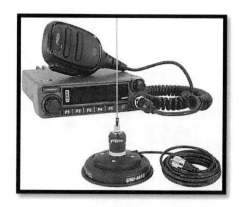

3. **Duplexer**: The duplexer is a device that enables the antenna to handle both transmission and reception at the same time, effectively separating the two frequency bands.

4. **Cabling and Connectors:** When it comes to cabling and connectors, it's crucial to prioritize quality. Opting for top-notch coaxial cables and connectors is a must to guarantee minimal signal loss and dependable connections.
5. **Power Supply:** A stable power source is necessary to ensure the repeater remains operational. It is advisable to have backup power, such as a generator or battery, in case of emergencies.
6. **Housing or Shelter**: If your repeater is installed outdoors, it is important to have a weather-resistant enclosure to safeguard the equipment.

Choosing the Perfect Spot for Your Repeater

The effectiveness of your GMRS repeater greatly depends on its location. Here are a few things to think about:

- **Elevation**: Maximizing antenna height improves coverage. Having a hilltop or tall building nearby can greatly enhance the repeater's range.
- **Consider accessibility**: Opt for a location that is convenient to reach for maintenance and troubleshooting purposes.
- **Power Source**: It is important to have a dependable power source at the location. If you're in a remote location, you might want to consider using solar panels or wind turbines to generate power.
- **Interference**: It is advisable to steer clear of areas with other radio transmitters or high-tension power lines, as they may lead to interference.

Setting up the Repeater

Once you have chosen the appropriate equipment and found the ideal location, you are ready to start the installation process.

Here are the steps to follow:

1. **Install the Antenna**: Place the antenna at the highest available spot and make sure it is firmly attached. Ensure the use of top-notch brackets and mounts to effectively minimize any potential movement during windy conditions.
2. **Connect the Duplexer:** Install the duplexer between the repeater and the antenna to connect them. The repeater can transmit and receive on different frequencies without any interference.
3. **Set up the Repeater Station**: Ensure the repeater station is properly set up by placing it in a weather-resistant enclosure if it will be located outdoors. Make sure to connect it to the duplexer and power supply.
4. **Connect the Power Supply**: Make sure the power source is reliable and can handle the power needs of the repeater. It would be advisable to consider incorporating a backup power source to ensure preparedness for unforeseen emergencies.

5. **Test the Repeater:** After making all the necessary connections, it is important to check if the repeater is working properly. Make sure to check the transmission range and ensure that there are no interference issues.

Once the installation is complete, the next step is to configure the repeater. Setting the correct frequencies, tones, and other parameters is essential.
Here is the step-by-step guide:
1. **Configure the Frequencies**: GMRS repeaters adhere to a consistent offset between the transmit and receive frequencies. The usual practice is to have a 5 MHz offset, where the receive frequency is lower than the transmit frequency. Make sure to set the appropriate frequencies to prevent any interference.
2. **CTCSS/DCS Tones Configuration**: Continuous Tone-Coded Squelch System (CTCSS) and Digital-Coded Squelch (DCS) are used to minimize interference caused by other repeaters. Configure these tones to ensure that only authorized users can access the repeater.
3. **Adjust Power Output:** Set the power output to a level that complies with regulations and ensures sufficient coverage. It's important to keep in mind that higher power levels can lead to interference.
4. **Emergency Alerts**: Certain GMRS repeaters can transmit emergency alerts or tones. If applicable to your setup, please configure these.

Testing and Troubleshooting

Now that everything is set up, it's time to put your GMRS repeater to the test. Presenting a fundamental testing checklist:
*   **Range Test:** Evaluate the communication range using various GMRS radios. Identify any areas where the signal strength is poor or non-existent.
*   **Interference Check**: Pay close attention to any interference or unwanted signals that may be present on your frequencies. Make sure to check for any issues and make necessary adjustments to your setup or frequencies if needed.
*   **User Communication Test:** Conduct a thorough evaluation of the repeater's communication capabilities by having multiple users engage in communication.
*   **Backup Power Test**: It is important to test your backup power source to ensure its functionality during power outages.

If you come across any problems during testing, here are some troubleshooting steps you can consider:
*   **Check Connections:** Make sure all cables and connectors are properly secured and in good condition.

*   **Review Configuration**: Take a second look at your frequency and tone settings to make sure they're accurate.
*   **Antenna Position:** If the signal strength is not optimal, you may want to consider adjusting the position or height of the antenna.

- **Power Supply**: Make sure the power supply is stable and capable of providing sufficient power.

GMRS Repeater Maintenance

Regular maintenance is crucial for ensuring the long-term durability and dependability of your GMRS repeater.

Here are a few suggestions to help you keep your setup in good condition:

- **Regular Inspections**: It is important to periodically inspect all components, such as the antenna, duplexer, cables, and power supply. Inspect for any indications of wear or damage.
- **Weatherproofing**: If your repeater is located outside, it is important to make sure that the enclosure is resistant to weather conditions and properly sealed.
- **Firmware Updates**: It is important to regularly update the firmware or software of your repeater to maintain its performance and security at the highest level.
- **Backup Power Maintenance**: Regularly testing your backup power source is crucial to ensure its reliability when it's needed.

Creating a Communication Plan

1. **Determine the Objective of Your Communication Plan**

Identifying the purpose is the initial step in creating a communication plan with GMRS. Consider the reasons behind your need for this communication network. Some common reasons include:
- **Emergency Preparedness**: Ensuring effective communication during natural disasters, power outages, or other emergencies.
- **Community Coordination**: Enhancing communication within a neighborhood or community group.
- **Family Safety**: Staying connected with loved ones during outings, camping trips, or other activities.

Understanding the objective of your plan will serve as a compass for your decision-making every step of the way.

2. **Get a GMRS License**

To operate GMRS radios within the bounds of the law, it is necessary to obtain a license issued by the FCC. The license remains valid for a decade and provides coverage for your entire family, encompassing your spouse, children, parents, and siblings. Here is a step-by-step guide to obtaining a GMRS license:
- **Create an FCC Account:** To create an FCC account, you can simply visit the FCC's website and follow the steps to create an account if you haven't done so already.
- **Submit a License Application**: Use the FCC's Universal Licensing System (ULS) to apply for a GMRS license. The application fee is approximately $70.

- **Receive your License**: Once your application is approved, you will be issued a license along with a distinctive call sign. It is necessary to use this call sign during radio communication.

3. **Choose Your GMRS Radios and Equipment**

After obtaining a GMRS license, the next crucial step involves choosing the right radios and equipment to suit your communication plan.

Take into account the following factors:

- **Range**: GMRS radios typically have a range of 1-5 miles, which can be further extended by using repeaters and external antennas.
- **Portability**: Handheld radios are ideal for communication on the move, while base stations provide extended power and range.
- **Features**: Consider radios that offer weather alerts, privacy codes, and a wide range of channels for versatile communication options.

Midland, Baofeng, and Motorola are among the top choices for GMRS radio brands. Make sure that the equipment you choose meets FCC regulations and has the required certifications.

4. **Establish Communication Channels**

GMRS radios provide a variety of channels for communication. For optimal communication without any disruptions, it is advisable to set up dedicated channels for various purposes. **Allow me to provide you with a suggested channel structure:**

- **Primary Channel**: Choose a primary channel for general communication.
- **Emergency Channel:** Dedicate a channel solely for emergencies.
- **Backup Channel:** Select an alternate channel if the primary channel is occupied or encountering interference.

It is crucial to ensure that all users of the GMRS network are informed about these channel assignments. It might be helpful to create a handy reference guide or laminated card that includes all the channel designations.

5. **Set Communication Protocols**

A successful communication plan depends on having well-defined protocols and procedures in place. It is crucial to establish guidelines for communication. **Here are some protocols to consider:**

- **Call Signs**: Remember to always use your GMRS call sign when communicating. It is important to promote the use of distinct identifiers to prevent any potential misunderstandings.
- **Radio Etiquette**: Learn the importance of proper radio etiquette, including clear communication, concise transmissions, and respectful listening.
- **Emergency Procedures**: Outlines the criteria for identifying emergencies and provides guidance on appropriate responses. Make sure to provide clear instructions on how to contact emergency services in case of any emergencies.
- **Regular Communication Drills**: It is important to conduct regular communication drills to ensure that everyone is well-prepared to use the radios and follow the protocols.

Clear protocols are crucial for smooth and successful communication, particularly in critical situations or times of heightened stress.

6. **Enhance Your Range with Integrated Repeaters**

Consider using repeaters to expand the reach of your GMRS communication network. A repeater is a device that receives radio signals and retransmits them, enabling communication over larger distances.

Here is a step-by-step guide on incorporating repeaters into your plan:

- **Selecting a Repeater Location**: Optimize the coverage of the repeater by locating it on a high point, such as a hill or tall building.
- **Obtain Permission**: Make sure you have the required permissions to install the repeater at your desired location.
- **Establish Repeater Frequencies**: GMRS has designated frequencies for repeater usage. Make sure your repeater is set to the appropriate frequencies to prevent any interference.
- **Test the Repeater**: After installation, it is important to verify that the repeater is functioning correctly and effectively extending your communication range.

Repeaters greatly enhance the reach of your GMRS network, enabling seamless communication over larger regions.

7. **Ensure regular maintenance and updates are implemented**

Maintaining and updating a communication plan with GMRS is crucial for its ongoing effectiveness.

Take a look at the following practices:

- **Equipment Checks**: It is important to regularly inspect radios and repeaters for any signs of wear or damage. Make any necessary replacements or repairs.
- **Software Updates**: Make sure to keep your radios or repeaters' firmware up-to-date for optimal functionality and security.
- **Training and Drills**: Regularly schedule training sessions and communication drills to ensure everyone remains knowledgeable about the equipment and protocols.
- **Review and Revise**: Regularly assess your communication plan to identify areas that can be enhanced. Make sure to update the plan as necessary to accommodate any changes in your group or environment.

Why is it compulsory to use a GMRS repeater

A GMRS repeater functions as a radio device that effectively boosts and extends the range of a GMRS transmitter by receiving, amplifying, and retransmitting the signal at a higher power or over a wider area. A repeater serves as a valuable tool for expanding the reach of GMRS radios, enabling seamless communication across vast distances or challenging terrains like buildings, hills, or dense forests. Repeaters are strategically positioned on high points such as mountaintops, towers, or tall buildings to optimize their coverage area.

Understanding the Significance of Range and Coverage

When GMRS radios are used in simplex mode, their range is limited as they can only transmit directly to another radio without any intermediary devices. The range can differ depending on various factors like terrain, obstacles, and radio power. In urban environments or areas with complex topography, the range of communication can be greatly diminished. A GMRS repeater overcomes this limitation by receiving the signal from a transmitting radio and retransmitting it at a higher power, effectively bridging the communication gap.

The extension of the range is essential for several reasons:

- **Safety and Emergency Communication**: In situations where safety is a concern, it is crucial to have dependable communication coverage across a wide area. GMRS repeaters allow users to stay connected with others, whether it's for coordinating emergency response or ensuring personal safety during outdoor activities.
- **Coordination and Efficiency**: GMRS repeaters offer a reliable communication network for businesses or groups that require coordination across large areas. They excel at facilitating coordination among teams, ensuring that everyone stays connected and informed.
- **Social and Family Connectivity**: GMRS repeaters provide a reliable means for families and social groups to stay connected during camping trips, road trips, or other outings. The connectivity fosters a sense of security and elevates the overall experience by enabling seamless communication for all.

Benefits of Using a GMRS Repeater

GMRS repeaters provide numerous benefits that make them a highly attractive option for a wide range of applications:

1. **Enhanced Communication Range**

GMRS repeaters greatly enhance the communication range of GMRS radios. This benefit is especially valuable for individuals who require communication over vast distances, like rural properties, agricultural lands, or outdoor recreational spaces.

2. **Enhanced Signal Clarity**

Repeaters can improve signal clarity by increasing the strength of the signal. This enhancement is particularly beneficial in urban settings where signal quality can be compromised by interference and obstacles. Using a GMRS repeater enhances communication by providing clearer and more reliable connections.

3. **Improved Dependability and Backup Systems**

When a GMRS repeater is added to a communication system, it enhances the network's strength and dependability. In situations where direct line-of-sight communication is interrupted, the repeater can serve as a reliable solution, ensuring uninterrupted communication by bridging the gap.

4. **Multiple User Support**

GMRS repeaters are specifically designed to accommodate multiple users at the same time, enabling seamless and effective communication within groups. This feature is extremely valuable for businesses, emergency response teams, and recreational groups that need to have coordinated communication among multiple individuals.

5. **Wide Range of Applications**

GMRS repeaters are incredibly versatile and adaptable, making them perfect for a wide range of applications. They have a wide range of applications, from personal use to commercial or public service purposes, and are commonly incorporated into larger communication networks.

Applications of GMRS Repeaters

GMRS repeaters find applications in a wide range of contexts, showcasing their versatility and usefulness.

Here are a few popular uses:

1. **Emergency and Public Safety**

Emergency response teams and public safety organizations rely on GMRS repeaters to ensure seamless communication during critical situations or when dealing with large-scale events. These repeaters are designed to ensure seamless communication for responders, even in the most demanding conditions.

2. **Exploring the Great Outdoors and Traveling**

Many families and groups find GMRS repeaters to be a valuable tool for staying connected during outdoor recreation or travel. Whether hiking in a national park or driving across the country in an RV, a GMRS repeater ensures a dependable communication network.

3. **Business and Industry**

GMRS repeaters are commonly used by businesses that operate across large areas or require coordination among teams to enhance communication. This application is widely used in industries like construction, transportation, and agriculture.

4. **Community and Social Groups**

GMRS repeaters are a valuable tool for community organizations and social groups to maintain communication during events or activities. This application emphasizes the importance of safety and encourages effective coordination among participants.

Regulatory Considerations

It is worth mentioning that GMRS repeaters in the United States are subject to regulatory requirements. The Federal Communications Commission (FCC) is responsible for regulating GMRS, and individuals are required to obtain a GMRS license to legally operate these radios or repeaters. The licensing process requires the submission of an application and payment of a fee. However, unlike certain other radio services, it does not entail a technical examination.

Advanced modulation schemes

To fully grasp the importance of advanced modulation schemes in GMRS, it is crucial to have a clear understanding of the role that modulation plays in radio communications. The process of encoding information into a carrier wave is known as modulation. Put simply, it entails modifying specific elements of a carrier signal, like its frequency, amplitude, or phase, to transmit data. The modulation scheme chosen has a significant impact on various aspects of the communication system. It determines the efficiency of data transmission, the clarity of the signal, and the system's ability to withstand interference and noise. GMRS systems typically use Frequency Modulation (FM) to encode data by varying the frequency of the carrier wave. FM is highly regarded for its ability to maintain signal quality even in the presence of noise and interference, making it a dependable option for GMRS communication. Nevertheless, with the rapid progress of technology and the growing need for greater communication bandwidth, there are more efficient modulation techniques available.

Advanced Modulation Schemes

Radio communication systems have seen the development of advanced modulation schemes to meet their changing requirements. These schemes prioritize the improvement of bandwidth efficiency, data rates, and signal clarity.

Presented below are a few instances of advanced modulation schemes that can significantly improve GMRS communications:

1. **Quadrature Amplitude Modulation (QAM):** QAM is a modulation scheme that combines amplitude modulation and phase modulation. The process entails modifying the amplitude and phase of a carrier signal to encode multiple bits of data. This technique is highly effective in achieving higher data rates and maximizing bandwidth efficiency, which has contributed to its widespread adoption in high-speed data communication. QAM has the potential to significantly improve the speed and effectiveness of communication in GMRS.
2. **Phase Shift Keying (PSK):** PSK is a modulation scheme that involves varying the phase of the carrier wave to transmit data. PSK comes in different variants, like BPSK and QPSK, which provide different levels of efficiency and data transmission rates. PSK offers superior noise and interference resistance in comparison to traditional FM, making it an ideal choice for GMRS applications that require clear signal quality.
3. **Orthogonal Frequency Division Multiplexing (OFDM):** This is a sophisticated modulation scheme that effectively splits a signal into numerous sub-carriers, allowing for separate modulation of each one. This technique enables the transmission of data at high rates, while also ensuring resilience against interference and multipath propagation. OFDM is widely used in modern communication systems such as Wi-Fi and LTE. OFDM in GMRS has the potential to improve bandwidth utilization and minimize signal fading.

Advantages of Advanced Modulation Schemes in GMRS

There are several significant benefits to be gained from adopting advanced modulation schemes in GMRS:

1. **Enhanced Data Rates**: Cutting-edge modulation schemes such as QAM and OFDM can facilitate higher data rates, allowing for the transmission of a greater amount of information within the given bandwidth. This can be particularly valuable in GMRS applications where data communication is crucial, such as in emergency response or business operations.
2. **Enhanced Signal Clarity**: PSK and other advanced modulation techniques provide increased resistance to noise and interference, resulting in clearer signals and fewer communication errors. Reliable communication is essential in GMRS, as it can have a significant impact on safety and business operations.
3. **Improved Bandwidth Use:** Advanced modulation schemes can enhance the utilization of available bandwidth, resulting in more efficient communication. Reduced congestion and improved spectrum management in GMRS can be achieved, especially in densely populated areas with limited radio frequency resources.
4. **Improved Resistance to Interference:** Advanced modulation schemes, such as OFDM, provide enhanced resistance to interference and multipath propagation. This is particularly useful in urban environments or areas with significant radio frequency interference.

Challenges and Considerations

Although GMRS can greatly benefit from advanced modulation schemes, it is important to be aware of the challenges and considerations associated with them:

1. **Regulatory Compliance**: GMRS is subject to regulations set by the Federal Communications Commission (FCC), which enforce strict guidelines on frequency usage and transmission power. It is crucial to adhere to these regulations when implementing advanced modulation schemes to prevent any potential interference with other radio services.
2. **Equipment Compatibility**: The use of advanced modulation schemes may necessitate the use of specialized equipment, resulting in potential cost increases for GMRS users. Ensuring a seamless transition to these new technologies requires compatibility with existing GMRS radios and infrastructure.
3. **Technical Complexity**: The implementation and troubleshooting of advanced modulation schemes often require specialized knowledge and expertise due to their greater technical complexity. For some GMRS users who are not familiar with advanced radio communication techniques, this can pose a challenge.

About Radio wave behavior and interference

The advent of radio communication has revolutionized human interaction, providing a medium for immediate exchange of information over vast distances. GMRS, also known as General Mobile Radio Service, is a highly popular communication system utilized for both personal and business communication purposes. Radio waves are a type of electromagnetic radiation that travels through the air at the speed of light. GMRS waves are generated by a transmitter, travel through the environment, and are received by a receiver.

Several factors influence the behavior of radio waves

1. **Frequency**: GMRS operates in the Ultra High Frequency (UHF) band, typically between 462 MHz and 467 MHz. The behavior of UHF waves in different environments is influenced by their shorter length compared to other radio frequencies. They excel in line-of-sight communication, although obstacles can pose a challenge.
2. **Line-of-Sight:** Clear line-of-sight is crucial for UHF radio waves, such as those used in GMRS, to travel effectively. Signal obstruction can occur due to hills, buildings, or dense foliage. On the other hand, waves with lower frequencies, like those found in the High Frequency (HF) range, can curve around obstacles, resulting in increased coverage over longer distances.
3. **Reflection and Refraction**: Radio waves can bounce off various surfaces, including buildings, water, and terrain. It is important to note that this reflection has the potential to cause signals to travel in unexpected directions, which can result in interference or a decrease in signal quality. Radio waves change direction as they pass through different mediums, such as layers of the atmosphere, which is known as refraction. The behavior described can have an impact on the signal's path, potentially affecting communication in either a positive or negative way.
4. **Diffraction:** Radio waves can bend around obstacles when they encounter them. Diffraction can be advantageous in certain situations, enabling GMRS signals to reach receivers even when there are partial obstructions in the line-of-sight. Excessive diffraction can weaken the signal, which can cause communication problems.

Issues with GMRS Communication Interference

Interference poses a major obstacle in radio communication, affecting the quality of signals and compromising communication reliability. Various factors can impact GMRS, such as:

1. **Co-Channel Interference**: This occurs when multiple radio transmitters operate on the same frequency, resulting in signals overlapping and competing with each other. In highly populated regions, co-channel interference can pose a significant problem, resulting in decreased clarity and heightened noise levels.
2. **Adjacent-Channel Interference:** Adjacent-Channel Interference occurs when radio transmitters operate on frequencies that are close to each other. This can result in the signals bleeding into adjacent channels and causing interference. Interference of this nature is frequently encountered in urban areas due to the high concentration of radio devices close by.
3. **Electromagnetic Interference (EMI):** This is a phenomenon that arises when external electronic devices emit electromagnetic fields, causing disturbances in radio

communication. EMI can be caused by various sources such as power lines, electrical equipment, and electronic devices. EMI can lead to issues such as static, noise, or signal loss in GMRS communication.

4. **Intermodulation Interference**: This occurs when multiple signals combine, resulting in the generation of additional frequencies that were not part of the original transmission. When radio transmitters are closed, it can result in unpredictable signal behavior and potential communication issues.

5. **Environmental Interference**: Radio wave propagation can be affected by external factors such as weather conditions and atmospheric disturbances. Instances of inclement weather, such as heavy rain, fog, or strong winds, may impact the quality and range of GMRS signals.

Addressing Interference in GMRS Communication

For reliable GMRS communication, it is crucial to have a good understanding of the factors that cause interference and to implement effective strategies to minimize its impact.

Here are some ways to reduce interference and improve the quality of your GMRS signal:

1. **Frequency Allocation**: It is important to ensure that GMRS transmitters operate on designated frequencies with sufficient spacing between channels to minimize interference from other channels. Frequency planning is crucial, particularly in busy environments.

2. **CTCSS and DCS:** Continuous Tone-Coded Squelch System (CTCSS) and Digital-Coded Squelch (DCS) are techniques employed to eliminate undesired signals. Users can avoid interference from other devices operating on the same frequency by configuring radios with specific codes.

3. **Appropriate Antenna Placement**: The placement of the antenna is vital for effective signal propagation. Optimizing the placement of antennas in elevated locations or areas with fewer obstructions can enhance line-of-sight communication and minimize interference caused by reflections or diffraction.

4. **Shielding and Grounding**: Proper shielding and grounding of radio equipment are essential for mitigating electromagnetic interference. The impact of external electronic devices is minimized, resulting in improved signal integrity.

5. **Use of Repeaters**: Repeaters are used to expand the coverage of GMRS communication by receiving and retransmitting signals. This can be beneficial for overcoming obstacles and enhancing signal strength in difficult environments. It is important to strategically position repeaters to optimize coverage and minimize interference.

6. **Weather Considerations**: Having a good grasp of how weather affects radio wave propagation can assist GMRS users in devising effective communication strategies. For instance, refraining from communication during severe weather or adjusting antenna orientation according to atmospheric conditions can enhance signal quality.

Mastering the art of proper channel etiquette and protocols

GMRS is a popular choice for families, outdoor enthusiasts, and small businesses that need reliable communication over longer distances, thanks to its increased capability. Nevertheless, it is important to recognize that having more power also means having more responsibility. Users must follow certain protocols and etiquette to prevent any disruptions and ensure effective communication.

Getting a GMRS License

Before we dive into channel etiquette, let's take a moment to go over the licensing process. GMRS does not require a technical examination, unlike amateur radio. Instead, you will need to submit FCC Form 605 and the necessary fee to the FCC. The license, once obtained, remains valid for ten years. It extends to all immediate family members, granting them the privilege to operate on GMRS frequencies without the need for any additional licensing. Getting a GMRS license helps to ensure that users are responsible for their communications, which in turn reduces the chances of interference and misuse of the frequencies. The FCC also benefits from maintaining a record of active GMRS users, as it plays a crucial role in maintaining order within the radio spectrum.

Proper Etiquette for GMRS Channels

Effective communication on GMRS channels relies heavily on proper etiquette, as these channels are shared by multiple users. Here are some important guidelines to follow:

1. **Use Clear Language:** When communicating on GMRS, it is important to use language that is clear and concise. Use clear and concise language to ensure that your message is easily understood by everyone. Communicate using clear and straightforward language so that your message can be easily understood by everyone on the channel.
2. **Identify Yourself:** Remember to begin each transmission by clearly stating your identity or the name of your group. It is important for others on the channel to be able to identify the speaker and for accountability to be promoted. Consider using a straightforward identifier such as your call sign, name, or organization.
3. **Keep Transmissions Short**: It is important to keep transmissions short to avoid monopolizing a channel and preventing others from using it. It's important to be concise and focused in your messages, without any unnecessary distractions. Consider breaking longer messages into smaller segments for better communication.
4. **Ensure Correct Use of Call Signs**: It is important to use the appropriate call signs when identifying yourself or others. The FCC issues unique combinations of letters and numbers for GMRS call signs. Proper use of call signs is crucial for maintaining order on the channel and ensuring clear identification of speakers.

5. **Note Channel Protocol:** Certain GMRS channels have been assigned for specific purposes, such as emergency communication or repeater use. It is important to familiarize yourself with these designations and utilize the appropriate channels for your specific requirements. Refrain from using emergency channels for non-urgent conversations and kindly adhere to repeater protocols.

6. **Pause for a Moment:** Before sending your message, take a moment to listen and make sure the channel is free. Interrupting someone else's conversation is generally seen as impolite and can lead to misunderstandings. When someone is speaking, it's important to wait for a pause in their transmission before using your mic.

7. **Reminder about Channel Sharing**: GMRS channels are public and can be used by multiple users simultaneously. Be considerate of others and refrain from dominating the channel. When you're in a group, it's a good idea to use a private frequency or a repeater to reduce interference with other users.

8. **Proper Use of Repeaters**: Repeaters can greatly enhance communication range, but it is important to follow proper etiquette when using them. It is important to adhere to the guidelines provided by the owner and to be mindful of any usage restrictions when using a repeater. Please be considerate and mindful of the purpose of the repeater. Some repeaters are specifically designated for emergency use, so it's important not to monopolize them.

GMRS Protocols for Efficient Communication

Aside from proper etiquette, adhering to specific protocols can enhance the quality of communication on GMRS channels.

Here are a few commonly used protocols to consider:

1. **Ensure Signal Strength:** GMRS operates in the UHF band, which can be influenced by various factors such as terrain, weather, and obstructions. Before initiating a discussion, it is advisable to verify your signal strength to guarantee effective and uninterrupted communication. If you're having trouble with interference or weak signals, you might want to try relocating to a higher spot or making some adjustments to your antenna.

2. **CTCSS or DCS Tones**: CTCSS and DCS are effective methods for minimizing interference on GMRS channels. By adjusting the tone on your radio, you can block out transmissions from other users who are not utilizing the same tone. It can be quite useful when using repeaters or operating in crowded areas.

3. **Monitor Emergency Channels:** GMRS has specific emergency channels (channels 1-7) dedicated to urgent communication. If you're operating on these channels, it's important to remain vigilant for emergency traffic and prioritize those in need. It is important to refrain from using these channels for casual conversation or non-emergency communication.

4. **Adhere to Repeater Guidelines**: Repeaters come with their own set of rules that must be followed, such as time limits, identification requirements, and usage restrictions. Follow these guidelines to ensure a seamless experience for all users and prevent any disruptions. If you have any questions about the repeater's rules, feel free to reach out to the owner or consult online resources for assistance.

5. **Equipment Maintenance**: Clear communication relies on the proper maintenance of your GMRS equipment. Make it a habit to regularly check your radio, antenna, and accessories to ensure they are in optimal working condition. Ensure that contacts are clean, inspect for any signs of damage, and replace any faulty components as necessary.

CHAPTER SIX
GMRS RADIO WORKSPACE SETUP

Overview

Setting up your GMRS Radio workspace is just as important as setting up your GMRS Radio as well. This chapter takes us on a roller coaster ride to revealing the processing of making this a reality as well as properly tuning a GMRS Antenna and how to boost GMRS radio power.

Setting up GMRS Workspace Radio

The GMRS system is perfect for workplace settings like construction sites, manufacturing plants, or agricultural operations, as it enables communication over greater distances compared to FRS.

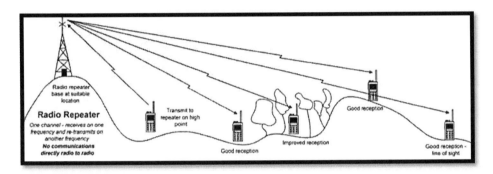

Step 1: Getting a GMRS License

To use a GMRS radio, it is necessary to acquire a license from the FCC. The license application is quite simple, and no exam is necessary. **Presenting a straightforward guide to obtaining your GMRS license:**

- **Check out the FCC Website**: Begin by visiting the FCC's Universal Licensing System (ULS) website. Sign up for an account if you haven't already, and then proceed to log in.
- **Complete the Application**: After logging in, navigate to the **"Apply for a New License"** section and select the **"ZA - General Mobile Radio (GMRS)"** option. Fill out the application form with your details.
- **License Fee Payment:** Once you have finished the application, a fee will be required for processing (currently approximately $35, but please note that this amount is subject to change). You have the option to make your payment online.
- **Receive your License**: Upon approval of your application and payment of the fee, you will be issued a GMRS license that remains valid for 10 years. The license extends to you and your immediate family members.

Step 2: Choosing the Appropriate Equipment

Once you have your license, the next important task is to choose the right GMRS equipment for your workspace.

Take into account the following factors when selecting your GMRS radios:

- **Type of Radios:** There are different types of radios available, including handheld, mobile, and base station formats. Handheld radios are convenient and perfect for communication while on the move. Mobile radios are specifically designed to be used in vehicles, while base stations are intended for fixed locations.
- **Communication Range:** The communication range of GMRS radios is influenced by various factors such as the terrain and environmental conditions. GMRS radios can communicate over several miles in open areas. The range may be shorter in urban or densely wooded areas.
- **Features**: Consider radios that offer a range of features to cater to your specific workspace requirements. These may include multiple channels, privacy codes, weather alerts, and VOX functionality for convenient hands-free communication.
- **Durability**: If you plan on using the radios in a challenging environment, it would be wise to opt for rugged and waterproof models.

Step 3: Setting up Communication Protocols

Now that you have your equipment ready, it's important to establish communication protocols to maximize the effectiveness and efficiency of your GMRS radios in the workspace. **Here are some guidelines to consider:**

- **Set Channels:** GMRS radios offer a variety of channels that can be designated for specific purposes. Take channel 1 for general communication and channel 2 for emergencies, for instance.
- **Using Privacy Codes:** Privacy codes, such as Continuous Tone-Coded Squelch System (CTCSS) or Digital-Coded Squelch (DCS), can effectively minimize interference caused by other radio users. Ensure a more streamlined communication experience by assigning distinct privacy codes to your channels, reducing the chances of receiving unwanted noise.
- **Establish Effective Communication Etiquette**: Ensure that your team is well-trained in proper radio communication etiquette. This includes using clear and concise language, identifying themselves before speaking, and keeping messages brief and focused.
- **Create Emergency Procedures**: Set up guidelines for handling emergencies. Make sure that all individuals are aware of the designated channel for emergencies and are knowledgeable about the appropriate actions to take during urgent situations.

Step 4: GMRS Radio Setup

After obtaining your license, acquiring the necessary equipment, and establishing communication protocols, it is now time to proceed with the setup of the GMRS radios in your workspace. **Here are the steps to follow for a seamless setup:**

- **Charge and Test Radios:** Ensure that the radios are fully charged and tested for functionality before distributing them to your team. Ensure proper functionality of radios by conducting a test communication to verify channel and privacy code settings.
- **Provide Radios and Accessories:** Provide radios to your team members along with any necessary accessories, like earpieces, belt clips, or carry cases. Make sure that all individuals are familiar with the correct operation of their radios.
- **Install Mobile Radios**: It is crucial to have mobile radios in vehicles installed by a professional or someone with experience to ensure proper installation. Ensuring proper installation is crucial for reliable communication and safety.
- **Establishing Base Stations:** When setting up base stations, it is crucial to identify an optimal location that allows for effective antenna placement, thereby maximizing the range of communication. Make sure to connect the base station to a power source and thoroughly test its functionality.

Step 5: Consistent Maintenance and Updates

It is essential to properly maintain your GMRS radios to ensure they last long and perform reliably. Here are some maintenance tips to consider:

- **Regular Inspections:** It is important to periodically check your radios for any signs of damage or wear. Replace any damaged components or accessories as necessary.
- **Revise Communication Protocols**: As your workspace changes, it is important to update your communication protocols to align with any modifications in workflow or personnel.
- **Recharge and Replace Batteries**: Rechargeable batteries have a finite lifespan. It is important to replace batteries when they no longer hold a charge effectively.
- **Training and Refresher Courses:** We conduct training sessions for new team members and periodic refresher courses for existing staff to reinforce communication protocols and emergency procedures.

Power source and battery management

GMRS radios utilize a variety of power sources, including disposable batteries and rechargeable battery packs. When deciding on a power source for the radio, it's important to consider the user's needs, budget and intended use.

Disposable Batteries

GMRS radios often rely on disposable batteries, like alkaline batteries, for their convenience. They are conveniently accessible, simple to replace, and have a lengthy shelf life. Handheld GMRS radios commonly use alkaline batteries due to their cost-effective performance. Nevertheless, the disposable nature of these products does raise valid environmental concerns regarding battery waste.

Rechargeable batteries

Rechargeable batteries offer a more sustainable option compared to disposable batteries. There are different chemistries available for these batteries, such as nickel-cadmium (NiCd), nickel-metal hydride (NiMH), and lithium-ion (Li-ion). Rechargeable batteries provide long-term cost savings since they can be recharged multiple times. GMRS radios commonly use rechargeable battery packs, offering a more environmentally friendly and economical power option.

Nickel-Cadmium (NiCd) Batteries

At one point, NiCd batteries were widely favored as a reliable option for rechargeable power. These devices have a strong build and can endure numerous charge cycles. On the other hand, NiCd batteries can experience a memory effect, resulting in a loss of capacity if they are not fully discharged before recharging.

Additionally, older battery technologies have a lower energy density compared to newer ones and pose environmental and disposal concerns due to the presence of toxic cadmium.

Nickel-Metal Hydride (NiMH) Batteries

NiMH batteries are a significant upgrade from NiCd batteries. They have a higher energy density and do not experience the memory effect, which makes them easier to maintain. NiMH batteries have a lower environmental impact and are less toxic compared to NiCd batteries.

Nevertheless, there is a possibility of experiencing some capacity loss over time and needing regular maintenance to uphold their performance.

Lithium-Ion (Li-ion) Batteries

Li-ion batteries are highly advanced rechargeable batteries that are widely used for GMRS radios. They possess an exceptional energy density, enabling extended battery life within a compact design. Li-ion batteries are not affected by the memory effect and have a lower self-discharge rate, which makes them perfect for portable devices. Li-ion batteries may have a higher initial price, but their exceptional performance and long lifespan make them a worthwhile investment. Li-ion batteries have safety concerns, particularly regarding overcharging and thermal runaway. However, modern safety features effectively address these risks.

Best Practices for Managing Batteries

For optimal battery life and reliable performance of GMRS radios, it is crucial to implement effective battery management techniques.

Here are some tips for optimizing battery life in GMRS devices:

- **Charging Your Device Correctly**

It is important to use the appropriate charger for the specific battery type when charging rechargeable batteries. It is important to avoid overcharging, as this can cause damage to the battery and shorten its lifespan. There are chargers available with built-in safety features to prevent overcharging, while others may require manual monitoring. It is crucial to charge batteries in a properly ventilated area to avoid any risk of overheating.

- **Preventing Deep Discharges**

It is important to note that NiCd batteries require complete discharges to prevent the memory effect, whereas Li-ion and NiMH batteries should not be deeply discharged. It's important to avoid deep discharges as they can harm the batteries and decrease their overall capacity. Recharging Li-ion batteries when they reach around 20-30% capacity is recommended for maintaining their longevity.

- **Proper Storage of Batteries**

Storing batteries correctly can help prolong their lifespan. It is important to store rechargeable batteries in a cool and dry location, away from direct sunlight. To ensure optimal storage conditions for longer periods, it is recommended to store Li-ion batteries at approximately 40-50% capacity. This helps prevent any potential degradation. It is recommended to remove batteries from GMRS radios when not in use for extended periods to prevent leakage or damage to the device.

- **Regular Maintenance**

It is important to regularly maintain batteries to ensure they remain in the best possible condition. Periodic conditioning of NiMH batteries can help restore their capacity. Li-ion batteries generally require minimal maintenance, although it is important to periodically inspect them for any indications of swelling or damage. It is important to promptly replace a battery that shows signs of damage or reduced performance to ensure the safety of the GMRS radio and the user.

- **Using Power-Saving Features**

GMRS radios often include power-saving features like automatic power-off and adjustable transmit power levels. Using these features can effectively preserve battery life when there is minimal activity. Lowering the transmit power level during short-distance communication can help conserve battery life.

- **Bringing Along Extra Batteries**

It is highly recommended to have spare batteries or a portable power bank for longer outdoor trips or in case of emergencies. Continued communication is guaranteed even in the event of a depleted primary battery. Make sure to check if the power bank is compatible with the charging requirements of the GMRS radio.

How to integrate GPS and location services

The Global Positioning System (GPS) is a reliable satellite-based navigation system that offers accurate location and time information, regardless of weather conditions, anywhere on or near the Earth. The integration of GPS with GMRS allows users to accurately determine their location and easily share it with others in real-time. This combination is especially valuable in outdoor settings, where traditional navigation methods may be less dependable.

Exploring the Potential of GMRS with GPS

Integrating GPS with GMRS offers numerous practical applications, such as:

1. **Outdoor Recreation**: Hikers, campers, and off-roaders can use GMRS radios with GPS to easily share their locations and navigate through remote areas with confidence. This integration enhances navigation and facilitates group cohesion.
2. **Emergency Response:** When it comes to emergencies, the coordination of first responders and search-and-rescue teams is crucial. That's why they rely on GMRS radios with GPS to effectively communicate and work together. This integration enables users to easily monitor their movements and effortlessly share location data, thereby enhancing the efficiency of search and rescue operations.

3. **Family Communication**: Using GMRS radios during outdoor activities can be enhanced with GPS integration, allowing families to easily track each other's locations and ensure everyone stays within a safe range.

Integrating GPS with GMRS

GPS integration with GMRS requires both hardware and software components. Here is a suggested approach for tackling this integration:

1. **Hardware Integration**: For seamless hardware integration, it is essential to have GMRS radios equipped with GPS receivers or external GPS modules that can easily connect to GMRS radios. Modern GMRS radios now include GPS capabilities, enabling users to easily share their locations through text or voice messages.

- **GPS Functionality**: Certain GMRS radios come equipped with built-in GPS, enabling users to easily track their locations and share them with others. The radios commonly include a display screen that provides the user with information about their location, altitude, and speed.

- **External GPS Modules**: In case your GMRS radio lacks a built-in GPS, an external GPS module can be used. These modules can connect to GMRS radios either through Bluetooth or wired connections, allowing for the transmission of GPS data to the radio.

2. **Software Integration**: After the hardware setup, the next crucial step involves incorporating GPS functionality into the software of the GMRS radio. This integration can include proprietary software from the radio manufacturer or third-party applications specifically designed for GPS and GMRS communication.

- **Manufacturer Software:** Certain GMRS radios are equipped with exclusive software that enables users to handle GPS data and customize communication settings. This software provides a range of useful features, including mapping, location sharing, and waypoint tracking.

- **Third-Party Applications**: Numerous third-party applications offer the ability to seamlessly integrate GPS with GMRS. These apps are compatible with smartphones or tablets and can connect to GMRS radios using either Bluetooth or wired connections. The app provides a range of advanced features, including real-time location sharing, route planning, and geofencing.

Tips for Seamlessly Combining GPS and GMRS

For a smooth integration of GPS and GMRS, it is important to keep in mind the following best practices:

- **Make the Right Hardware Choice**: Opt for GMRS radios that come with built-in GPS or are compatible with external GPS modules. Take into account factors such as range, battery life, durability, and any additional features.

- **Ensure Compatibility**: Make sure to check the compatibility of any external GPS modules or third-party applications with your GMRS radios. Make sure to regularly check for software and firmware updates to ensure compatibility.
- **Secure Data Transmission**: When sharing location data, it is crucial to prioritize the security of communication to prevent any unauthorized access. Ensure the safeguarding of sensitive information by implementing encryption and employing various security measures.
- **Ensure Software is Up to Date:** It is important to regularly update the software of your GMRS radio and any associated applications. By keeping your system up to date, you can benefit from the most recent features, bug fixes, and security patches.
- **Test before Use**: Before using your GMRS radios with GPS integration, it is crucial to test them to ensure they are functioning properly. Make sure you can easily share location data and communicate efficiently.
- **Be aware of Regulatory Requirements**: Make sure to adhere to FCC regulations for GMRS use and GPS integration. It is important to acquire the required licenses and follow the prescribed communication protocols.

How to properly tune a GMRS Antenna

The tuning of an antenna greatly affects its performance. The antenna must be properly tuned to ensure resonance at the desired frequency, which enables optimal signal transfer between the radio and the antenna. These factors contribute to enhanced transmission and reception, minimized signal loss, and an overall improvement in communication.

Tools and Equipment

To properly tune a GMRS antenna, specific tools and equipment are required. Here are some of the necessary items needed:

1. **Standing Wave Ratio (SWR) Meter**: An SWR meter is used to measure the ratio of reflected transmitted power, which is an important metric for tuning antennas.
2. **Antenna Analyzer**: The Antenna Analyzer provides a thorough analysis of the antenna's performance, covering impedance and resonance.
3. **Coaxial Cable and Connectors**: It is crucial to use high-quality coaxial cable to minimize signal loss. Additionally, selecting the appropriate connectors is important to ensure proper connections between the radio, antenna, and tuning equipment.
4. **Adjustable Antenna**: GMRS antennas can be adjusted for precise tuning. If your antenna cannot be adjusted, you might have to consider making some modifications or choosing an alternative antenna.

Tuning a GMRS Antenna

Here are the steps to tune a GMRS antenna

Step 1: Set Up the Equipment

- **Properly Position the Antenna**: It is important to securely mount the antenna in its intended operating position. This will effectively replicate real-world conditions.
- **Connect the SWR Meter:** Position the SWR meter in the pathway connecting the radio and the antenna. To properly connect the radio, make sure to connect its output to the **"Transmitter"** port on the SWR meter. Then, ensure that the antenna is connected to the **"Antenna"** port.
- **Turn On the Radio**: Begin by setting the radio to a GMRS frequency, ideally in the middle of the frequency range (around 465 MHz), to initiate the tuning process.

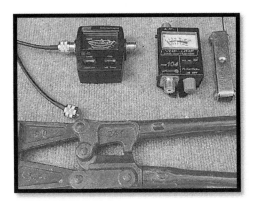

Step 2: Measure the SWR

- **Send a Signal:** Activate the radio and send a signal while monitoring the SWR reading on the meter. A lower SWR suggests improved tuning.
- **Verify the Reading:** Ideally, the SWR should be as close as possible to 1:1, indicating very little reflected power. If the SWR reading is above 2:1, it indicates that some adjustments may be needed for the antenna.

SWR Reading	% OF LOSS	ERP*	Power Output in Watts	Power Loss in Watts
1.0:1	0.0%	100.0%	100.00	0.0
1.1:1	0.2%	99.8%	99.8	0.2
1.2:1	0.8%	99.2%	99.2	0.8
1.3:1	1.7%	98.3%	98.3	1.7
1.4:1	2.8%	97.2%	97.2	2.8
1.5:1	4.0%	96.0%	96	4.0
1.6:1	5.3%	94.7%	94.7	5.3
1.7:1	6.7%	93.3%	93.3	6.7
1.8:1	8.2%	91.8%	91.8	8.2
2.0:1	11.1%	88.9%	88.9	11.1
2.2:1	14.1%	85.9%	85.9	14.1
2.4:1	17.0%	83.0%	83	17.0
2.6:1	19.8%	80.2%	80.2	19.8
3.0:1	25.0%	75.0%	75	25
4.0:1	36.0%	64.0%	64	36
5.0:1	44.4%	55.6%	55.6	44.4
6.0:1	51.0%	49.0%	49	51
7.0:1	56.3%	43.8%	43.8	56.3
8.0:1	60.5%	39.5%	39.5	60.5
9.0:1	64.0%	36.0%	36	64
10.0:1	66.9%	33.1%	33.1	66.9

Step 3: Fine-tune the Antenna

- **Lengthen or Shorten the Antenna**: Adjusting the length of the antenna can help address high SWR levels. The resonant frequency of an antenna can be affected by its length. A shorter antenna tends to have a higher resonant frequency, while a longer antenna tends to have a lower resonant frequency. Make small adjustments to prevent over-tuning.

- **Double-check the SWR:** Once you've made the necessary adjustments, it's important to measure the SWR again to determine if the tuning has been enhanced. Keep repeating this procedure until you reach an SWR that is as close to 1:1 as you can get.
- **Optimize for Multiple Frequencies**: Ensure the SWR of the antenna remains within acceptable limits across the entire range of GMRS frequencies if you plan to use it across multiple frequencies.

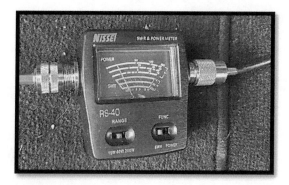

Step 4: Ensure the Antenna is Secure
- **Tighten All Connections**: Ensure all connections are tight and secure after completing the tuning process. Properly established connections are crucial for maintaining signal integrity and optimal performance.

- **Ensure Mount Stability:** Inspect the antenna mount for stability and tighten any bolts or screws if necessary.

Understanding what SWR is about and how to set GMRS Radio SWR

Understanding the Standing Wave Ratio (SWR) is crucial in radio communication, especially for individuals using General Mobile Radio Service (GMRS) equipment. Put simply, SWR quantifies how effectively power is transmitted from a radio transmitter to its antenna. When the SWR is good, it means that the RF energy from the transmitter is effectively reaching the antenna. On the other hand, a poor SWR indicates that a considerable amount of energy is being reflected in the transmitter. SWR, or Standing Wave Ratio, is a measure that helps determine the level of reflected power in a radio transmission system. The text discusses the comparison between the forward power and the reflected power, highlighting their significance in terms of energy transmission and potential inefficiencies. A SWR of 1:1 signifies ideal matching, with complete power transmission and no reflection. However, higher SWR values can indicate more reflection, resulting in lower signal quality, shorter transmission range, and potential damage to the transmitter over time.

What is the Significance of SWR?

The significance of SWR cannot be understated. First and foremost, it has a direct impact on the performance of the radio system. Having a low SWR is crucial for optimal performance as it allows the transmitter to efficiently deliver energy to the antenna. This leads to stronger signals and an improved communication range. Additionally, a high SWR can lead to potential harm to the radio's transmitter. When energy is reflected, it has the potential to overheat the transmitter's components, leading to potential permanent damage. Additionally, maintaining an optimal SWR is crucial for meeting regulatory standards, as excessive reflected power can potentially disrupt other communication systems.

Reasons for High SWR

Multiple factors can contribute to a GMRS radio system experiencing high SWR:

- **Antenna Mismatch:** One of the most common causes is when the transmitter's impedance does not match the impedance of the antenna. The antenna for GMRS radios must match the 50-ohm impedance typically used in these systems.
- **Faulty Connections**: Loose or corroded connections between the transmitter, coaxial cable, and antenna may result in reflections.
- **Damaged Coaxial Cable**: In the unfortunate event that the coaxial cable sustains damage or has subpar shielding, it may result in reflections.

- **Antenna Placement**: Improperly positioning the antenna or placing it close to metal structures can result in an increased SWR.

Measuring SWR

To measure SWR, you will require the use of an SWR meter. This device is positioned between the transmitter and the antenna, enabling you to accurately measure both the forward and reflected power.

Here is a detailed guide on how to measure SWR on a GMRS radio system:

1. **Switch off the radio:** Prioritizing safety. Make sure to turn off the radio before making any connections.
2. **Connect the SWR Meter:** Place the SWR meter in line with the transmitter and the antenna. Attach the transmitter to the "**TX**" port on the meter, and connect the antenna to the "**ANT**" port.
3. **Choose a frequency to test:** Select the frequency. Testing across a range of frequencies within the GMRS band is recommended for consistent performance.
4. **Set the SWR Meter**: Ensure the radio is turned on and follow the instructions provided to set up the SWR meter. Usually, this requires establishing a benchmark for the forward power.
5. **Measure SWR:** To measure SWR, simply key the radio's microphone to transmit and read the SWR value on the meter. An optimal SWR should be below 2:1, with 1:1 being the desired goal.
6. **Test across Frequencies:** Testing SWR across a range of frequencies within the GMRS band is crucial for achieving optimal performance.

Reducing SWR

If you discover that your SWR is too high, there are a few measures you can take to lower it:

- **Check Connections:** Make sure all connections are secure and free from any signs of corrosion. Make sure to re-seat any connectors if necessary.
- **Check the Coaxial Cable**: Take a close look at the cable to identify any signs of damage or inadequate shielding. If needed, replace it.
- **Adjusting the Antenna**: If the antenna is adjustable, you might need to fine-tune its length or position. Occasionally, making adjustments to the antenna's angle or height can greatly enhance SWR.
- **Use a Different Antenna**: Consider replacing your current antenna with one that is designed for GMRS frequencies or of higher quality.
- **Optimize Antenna Placement**: Make sure the antenna is positioned in a clear area, away from any metal structures, and ideally mounted at a higher elevation.

How to boost GMRS Radio Power

The use of GMRS radios in the United States is regulated by the Federal Communications Commission (FCC). As per FCC guidelines, GMRS radios are allowed to operate at a maximum power output of 50 watts. The power output of FRS radios, which is limited to 2 watts, is considerably lower in comparison. It is important to adhere to the regulatory limits when operating GMRS radios to avoid any potential fines or legal complications, despite the flexibility they offer.

Deciding on the Perfect GMRS Radio

For optimal performance and extended coverage, it is important to choose a GMRS radio that is specifically engineered to deliver maximum power and range. Consider searching for radios with a higher wattage capacity, as this can enhance the range and signal strength. Midland, Motorola, and Uniden are well-known brands that offer a range of GMRS radios with different power levels, giving you the flexibility to select the one that fits your requirements. **When choosing a GMRS radio, it's important to take into account various features:**

- **Power Output**: Choose radios with higher wattage that stay within legal limits.

- **Antenna Quality**: The quality of the antenna plays a crucial role in determining the range and signal clarity.
- **Increased Channels and Privacy Codes**: The availability of more channels and privacy codes provides users with enhanced flexibility and minimizes the chances of interference.
- **Weather Resistance**: When using radios outdoors, it's important to choose models that are resistant to water and dust.

Upgrading the Antenna

Upgrading the antenna is a highly effective method for increasing GMRS radio power. The antenna is an essential component for signal transmission and reception, and an upgraded antenna can greatly enhance the range and clarity of the signals.

Take into account the following factors when upgrading your GMRS radio antenna:

- **Consider the Length and Gain**: Opting for a longer antenna with higher gain can enhance signal strength and expand the range. Make sure to search for antennas that are specifically designed for GMRS frequencies to ensure they are compatible.
- **Antenna Placement**: Placing the antenna at a higher position can improve the reach of the signal. For optimal performance when using a mobile GMRS radio in a vehicle, it is recommended to mount the antenna on the roof or a similar elevated location.
- **External Antennas**: Certain GMRS radios offer the option to connect external antennas, which allows for greater flexibility in selecting the antenna. Mounting external antennas on masts or towers is recommended to achieve maximum height and range.

Using a Repeater System

GMRS radios can use repeaters, which greatly enhance the range of communication. A repeater serves as a station that effectively boosts the power of signals received from a GMRS radio, enabling communication to extend over larger distances. Repeaters are frequently used by GMRS radio enthusiasts to establish networks for community or emergency communication.

Learn how to effectively enhance the power of your GMRS radio with a repeater system:

- **Locating a Repeater**: Discover GMRS repeaters in your vicinity. There are websites available, such as myGMRS.com that provides a comprehensive list of repeaters located throughout the United States. Make sure to obtain the necessary authorization to use the repeater, as certain ones may require membership or specific access codes.
- **Programming Your Radio**: Set up your GMRS radio to establish communication with the repeater. Setting the correct frequency, tone, or access code is crucial in this process. Refer to the user manual of your radio for detailed instructions.

- **Proper Etiquette for Using a Repeater**: When using a repeater, it is important to adhere to the appropriate etiquette. Introduce yourself and follow any guidelines established by the owner or group of the repeater. Refrain from engaging in unnecessary conversations and show consideration for other users.

Reducing Interference

Interference can have a significant impact on the performance of GMRS radios. To maximize power and range, it is crucial to minimize any potential interference caused by electronic devices, structures, or natural obstacles.

Here are a few suggestions to help minimize interference:

- **Avoiding Obstructions**: Ensure that your GMRS radio and antenna are positioned away from any potential obstacles such as large buildings, metal structures, or dense foliage. These obstacles have the potential to weaken signals and limit the range.
- **Channel Selection:** Opt for less crowded channels to minimize interference from other GMRS users. It's important to keep in mind that certain channels have specific purposes and should be used accordingly.
- **Weather Considerations:** Radio signals can be influenced by various weather conditions, including rain, fog, or atmospheric disturbances. Take note of these factors and adapt your communication strategy accordingly.

How to Maintain Your GMRS Radio

Proper maintenance is essential for optimal performance of your GMRS radio. Maintaining the radio and its components is crucial for optimal power output and signal quality.

Here are some maintenance practices to consider:

- **Battery Maintenance**: Regularly monitor battery levels and recharge or replace them as necessary. Insufficient battery power can harm the performance of your radio, affecting both its power and signal strength.
- **Cleaning**: It is important to maintain the cleanliness of your GMRS radio and antenna to ensure optimal performance and prevent any issues caused by dirt or debris. It is advisable to use a gentle cloth when cleaning the radio to prevent any potential damage caused by harsh chemicals.
- **Software Updates**: Certain GMRS radios may need software updates to ensure they perform at their best. Make sure to visit the manufacturer's website to see if there are any updates available. Follow the provided instructions to install them.

Legal Compliance

It is important to always adhere to FCC regulations when increasing the power of GMRS radios. Failure to comply with these regulations may lead to penalties, seizure of equipment, or potential legal ramifications.

When optimizing GMRS radio performance, it is important to:

- **Adhere to Power Limits**: Ensure that you do not surpass the maximum power output permitted by the FCC. Amplifiers or other devices that artificially enhance power are used in this.
- **Operate with Licensed Equipment**: It is important to note that GMRS radios must be used with a proper license to ensure legal operation. Make sure you have the correct license and follow its terms.
- **Adhere to Privacy and Etiquette**: It is important to follow GMRS communication rules and show respect for the privacy of other users. It is important to refrain from using private frequencies without proper authorization or causing any disruptions to emergency channels.

Enhancing GMRS Radio Range

Upgrade to High-Gain Antennas

The antenna plays a vital role in the functionality of every radio system. High-gain antennas can greatly enhance signal strength and extend the range of coverage.

Take into account the following factors when choosing an antenna:

- **Gain**: A higher-gain antenna allows for a more focused energy direction, resulting in an increased range in that specific direction. This is a helpful tool for communicating over long distances, although it may have some limitations in terms of coverage in certain directions.
- **Antenna Type**: Yagi and dipole antennas are commonly used to extend the range. Yagi antennas provide focused, long-range communication capabilities, while dipole antennas have a more widespread coverage.
- **Antenna Height:** The height of your antenna is a key factor in determining its range. By elevating your antenna, you can ensure unobstructed communication, enhancing line-of-sight connectivity.

Use Repeaters

Repeaters are incredibly useful for expanding the range of GMRS radios. The function of a repeater is to receive a signal and transmit it at a higher power level or from a more advantageous location, thereby enabling communication over greater distances.

Here are some helpful tips for using repeaters:

- **Location**: Place the repeater in an elevated area, like a hilltop or tall building, to optimize coverage.
- **Frequency Coordination**: Make sure your repeater operates on a frequency that avoids interfering with other radio systems.
- **Access Control:** Ensure that access controls are in place to prevent unauthorized use and maintain the repeater's efficiency.

Maximize Radio Settings

Making adjustments to your GMRS radio settings can also enhance its range. Here are some factors to take into account:

- **Power Level**: Many GMRS radios provide the option to adjust the power settings. For maximum range, it is recommended to use the highest power setting. It's important to keep in mind that using more power will result in a quicker drain on the battery. Therefore, it's crucial to find a balance between power consumption and battery life.
- **Squelch Control**: The Squelch Control feature effectively eliminates any background noise that may be present when there is no signal detected. Modifying squelch settings can enhance the clarity of the signal, although it may have an impact on the range. Discover the ideal configuration for your surroundings.
- **CTCSS/DCS Codes:** These codes are used to minimize interference from other radios that are operating on the same frequency. They are an effective way to ensure clear communication. These codes can help ensure effective communication while still maintaining a wide range of coverage.

Minimize Interference

Interference can have a substantial effect on the range of GMRS radios.

Here are some strategies to reduce interference:

- **Select Clear Frequencies**: Steer clear of frequencies that experience heavy traffic or interference from other radio systems. Conduct a frequency scan to determine the channels with the best signal quality.

- **Minimize Nearby Electronic Noise**: Ensure that radios are kept at a distance from electronic devices that may cause interference, such as computers, televisions, and other wireless devices.
- **Opt for Shielded Cables**: To minimize signal degradation, it is advisable to use shielded cables when connecting external antennas or repeaters.

Environmental Plan

The GMRS radio range is greatly influenced by the environment. Take into account these environmental factors and adjust accordingly:

- **Terrain**: Hills, mountains, and other natural obstacles may affect the range. Ensure optimal communication by positioning yourself and your antenna in a way that minimizes obstructions and maximizes line-of-sight.
- **Weather Conditions:** Rain, fog, and other weather conditions may impact radio signals. Take into consideration the potential impact of weather conditions on your communication range and make any necessary adjustments.
- **Urban Areas:** Signals can be affected by buildings and other man-made structures. When operating in an urban environment, it may be helpful to use higher-gain antennas or repeaters to overcome any obstacles you may encounter.

Enhance Your Radio Communication Practices

GMRS radio range can also be influenced by user practices. Here are some helpful tips for effective communication:

- **Ensure a Clear Line of Sight:** Whenever feasible, it is important to maintain an unobstructed line of sight between radios. Clear any obstacles and locate areas with good communication access.
- **Proper Radio Handling:** Ensure that you correctly hold the radio, with the antenna kept vertical and at a safe distance from your body. Signal strength can be diminished by improper handling.
- **Communication Protocol**: It is important to establish a clear communication protocol with other users to avoid confusion and ensure efficient communication.

CHAPTER SEVEN
GMRS ADVANCED FUNCTIONS

Overview

Chapter seven talks about GMRS's advanced functions such as CTCSS and DCS codes, group call features, and more.

CTCSS and DCS Codes

Methods such as the Continuous Tone-Coded Squelch System (CTCSS) and Digital-Coded Squelch (DCS) are used to regulate the signals that a radio responds to. They serve as filters that ensure a radio only opens its squelch when it detects a specific tone or digital code. The selective filtering feature enables multiple users to effectively share the same frequency without any interference, resulting in a significant reduction of unwanted noise and unnecessary chatter.

Understanding CTCSS

Standard CTCSS Tones			
No.	Tone	No.	Tone
1	67.0	26	156.7
2	69.3	27	159.8
3	71.9	28	162.2
4	74.4	29	165.5
5	77.0	30	167.9
6	79.7	31	171.3
7	82.5	32	173.8
8	85.4	33	177.3
9	88.5	34	179.9
10	91.5	35	183.5
11	94.8	36	186.2
12	97.4	37	189.9
13	100.0	38	192.8
14	103.5	39	196.6
15	107.2	40	199.5
16	110.9	41	203.5
17	114.8	42	206.5
18	118.8	43	210.7
19	123.0	44	218.1
20	127.3	45	225.7

CTCSS also referred to as **"sub-audible tones,"** uses analog tones to effectively filter radio communications. When CTCSS is enabled, a low-frequency tone is transmitted alongside your voice or data. The frequency of this tone usually falls between 67.0 Hz and 254.1 Hz. When radios are programmed with CTCSS codes, they will only open their squelch when they detect a tone that matches, enabling users to have private communication on a frequency that is shared. CTCSS is a widely used feature in two-way radios to enhance security measures. As an illustration, when two groups are using the same frequency, CTCSS enables them to maintain distinct conversations. Each group has the option to choose a unique CTCSS tone, which helps prevent their conversations from overlapping. This feature is especially valuable in settings with multiple radios, like construction sites, warehouses, or outdoor events.

Understanding DCS

DCS (Digital Code) TONE TABLE: 105 codes

No	Dcs Code	No	Dcs Code	No	Dcs Code	No	Dcs Code
01	023	31	165	61	356	91	627
02	025	32	172	62	364	92	631
03	026	33	174	63	365	93	632
04	031	34	205	64	371	94	645
05	032	35	212	65	411	95	654
06	036	36	223	66	412	96	662
07	043	37	225	67	413	97	664
08	047	38	226	68	423	98	703
09	051	39	243	69	431	99	712
10	053	40	244	70	432	100	723
11	054	41	245	71	445	101	731
12	065	42	246	72	446	102	732
13	071	43	251	73	452	103	734
14	072	44	252	74	454	104	743
15	073	45	255	75	455	105	754
16	074	46	261	76	462		
17	114	47	263	77	464		
18	115	48	265	78	465		
19	116	49	266	79	466		
20	122	50	271	80	503		
21	125	51	274	81	506		
22	131	52	306	82	516		
23	132	53	311	83	523		
24	134	54	315	84	526		
25	143	55	325	85	532		
26	145	56	331	86	546		
27	152	57	332	87	565		
28	155	58	343	88	606		
29	156	59	346	89	612		
30	162	60	351	90	624		

DCS, however, is a digital approach to squelch control. DCS utilizes a digital code to control the squelch, rather than sending a continuous analog tone. The digital code is significantly shorter and is composed of a sequence of bits that form a distinct pattern. The codes are more intricate than CTCSS, offering a wider array of potential combinations. DCS offers a wide range of codes, providing enhanced flexibility and security. This system is highly resistant to interference or accidental code matching, making it perfect for crowded radio environments where multiple users share the same frequency.

Applications of CTCSS and DCS in GMRS

Understanding CTCSS and DCS codes is crucial for maximizing the effectiveness and convenience of GMRS radios. **Here are some important applications of these codes in GMRS communications:**
 1. **Interference Reduction**
Interference can become a significant problem when multiple users share the same frequency. CTCSS and DCS codes enable users to create separate communication channels within the same frequency range. Through the use of various CTCSS tones or DCS codes, individuals can effectively prevent any disruptions caused by other radio users, thus guaranteeing a seamless and uninterrupted communication experience.
 2. **Privacy and security**

GMRS radios operate on public frequencies, but the use of CTCSS and DCS adds an extra level of privacy and security. Setting unique codes allows users to ensure that only radios with matching codes can hear their transmissions. This feature is especially beneficial for families or small businesses seeking to uphold a certain degree of privacy in their communications.

3. **Community Events and Recreational Use**

CTCSS and DCS codes are extremely useful for community events, outdoor activities, or group outings. They facilitate effective communication and coordination among various teams or groups, promoting clarity and organization. For instance, during a big family camping trip, various CTCSS tones can be utilized for different activities like hiking, fishing, and cooking. This ensures effective communication without any interference.

4. **Emergency Preparedness and Coordination**

During emergencies, effective communication is essential. Clear communication channels are crucial for emergency response teams, especially in busy radio environments. CTCSS and DCS codes play a vital role in ensuring this clarity. Emergency response units often utilize distinct codes to prevent any confusion and maintain clear communication among their teams, free from interference from other responders or public radio users.

Adjusting CTCSS and DCS Codes on GMRS Radios

GMRS radios typically offer the option to configure CTCSS and DCS codes for both transmitting and receiving. Typically, you would access the radio's menu system and choose the desired code from a list of available options.

Configuring CTCSS Codes

Setting a CTCSS code usually involves the following steps:

1. Explore the radio's menu or settings.
2. Find the CTCSS option in the menu.
3. Choose the preferred CTCSS tone from the list of frequencies provided.
4. Proceed to confirm your selection and exit the menu.

Once configured, the radio will exclusively recognize transmissions that include the corresponding CTCSS tone, effectively disregarding any other signals.

Configuring DCS Codes

Setting DCS codes follows a similar process to CTCSS:

1. Find the menu or settings on the radio.
2. Locate the DCS option.
3. Select the DCS code you want from the list of available codes.
4. Proceed to confirm your selection and exit the menu.

With DCS enabled, the radio will only respond to transmissions that include the corresponding digital code. This feature guarantees clear and interference-free communication.

Factors to Keep in Mind

Although CTCSS and DCS codes are quite effective in minimizing interference and ensuring privacy, it is important to be aware of their limitations:

1. **Not a Security Guarantee**: CTCSS and DCS do not provide encryption for transmissions. They simply serve as filters for squelch control. Transmissions can be intercepted by anyone who has a scanner or a radio set to the same frequency, regardless of whether they possess the correct code.
2. **Limited Number of Codes**: There is a finite number of available combinations for the codes offered by CTCSS and DCS, despite their range. In crowded radio environments, it is possible for users to accidentally choose the same code, which can result in interference.
3. **Compatibility**: Some GMRS radios do not offer support for both CTCSS and DCS codes. Compatibility with other radios may be affected if older models only support one or the other.

Scanning Modes and Features

Scanning is an essential feature in GMRS radios that enables users to efficiently monitor multiple channels or frequencies. **Scanning modes prove to be highly beneficial for users who want to efficiently manage multiple conversations or monitor the GMRS spectrum for any activity.**

- **Channel Scanning**: This mode effortlessly cycles through pre-programmed channels, pausing when it detects an active transmission. Channel scanning is perfect for users who wish to keep an eye on multiple channels for any communication activity. It is frequently utilized by groups who need to coordinate across multiple channels or when monitoring emergency frequencies.
- **Priority Channel Scanning**: Users can easily designate a specific channel as a priority with this convenient feature. During scanning, the radio will regularly monitor the priority channel, even if it is currently tuned to a different active channel. This is a helpful way to stay informed about a central communication channel while also keeping an eye on other channels for any activity.
- **Dual-Watch Scanning**: This mode allows users to monitor two channels at the same time. This feature is especially beneficial for individuals who need to stay connected on one channel while also monitoring another. This mode is frequently utilized in situations that require immediate response or when managing extensive groups.
- **CTCSS/DCS Scanning:** The scanning feature for CTCSS/DCS allows for the reduction of interference by selectively allowing signals with specific tones or codes to be heard. By

using CTCSS/DCS scanning, users can easily identify active channels that match specific tones. This feature allows for a more streamlined communication experience, free from any unnecessary noise and distractions.

Advanced Features

GMRS radios offer more than just basic communication capabilities. They are equipped with a range of advanced features that improve their functionality and make them more user-friendly.

- **Repeater Capability**: Numerous GMRS radios are equipped with repeater operations. Repeaters play a crucial role in expanding the reach of communication by receiving a signal on one frequency and retransmitting it on another. This feature is essential for users who operate in expansive areas or require extended communication coverage.
- **Weather Alerts**: Certain GMRS radios are equipped with weather alert features, enabling users to receive crucial emergency weather updates from NOAA Weather Radio. This feature is extremely useful for outdoor activities, camping, or in areas that are susceptible to harsh weather conditions.
- **Emergency Channels and SOS Features**: GMRS radios frequently come equipped with dedicated emergency channels or SOS features, allowing for a swift and effortless method of sending distress signals. These features are crucial in emergency scenarios where prompt communication is vital.
- **Voice-Activated Transmission (VOX):** The Voice-Activated Transmission (VOX) feature enables hands-free operation as the radio automatically transmits when it detects sound. VOX is perfect for individuals who want to stay hands-free while communicating, whether it's while driving, hiking, or working.
- **Privacy Codes:** GMRS radios commonly offer privacy codes using CTCSS and DCS. The codes provided effectively minimize interference by filtering out any unwanted signals, enabling users to communicate with greater privacy within their group.
- **Battery Saver Modes and Battery Monitoring:** GMRS radios often include battery saver modes that help conserve power when the radio is not in use, thus extending battery life. Users are kept informed about the battery's charge level through battery monitoring features, which help prevent unexpected power loss during crucial communications.
- **Customizable Settings and Programmable Channels**: Advanced GMRS radios provide users with the flexibility to personalize their experience. Users can program specific channels, set custom tones, and adjust various other parameters to suit their needs. GMRS radios offer a high level of flexibility, making them ideal for a variety of uses, from everyday communication to more intricate network setups.

Applications and Use Cases

GMRS radios are incredibly versatile, thanks to their advanced functions and scanning modes. This makes them suitable for a wide range of scenarios.

- **Outdoor Adventures**: GMRS radios are highly favored by hikers, campers, and outdoor enthusiasts. With the ability to communicate over long distances and the inclusion of weather alerts and emergency features, these devices are perfect for staying connected and ensuring safety during outdoor activities.
- **Emergency Response and Preparedness**: GMRS radios are commonly utilized in emergency response situations because of their repeater support and availability of emergency channels. In emergencies, it is crucial to have the ability to scan for multiple channels and maintain priority communication.
- **Family Communication**: GMRS radios are a popular option for family communication, particularly during trips or events when cell phone coverage may be limited. Families can effortlessly stay connected and communicate across various channels with the help of advanced scanning modes.
- **Event Coordination**: GMRS radios are highly effective communication tools for coordinators and staff during large events or gatherings. With its advanced scanning modes and repeater capabilities, this device enables smooth and uninterrupted communication even in large venues.
- **Enhancing Community and Neighborhood Communication:** GMRS radios offer a valuable tool for neighborhood watch programs and community events. Efficient and secure communication is guaranteed with the ability to scan channels and use privacy codes.

Group Calls Features

Before we delve into the group call features, let's take a moment to review what GMRS is and how it functions. GMRS operates within the ultra-high frequency (UHF) band, specifically between 462 and 467 MHz. The service is overseen by the Federal Communications Commission (FCC), and users are required to obtain a license to legally operate a GMRS radio. Users and their immediate family members are permitted to use GMRS frequencies for personal or business-related communication under this license. GMRS radios provide a variety of channels, usually 22 primary channels, some of which can be used with the Family Radio Service (FRS), a lower-power radio service that doesn't need a license. GMRS and FRS radios have a key distinction: GMRS permits higher power output and the use of repeaters to expand communication range.

Group Call Features in GMRS

GMRS offers great flexibility for group communication, making it a key advantage. This is particularly beneficial for families, outdoor enthusiasts, emergency response teams, and small businesses.

Now, let's delve into the various group call features available in GMRS radios:

1. **Sub-Channels and Privacy Codes**
GMRS radios commonly use sub-channels and privacy codes to facilitate group communication while minimizing interference from other users sharing the same frequency. You can use sub-

channels, such as Continuous Tone-Coded Squelch System (CTCSS) or Digital-Coded Squelch (DCS), to effectively eliminate unwanted transmissions. When a group uses a particular sub-channel or privacy code, their radios will exclusively respond to transmissions that employ the identical code. This feature helps minimize any potential disruptions caused by other radio users who may be operating on the same frequency but use separate sub-channels.

2. Group Calls

Group calls can be easily set up on GMRS radios. This feature enables users to easily communicate with all members of a designated group at once, eliminating the need to address each individual separately. Group calls are incredibly valuable in scenarios that demand quick and efficient communication with multiple individuals, like when embarking on a hiking trip, going camping, or dealing with emergencies. To start a group call, the radio operator chooses a particular channel and sub-channel, making sure that all group members are tuned to the same settings. After a transmission is sent, the message will be received by all radios in the group.

3. Repeater Support

Repeaters are devices that receive a signal on one frequency and retransmit it on another, typically with increased power. GMRS radios that have repeater support are capable of communicating over significantly greater distances by strategically using repeaters placed throughout an area. This feature is incredibly valuable for facilitating group communication in various settings, like a sprawling campground or an outdoor event. For effective group communication using repeaters, all members must be tuned to the same repeater frequency and sub-channel. Messages are transmitted and received accurately across the network.

4. Emergency Channels and Alerts

GMRS radios frequently include dedicated emergency channels and alert features. These features enable users to swiftly send distress signals or call for assistance during an emergency. Emergency channels are essential for effectively notifying all members of a group about emergencies, guaranteeing that everyone is well-informed and capable of responding accordingly. Emergency alerts can be activated by pressing a designated button or using a specific command on the radio. During a crisis, the alert will be received by all radios tuned to the same emergency channel, enabling swift coordination among group members.

5. Scanning and Monitoring

The GMRS radios come equipped with scanning and monitoring features that enable users to listen to multiple channels or sub-channels at the same time. This feature is highly beneficial for group communication, as it enables users to effortlessly keep track of multiple groups or channels, ensuring they are always up-to-date with ongoing activities or emergencies. Scanning allows users to discover active channels where communication is happening, while monitoring allows them to listen to specific channels without transmitting. These features are highly beneficial in group settings where coordination and communication are of utmost importance.

Practical Applications of GMRS Group Call Features

The practical applications of the advanced group call features in GMRS radios are extensive. Here are some situations where these features are especially helpful:

- **Engaging in outdoor activities**

GMRS radios are a dependable choice for families or groups who enjoy outdoor activities like hiking, camping, or hunting. Group calls are a great way for participants to stay connected and coordinate their activities. During a hiking trip, group calls can be used to ensure everyone stays on track or to quickly notify others in case of an injury or if someone gets lost.

- **Emergency Response and Preparedness**

GMRS radios are an essential tool for emergency response and disaster preparedness. Group calls on emergency channels facilitate rapid communication among family members or response teams during a crisis. Repeaters are a valuable tool for expanding communication range, enabling responders to effectively cover larger areas in times of emergencies.

- **Effective Communication within the Community**

GMRS radios are commonly used for neighborhood watch programs or community communication purposes. Group calls enable neighbors to effectively coordinate security efforts and exchange vital information regarding community events. Through the utilization of sub-channels and privacy codes, groups can effectively maintain the confidentiality and security of their communication.

- **Business and Worksite Communication**

GMRS group call features can be a valuable asset for small businesses and worksite teams. As an illustration, construction teams can utilize group calls to effectively coordinate tasks and prioritize safety on the worksite. In the same way, businesses that have multiple locations can use repeaters to ensure seamless communication across a wider geographical range.

- **Family Communication**

GMRS radios are a great tool for families to stay connected while traveling or enjoying outdoor activities. Group calls are a convenient way for family members to stay connected and organize their schedules, promoting better coordination and ensuring the well-being of everyone involved.

Multi-user and group communication in GMRS

GMRS is known for its impressive ability to facilitate communication among multiple users. GMRS enables more intricate communication patterns involving multiple users, unlike traditional walkie-talkies that only support one-on-one interactions. This is especially helpful in situations like family outings, group events, or business operations where effective coordination among multiple participants is necessary.

1. **Channel Sharing and Selective Calling**

GMRS allows multiple parties to communicate on the same frequency by sharing channels. GMRS radios often come equipped with features such as selective calling or sub-audible tones to enhance communication efficiency. Users can utilize these features to customize the tones of their radios, ensuring that only individuals with corresponding tones can receive the transmission.

This approach is highly effective in reducing interference from other users on the same channel and is widely used in both family and business environments.

2. **Group Communication and Repeater Systems**

Repeater systems play a crucial role in facilitating multi-user communication in GMRS. Repeaters serve as stationary stations that receive transmissions on one frequency and then retransmit them on another, effectively expanding the reach of communication. This setup is advantageous for group communication, enabling users across a wide area to connect through a single repeater. Through collaboration with a nearby GMRS repeater network, a collective of users can effectively communicate over a wide area, making it easier to manage large-scale events or business activities.

Group Communication in GMRS

GMRS is specifically designed to facilitate group communication, making it an ideal option for families, organizations, and businesses that prioritize dependable and efficient communication. **Here are some advanced functions that can enhance group communication in GMRS:**

1. **CTCSS and DCS for Group Identification**

CTCSS and DCS are popular features found in GMRS radios that allow for effective group communication. These systems enable users to allocate specific codes or tones to their radios, guaranteeing that only individuals with corresponding codes can listen to the transmission. This feature is especially valuable in busy environments where different groups share the same frequency. CTCSS and DCS are effective in reducing interference and promoting clear communication within a group.

2. **Tone Codes for Privacy and Coordination**

Understanding tone codes is crucial for effective GMRS group communication. The codes effectively ensure privacy by selectively blocking transmissions from other users operating on the same frequency. Users can establish a unique tone code for their group, which restricts communication to only those who possess the same code. This feature promotes better coordination among group members and is commonly used in outdoor activities such as hiking, camping, or off-roading, where multiple groups may be using GMRS.

3. **Dual-Watch and Scanning Functions**

GMRS radios that come equipped with dual-watch and scanning functions provide a high level of flexibility when it comes to group communication. With a dual watch, users can effortlessly monitor two channels at the same time, ensuring they stay connected to their primary group while also staying alert to any activity on secondary channels. On the other hand, scanning allows users to conveniently monitor multiple channels by cycling through them. This feature is beneficial for users who require communication with multiple groups or the ability to monitor a wider area.

Advanced Functions for Enhanced GMRS Communication

With the advancement of GMRS technology, there have been notable improvements in multi-user and group communication, thanks to the emergence of additional features and functions. Now, let's delve into the advanced functions that make GMRS communication more effective.

1. **Digital Displays and User-Friendly Interfaces**

Modern GMRS radios are often equipped with digital displays and user-friendly interfaces, which makes them incredibly user-friendly and easy to operate. The digital displays offer a comprehensive view of the current channels, tone codes, battery levels, and other important data, ensuring that you have all the information you need at your fingertips. This feature enhances communication and coordination among multiple users, making it easier to select channels and coordinate as a group.

2. **Emergency Channels and NOAA Weather Alerts**

GMRS radios also offer emergency channels and NOAA weather alerts, providing essential safety features for groups. Emergency channels are specifically designed to facilitate urgent communications, enabling users to swiftly transition to emergency mode whenever necessary. NOAA weather alerts provide up-to-date weather information; ensuring users are well-informed about any changes in conditions. These functions play a vital role in outdoor activities, business operations, and emergency preparedness.

3. **Convenient and Easy-to-Use Hands-Free Operation and Voice Activation**

GMRS is made even more efficient with the addition of hands-free operation and voice activation (VOX), which are advanced features that improve communication. You can communicate without the need to physically hold the radio, making it perfect for situations where both hands are occupied. When it comes to communication in fast-paced environments, voice activation, also known as VOX, can be a game-changer. It allows the radio to automatically transmit as soon as it picks up the user's voice, making communication more efficient.

GMRS in Practical Scenarios: Using Multi-User and Group Communication

Let's explore some practical scenarios where multi-user and group communication in GMRS are crucial to fully grasp their significance.

1. **Family Outings and Group Camping**

GMRS is a commonly chosen option for family outings and group camping trips. Families can establish a private channel by using CTCSS or DCS codes, which guarantees that only their members will be able to communicate on that particular frequency. This setup promotes effective coordination, enabling parents to easily monitor their children and ensuring seamless connectivity for everyone. In addition, the scanning function allows families to stay informed about other campers' activities by monitoring other channels.

2. **Exciting Off-Road Adventures and Thrilling Trail Rides**

GMRS's multi-user and group communication capabilities truly excel in off-road adventures and trail rides. The communication range is extended by repeater systems, enabling off-road enthusiasts to stay connected across vast areas. By using tone codes and selective calling, groups can effectively maintain private communication without any disruptions from other users sharing the same frequency. You can easily coordinate with other groups and keep track of their trail partners using the dual-watch and scanning functions.

3. **Business Operations and Event Coordination**

GMRS is commonly used by businesses and event organizers to facilitate multi-user communication and group coordination. For any type of setting, whether it's a construction site, a music festival, or a large-scale event, GMRS provides organizers with the ability to establish communication networks that have designated channels for different teams. The range of communication is enhanced by repeater systems, while tone codes and selective calling help maintain clear and organized communication. Efficient communication is made possible through hands-free operation and voice activation, enabling workers to stay focused on their tasks without any interruptions.

CHAPTER EIGHT
GMRS FOR EMERGENCIES AND PREPAREDNESS

Overview

In this chapter, you will learn how beneficial it is for GMRS Radios in emergencies and how best to prepare and connect to emergencies

GMRS in Disaster Preparedness and Emergency Response

GMRS radios are a popular choice among families and groups for convenient communication over short distances. They prove to be highly useful during outdoor activities such as camping, hiking, and hunting. The system is becoming increasingly popular for emergency preparedness, providing a reliable and user-friendly communication option for disaster situations. During disasters, conventional communication systems can be severely disrupted, making cell phones and the internet unreliable or completely unusable. GMRS can be a vital communication resource for individuals and communities in these types of situations.

Here are some important aspects of GMRS's role in disaster preparedness:

1. **Reliability and Independence**
GMRS operates autonomously from cellular networks and internet infrastructure, ensuring its resilience against disruptions caused by natural disasters, power outages, or cyberattacks. GMRS users can maintain communication independently, ensuring reliable emergency communication even when other systems are compromised.

2. **Adaptability and Range**
GMRS radios are versatile and can be used in a wide range of settings, from bustling cities to secluded wilderness areas. They are incredibly versatile tools for disaster preparedness due to their portability and ease of use. Handheld GMRS radios can be carried by individuals, while vehicles can be equipped with more powerful mobile units. Users of GMRS have the advantage of being able to easily adjust to different situations and effectively communicate in a variety of settings.

3. **Effective Collaboration**
GMRS enables seamless communication within communities, allowing families and neighbors to stay connected during critical situations. Establishing a network of GMRS users allows communities to effectively coordinate disaster response efforts, exchange vital information, and provide mutual support. The community-based approach has the potential to greatly improve disaster preparedness and resilience through fostering cooperation and collaboration.

4. **Access to Repeaters**

GMRS licenses enable users to use repeaters, which are stations capable of receiving a signal and transmitting it at a higher power. Repeaters greatly enhance the communication range of GMRS radios, allowing users to easily connect with others over much larger distances. This capability is extremely valuable in disaster scenarios, as it allows for effective communication across a wider area, which is crucial for coordinating response efforts.

GMRS in Emergency Response

GMRS also plays a vital role in emergency response, in addition to disaster preparedness. In the following sections, we will delve into how GMRS is used to assist emergency responders, first responders, and search and rescue operations.

1. **Effective Collaboration Among Responders**

GMRS enables effective communication and coordination among emergency responders, including fire departments, police, and emergency medical services. GMRS enables responders to effectively share information, coordinate activities, and respond to emergencies by offering a reliable communication platform. Effective coordination is crucial to ensure a prompt and well-organized response to disasters and emergencies.

2. **Search and Rescue Operations**

GMRS is highly beneficial for search and rescue operations, enabling teams to effectively communicate across vast areas. Repeater technology is crucial for expanding communication range, allowing search and rescue teams to effectively cover larger areas while maintaining a constant connection with their base of operations. GMRS can also be used for effective communication with volunteers and community members who are assisting in search and rescue operations, thereby ensuring a well-coordinated response.

3. **Communication with Affected Populations**

In times of crisis, it is of utmost importance to establish and maintain effective communication with the people affected. This enables us to provide them with vital information, issue necessary warnings, and efficiently coordinate evacuation or sheltering operations. GMRS is a reliable communication system that can effectively connect people in areas where other methods may not be as dependable. This clear and effective communication enables emergency responders to keep individuals informed and prioritize their safety during disaster response efforts.

4. **Backup Communication for Critical Services**

GMRS is a valuable backup communication system for critical services like hospitals, utility companies, and emergency shelters. In situations where primary communication systems are no longer functional, GMRS can serve as a reliable backup method of communication. This allows for the coordination of essential services and the uninterrupted continuation of operations. The redundancy plays a vital role in ensuring stability during emergency response and recovery operations.

Challenges and Considerations

Although GMRS provides numerous advantages for disaster preparedness and emergency response, it is important to be aware of the challenges and considerations:

1. **Licensing Requirements**

Obtaining a license from the FCC is necessary for GMRS, which might discourage certain users from embracing the system. The licensing process requires a fee and the completion of an online form, which can be a challenge for certain individuals. Efforts to increase awareness about the advantages of GMRS and streamline the licensing process may motivate more individuals and communities to use the system for disaster preparedness.

2. **Limited Frequency Bandwidth**

GMRS operates within a restricted frequency range, which can result in congestion in densely populated regions. The system's effectiveness can be impacted during large-scale emergencies when there is a high volume of users trying to communicate at the same time. Effective coordination among GMRS users and the use of repeaters can greatly alleviate this challenge.

3. **Training and Education**

To fully capitalize on the advantages of GMRS, users must possess a comprehensive understanding of radio operation and the effective use of the system. Training and education play a crucial role in ensuring effective communication and minimizing interference among GMRS users. Users can enhance their disaster preparedness and emergency response skills by utilizing community-based training programs and resources for GMRS.

4. **Coordination with Other Communication Systems**

GMRS is just one of the many communication systems used in disaster preparedness and emergency response. Effective response to emergencies requires coordination with other systems, including amateur radio, public safety radio, and satellite communication. Establishing protocols for interoperability and communication among different systems can greatly improve overall disaster preparedness.

GMRS for Neighborhood Watch and Community Safety

Benefits of GMRS for Neighborhood Watch

Ease of Use

GMRS is known for its user-friendly nature. GMRS radios are known for their user-friendly nature and typically do not require extensive technical expertise, unlike more complex radio systems. These devices are perfect for neighborhood watch programs, as they are user-friendly and don't require any technical expertise.

Dependable Communication

GMRS radios are crafted to ensure dependable communication. These radios provide superior range and clarity compared to traditional Family Radio Service (FRS) radios, making them ideal for organizing neighborhood watch activities and reporting any suspicious behavior. GMRS radios use UHF frequencies, which greatly reduce the likelihood of interference. This means that you can enjoy uninterrupted communication, even in areas with high population density.

Group Communication

GMRS enables effective group communication, making it a valuable tool for neighborhood watch programs. Participants have the convenience of seamless communication, allowing them to efficiently coordinate patrols and promptly respond to emergencies. This feature encourages a strong sense of community and teamwork among participants in the neighborhood watch program.

Emergency Preparedness

GMRS radios are a valuable asset to have in any emergency preparedness plan. During times of disaster or crisis, traditional communication networks may become unavailable or overwhelmed. GMRS radios offer a dependable solution, enabling neighborhood watch members to maintain communication with one another and emergency services. This capability is essential for maintaining community safety during emergencies.

Best Practices for GMRS in Neighborhood Watch and Community Safety

- **Regular Maintenance and Testing**

Regular maintenance and testing are essential for ensuring the proper functioning of GMRS radios. It is important to perform regular checks on batteries, antennas, and radio communication ranges to ensure everything is in proper working order. Regular testing is crucial for identifying potential issues promptly, and ensuring that radios are always prepared for use.

- **Respecting Privacy and Legal Boundaries**

Although GMRS radios serve a practical purpose in facilitating communication, it is crucial to uphold privacy and adhere to legal boundaries. It is important to refrain from using radios for surveillance or recording conversations without obtaining consent. Furthermore, it is important to follow FCC regulations regarding GMRS use to prevent any potential fines or legal repercussions.

- **Advocating for Inclusivity and Diversity**

Neighborhood watch programs should actively encourage inclusivity and embrace diversity. Promote inclusivity and engagement among all members of the community, regardless of their background or demographics. This approach promotes a more thorough and efficient neighborhood watch program, improving community safety for all.

- **Establishing Clear Roles and Responsibilities**

To ensure the effectiveness of a neighborhood watch program, it is crucial to define and assign specific roles and responsibilities to all participants. Assigning patrol duties, communication roles, and emergency response tasks are all part of the process. Having clearly defined roles is crucial for ensuring that all team members have a clear understanding of their responsibilities and can effectively carry out their duties, whether it's during routine patrols or emergencies.

- **Encouraging Feedback and Improvement**

Lastly, it is important to seek feedback from neighborhood watch participants to consistently enhance the program. It is important to consistently seek feedback on communication protocols, training, and overall effectiveness. Take this feedback into consideration to make adjustments and implement changes that will improve the safety and cohesion of the community.

Connecting GMRS to Other Emergency Services

During times of natural disasters, accidents, or other emergencies, the importance of effective communication cannot be overstated. It serves as a crucial lifeline for coordinating efforts and ensuring safety. GMRS has become increasingly popular among emergency response teams and amateur radio enthusiasts due to its reliable communication capabilities. Establishing strong connections between GMRS and other emergency services is crucial for maximizing its effectiveness in emergency scenarios. This essay delves into the integration of GMRS with broader emergency response networks, aiming to enhance public safety and emergency management. GMRS operates on a specific set of frequencies that have been assigned by the Federal Communications Commission (FCC). GMRS licensing is more accessible compared to traditional amateur radio services, as it does not require specialized knowledge and licensing. It enables families and groups to easily communicate over long distances using affordable equipment, making it a popular choice for personal use and community-based emergency response. GMRS has a shorter range compared to certain other radio services, typically spanning only a few miles. When repeaters are strategically positioned on elevated areas such as hills or towers, the range can be greatly expanded. Repeaters play a crucial role in extending the communication range for GMRS users by receiving and rebroadcasting signals. GMRS is a valuable tool in emergency preparedness due to its ability to cover more ground.

GMRS in Emergency Situations

Effective communication is crucial in emergencies to ensure the smooth coordination of rescue operations, guide individuals to safety, and disseminate vital information. GMRS radios are incredibly user-friendly, requiring very little setup. This makes them ideal for first responders and community groups who need to establish communication networks in a hurry. During natural disasters such as hurricanes, tornadoes, earthquakes, or wildfires, the communication infrastructure, including cellular networks, can suffer damage or become overwhelmed. GMRS offers a dependable communication system that remains operational in such circumstances. GMRS is a highly reliable option for disaster preparedness and emergency response plans.

Integrating GMRS with Other Emergency Services

GMRS is not only effective for local communication, but it also gains significant strength when integrated into larger emergency response networks.

There are multiple ways to integrate GMRS with other emergency services:

1. **Working together with local emergency response teams**

To facilitate smooth communication during emergencies, GMRS users need to work together with local emergency response teams, including fire departments, police, and emergency medical services (EMS). This collaboration focuses on the sharing of communication plans and the prevention of interference with other essential services by GMRS frequencies. Regular joint training exercises and emergency drills can facilitate a better understanding of protocols between GMRS users and emergency responders. Through collaboration, GMRS operators can acquire the skills to aid first responders by transmitting information, offering assistance, and serving as supplementary communication hubs.

2. **Collaboration with Amateur Radio Operators**

Hams, or amateur radio operators, are essential for emergency communication. Their expertise lies in handling intricate communication networks and using state-of-the-art equipment. Connecting GMRS and amateur radio operators can greatly improve the range and capabilities of both systems. By using cross-band repeaters or gateway systems, it is possible to establish a connection between GMRS signals and amateur radio frequencies, enabling a wider range of communication. This integration is incredibly valuable in situations of large-scale emergencies, where effective coordination across multiple jurisdictions is crucial. Through partnerships with amateur radio clubs and organizations, GMRS users can expand their coverage and access a wider emergency response network.

3. **Integration with Emergency Operations Centers (EOCs)**

During disasters, Emergency Operations Centers (EOCs) function as central command points. They efficiently coordinate resources, effectively manage information, and skillfully direct emergency response efforts. Integrating GMRS communication with EOCs enables the transmission of real-time information from the field, leading to improved resource allocation and decision-making. GMRS operators play a crucial role in emergency response by serving as field agents who relay vital information to EOCs and other response agencies. This direct communication channel allows EOCs to stay well-informed about conditions on the ground, enabling them to make better decisions during emergencies. GMRS users can establish contact with local EOCs and participate in training sessions to understand their protocols and procedures, which will help achieve this integration.

4. **Public-Private Partnerships**

Public-private partnerships have the potential to improve the integration of GMRS into wider emergency response networks. Collaboration between companies specializing in communication equipment or emergency services, local governments, and GMRS users can lead to the development of a unified communication system. These partnerships can help with the installation of GMRS repeaters in key locations, like schools, community centers, or corporate buildings. Establishing these infrastructure points enhances the resilience of GMRS networks, ensuring uninterrupted communication during emergencies.

5. **Education and Community Outreach**

For GMRS to serve as a reliable emergency communication tool, community members must have a clear understanding of its capabilities and be well-versed in its usage. Education and community outreach play a crucial role in raising awareness about GMRS's importance in emergency preparedness. Local governments and emergency response organizations have the opportunity to provide valuable training sessions and workshops to educate the public on the effective use of GMRS radios in emergencies. The sessions will include topics such as basic radio operations, emergency protocols, and the significance of working together with other emergency services. In addition, GMRS users have the opportunity to create community-based groups that focus on promoting emergency preparedness and communication. These groups can coordinate practice sessions and drills to ensure that all individuals are well-prepared in case of a disaster.

CHAPTER NINE
GMRS ACCESSORIES AND PROGRAMMING

Overview

Chapter nine further discusses GMRS Radio accessories, GMRS antennas, the factors to consider when choosing them, the recommended GMRS equipment, and others.

List of GMRS Accessories

There is a wide range of accessories available to enhance the functionality of GMRS radios.

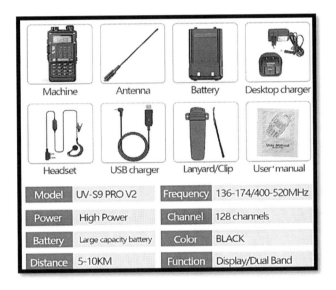

Model	UV-S9 PRO V2	Frequency	136-174/400-520MHz
Power	High Power	Channel	128 channels
Battery	Large capacity battery	Color	BLACK
Distance	5-10KM	Function	Display/Dual Band

1. **Antennas**

Antennas are essential for optimizing the range and performance of GMRS radios. There are various types available, such as whip antennas, gain antennas and external antennas.

- **Whip Antennas**: These antennas are designed to be flexible and lightweight, making them perfect for those who need portability and mobility. Whip antennas are a great choice for handheld GMRS radios, providing a solid combination of performance and durability.
- **Gain Antennas**: Gain antennas are specifically designed to enhance the effective radiated power of GMRS radios, enabling seamless long-range communication. They are commonly used in base stations or mobile setups.
- **External Antennas**: External antennas are commonly installed on vehicles or stationary structures. They provide an extended range and are highly beneficial for users who require dependable communication over long distances.

2. **Microphones**

Microphones play a crucial role in ensuring communication is clear and effective. GMRS radios offer a range of microphone options to cater to various requirements.

- **Handheld Microphones**: These are commonly used with mobile GMRS radios. They are user-friendly and usually come with a convenient push-to-talk (PTT) button.
- **Speaker Microphones**: Speaker microphones are designed to provide convenience and ease of use by combining a microphone and a speaker into a single unit. This allows users to communicate without the need to hold the radio, enhancing their overall experience. These are frequently used in public safety and outdoor pursuits.
- **Lapel Microphones**: Lapel microphones are compact and can easily be attached to clothing, allowing for convenient hands-free operation. They are commonly utilized in business or professional environments.

3. **Headsets**

Headsets offer a convenient way to communicate without the need for hands with GMRS radios. They are highly favored by individuals who value the ability to communicate discreetly or keep their hands free from other activities.

- **In-Ear Headsets:** These are crafted to be lightweight and provide optimal comfort. In-ear headsets are perfect for individuals who require discreet communication or find themselves in loud surroundings.
- **Over-Ear Headsets**: Over-ear headsets are known for their superior noise isolation, making them ideal for use in noisy settings or outdoor environments.
- **Bone Conduction Headsets:** These headsets utilize bone conduction technology to transmit sound, enabling users to stay aware of their surroundings while communicating. They are valuable for users seeking situational awareness.

4. **Batteries and Chargers**

GMRS radios rely heavily on batteries and chargers to ensure their continuous operation. Various batteries and chargers come with different levels of capacity and convenience.

- **Rechargeable Batteries**: These batteries are designed for recharging, which reduces the need for frequent replacements. They are frequently utilized in portable GMRS radios.
- **Battery Packs:** Battery packs provide extended battery life, making them ideal for users who require longer operating times without the need for frequent recharging.
- **Charging Stations:** Users can conveniently charge multiple GMRS radios or batteries at the same time with charging stations. They are perfect for organizations or groups that use multiple radios.

5. **Mounting Accessories**

You can easily attach GMRS radios to vehicles, equipment, or fixed locations using mounting accessories for a secure connection.

- **Vehicle Mounts:** These mounts are specifically designed to securely attach GMRS radios to vehicles, ensuring easy access to communication equipment.
- **Base Station Mounts:** Base station mounts are essential for securely installing GMRS radios in fixed locations, such as offices or homes. They offer a sense of stability and organization for radio setups.

6. **Carrying Cases and Holsters**

Carrying cases and holsters provide excellent protection for GMRS radios, ensuring their safety and enhancing their portability.

- **Soft Cases:** Soft cases are crafted from flexible materials and provide a modest level of protection against scratches and minor impacts. These items are light in weight and convenient to transport.
- **Hard Cases**: Hard cases offer a durable solution, featuring rigid shells that can endure rough handling. They are perfect for users who require added durability.
- **Holsters**: Holsters provide a convenient way to attach GMRS radios to belts or other gear for quick and easy access. They are frequently used by security personnel and individuals who enjoy outdoor activities.

7. **External Speakers**

External speakers significantly improve the audio quality of GMRS radios, allowing for clearer communication even in loud surroundings.

- **Portable External Speakers**: These speakers are compact and perfect for on-the-go use. They are great for handheld GMRS radios when you require extra volume.
- **High-Power External Speakers**: These speakers are specifically designed to deliver exceptional volume and clarity, making them perfect for loud environments. They are commonly used in vehicles or base stations.

8. **Data Cables and Programming Software**

You can easily customize GMRS radios and manage frequency programming with the help of data cables and programming software.

- **USB Data Cables:** USB data cables are used to connect GMRS radios to computers, allowing for programming and configuration. They are crucial for users who wish to personalize their radio settings.
- **Programming Software:** Programming software enables users to make adjustments to GMRS radio settings, including frequencies, channels, and power levels. This software is commonly used by experienced users or radio technicians.

9. **Repeater Systems**

Repeater systems enhance the coverage of GMRS radios by transmitting signals over longer distances. They are frequently used in organizations or communities that need extensive communication coverage.

- **Stand-Alone Repeaters**: These repeaters can be conveniently installed in strategic locations to extend communication range.
- **Mobile Repeaters:** Mobile repeaters are specifically designed to be used in vehicles, providing convenient and adaptable communication coverage.

List of GMRS Antennas

Antennas play a crucial role in connecting a GMRS radio to its surroundings. The performance of radio signals is directly influenced by the design, size, and installation of these devices, as they serve as the means of transmitting and receiving. There are different types of GMRS antennas available, each designed for specific applications and with their unique characteristics. When choosing an antenna that is right for you, it's important to take into account various factors such as frequency range, gain, polarization, height, and the terrain in your surroundings.

Types of GMRS Antennas

There is a wide range of GMRS antennas available, each tailored to meet specific requirements.

Here's a detailed list to assist you in making an informed decision:

1. **Whip Antennas**

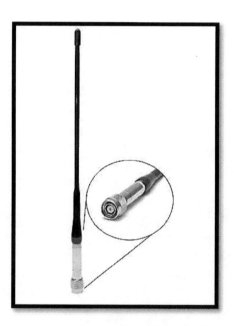

Whip antennas are widely used and easily identifiable GMRS antennas. They are usually flexible antennas that can be attached to handheld or mobile GMRS radios. Whip antennas are widely favored due to their small size and user-friendly nature. They provide a decent gain, usually ranging from 2 dBi to 5 dBi, and are appropriate for distances that are not too long. These antennas are ideal for mobile operations or handheld devices where portability is crucial. They are commonly used by individuals who enjoy hiking, camping or are engaged in emergency response scenarios. Although their range is more limited compared to other antenna types.

2. **Ground Plane Antennas**

Ground plane antennas are commonly used for stationary GMRS base stations. The antenna is constructed with a vertical radiator and radial elements that extend outward, resulting in a stable design and excellent omnidirectional coverage. Ground plane antennas provide a higher gain, typically ranging from 3 dBi to 6 dBi, which makes them well-suited for longer-range communication.

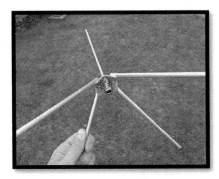

These antennas are commonly installed on masts or rooftops, allowing for a wider coverage area. These radios are perfect for users who need dependable communication over a larger area, like families with GMRS base stations at home or emergency responders coordinating over a wider range.

3. **Yagi Antennas**

Yagi antennas are designed to concentrate signal strength in a specific direction, making them highly effective for directional communication. The components of these structures include a reflector, a driven element, and directors. Yagi antennas are specifically engineered to achieve optimal gain, typically ranging from 6 dBi to 15 dBi. This enables substantial amplification of signals in the intended direction.

Yagi antennas are most suitable for point-to-point communication or when there is a need to reach specific areas with a strong signal. They are frequently used in urgent scenarios that require long-distance communication or for establishing a connection with a designated repeater station.

4. **Dipole Antennas**

The design of dipole antennas is quite straightforward, with two conductive elements extending outward from a central feed point. The antennas provide a wide coverage area in all directions, offering a moderate gain of approximately 2 dBi to 4 dBi. Dipole antennas are commonly utilized in a variety of applications, including handheld devices and base stations.

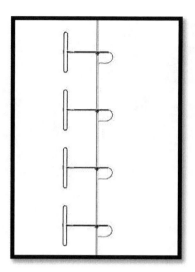

Dipole antennas offer great versatility and can be easily mounted in different configurations, whether it's horizontally or vertically. They are effective for general-purpose communication and perform admirably in areas with fewer obstructions.

5. **J-Pole Antennas**

The design of J-pole antennas is quite fascinating, as it closely resembles the shape of the letter "**J**." These antennas are made up of a single vertical element and a smaller parallel feedline element, resulting in a well-balanced structure. J-pole antennas provide a wide coverage area in all directions, offering a decent to strong signal gain, typically ranging from 3 dBi to 6 dBi.

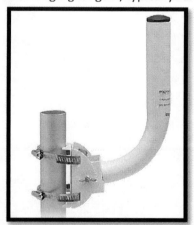

These antennas are highly sought after for GMRS base stations because of their simple design and ease of assembly. They are commonly utilized in stationary applications that require a stronger signal, like emergency communication centers or for ham radio enthusiasts who are switching to GMRS.

6. **Mobile Antennas**

Mobile antennas are specifically designed for use on vehicles, making them perfect for GMRS users who are always on the move. They can be easily attached to car roofs, hoods, or other vehicle surfaces. Mobile antennas provide reliable communication while on the move with moderate gain, typically between 2 dBi and 5 dBi, and omnidirectional coverage. These antennas are highly sought after by individuals who enjoy outdoor activities, professionals in emergency response, and individuals who need reliable mobile communication. These products are specifically engineered to endure the harsh conditions and vibrations that come with being used in vehicles, ensuring their exceptional durability and longevity.

Factors to Consider When Choosing a GMRS Antenna

When choosing a GMRS antenna, it's important to take into account various factors to ensure optimal performance that meets your specific requirements.

Here are some important aspects to consider:

1. **Antenna Gain**

The concept of gain relates to the antenna's capacity to concentrate or enhance a signal. Antennas with higher gain offer a boost in range and signal strength, although they tend to have a more focused direction. Low-gain antennas provide a broader coverage area, although their range is limited. Select an antenna that best suits your communication needs by considering its gain.

2. **Polarization**

The orientation of the electric field in a radio wave is known as polarization. GMRS antennas can be polarized either horizontally or vertically. For optimal signal reception, it is important to align the polarization of your antenna with the antennas of other devices you will be communicating with. GMRS applications typically use vertical polarization more frequently.

3. **Antenna Height**

The range and effectiveness of an antenna are influenced by the height at which it is mounted. Antennas that are positioned at higher elevations above the ground generally offer a wider range and experience less interference. Take into account the installation location and the necessary height for optimal performance.

4. **Environmental Factors**

The performance of antennas can be influenced by various environmental factors, including terrain, buildings, and other obstacles. In areas with numerous obstructions, it may be beneficial to utilize a higher-gain or directional antenna to mitigate interference.

5. **Antenna Durability**

Having a durable antenna is essential, particularly when it comes to outdoor or mobile use. Make sure the antenna is constructed using durable materials that can withstand various weather conditions, UV exposure, and other environmental factors.

6. **Installation Complexity**

Certain antennas may necessitate more intricate installation processes compared to others. Take into account your technical expertise and the resources at your disposal when selecting an antenna. Installing whip antennas is a breeze, whereas Yagi antennas demand a more intricate process of mounting and alignment.

Recommended GMRS Equipment

There is a wide range of GMRS equipment available, with each device designed for specific situations. **Now, let's explore the most prevalent types of GMRS equipment and how they can be used:**

1. **Handheld Radios (Walkie-Talkies):** Handheld radios, also referred to as walkie-talkies, are incredibly popular GMRS devices. These devices are highly portable, user-friendly, and perfect for outdoor adventures, family excursions, and emergency preparedness. When choosing a handheld radio, it's important to take into account the following features:
   - **Range**: The range of GMRS radios can vary depending on factors such as terrain and obstructions. Manufacturers frequently boast about distances of up to 30 miles, although real-world conditions may significantly decrease this range. Consider radios with a higher power output (usually 1-5 watts) to enhance the range.
   - **Channels**: GMRS radios come equipped with 22 channels, some of which are shared with FRS. Make sure the radio is compatible with other devices by supporting all GMRS channels.
   - **Durability**: When using radios outdoors, it's important to select models with sturdy casings that can withstand water and shocks.
   - **Battery Life:** Having a longer battery life is essential for those longer outings. Take into account radios that come with rechargeable batteries and the added convenience of being able to use alkaline batteries as a backup.
2. **Mobile Radios:** Mobile radios are typically installed in vehicles and provide a greater power output and range compared to handheld radios. They are perfect for off-road adventures, caravanning, or staying connected on the go. Important factors to take into account are:
   - **Power Output:** Mobile radios can output up to 50 watts, resulting in enhanced range and clarity.
   - **Antenna Options:** Mobile radios commonly use external antennas, providing the flexibility to tailor them to your vehicle and the surrounding landscape.
   - **Mounting and Installation**: Make sure the radio can be securely mounted in your vehicle and that the installation process is straightforward.
   - **Repeater Capability**: Certain mobile radios can access GMRS repeaters, which can extend communication range by relaying signals over longer distances.
3. **Base Stations:** Base stations are stationary radios that are commonly used at home or in a central location. They serve a variety of purposes, such as facilitating the organization of large-scale events, enabling effective emergency communication, and maintaining

contact with mobile units. Base stations have similarities to mobile radios, such as a higher power output and the use of external antennas.

4. **Repeaters**: Repeaters are incredibly useful for extending the range of your radio network, providing a significant boost in power. They operate by receiving and retransmitting signals at a higher power, enabling communication over vast distances. Repeaters are widely utilized by emergency services, amateur radio operators, and GMRS enthusiasts. Take these factors into account when configuring a repeater:

- **Location**: Place the repeater in a high spot, like a hilltop or tall building, to ensure the best coverage.
- **Power Supply:** Make sure you have a dependable power source and a backup plan in case of any outages.
- **Licensing and Coordination**: Repeater operation necessitates coordination with other users to prevent any potential interference. You might want to think about joining a local GMRS group for some extra help.

GMRS Equipment Accessories

Aside from the main radios, there are a variety of accessories available to enhance your GMRS communication experience. Here are some examples:

1. **Antennae**: Enhancing your radio's antenna can greatly enhance its range and signal quality. Longer whip antennas can enhance the performance of handheld radios. Gain antennas designed for vehicle use are advantageous for mobile radios.

2. **Headsets and Microphones:** Hands-free communication is crucial for a wide range of activities. For added convenience, you may want to consider using headsets or microphones that have push-to-talk (PTT) functionality. These accessories are essential for effective team coordination during events or emergencies.

3. **Batteries and Chargers**: Ensuring that your radios are always charged is crucial for maintaining dependable communication. Consider looking for radios that come with rechargeable batteries and think about getting external chargers for faster recharging. Certain radios offer the convenience of USB charging, allowing for flexibility when using power banks or car chargers.

4. **Carrying Cases and Holsters:** Safeguard your radios with sturdy carrying cases or holsters. These accessories are designed to enhance the convenience and durability of transporting your radios, ensuring their protection during outdoor activities.

5. **Programming Software and Cables**: If you have multiple radios or a repeater system, programming software and cables are necessary for customizing frequencies, tones, and settings. You can optimize your communication network for maximum performance.

Deciding on the Appropriate GMRS Equipment

Choosing the right GMRS equipment from a wide range of options can be overwhelming. Here are some helpful tips for selecting the most suitable GMRS equipment for your specific requirements:

1. **Identify Your Use Case**: Determine the main purpose for your GMRS equipment. If you're planning outdoor activities, handheld radios might be suitable. Mobile radios are the perfect choice for vehicle-based communication. Base stations and repeaters are ideal for large-scale communication networks.
2. **Take into account your surroundings**: Evaluate the landscape and any obstacles in your vicinity. Effective communication in dense forests, urban environments, and mountainous regions may necessitate the use of more powerful radios or repeaters.
3. **Assess Your Budget:** The cost of GMRS equipment can vary depending on factors such as power output, features, and durability. Establish a budget and discover equipment that fulfills your requirements without straining your finances. Remember to consider the licensing fees, which remain valid for 10 years.
4. **Consider Reviews and Recommendations**: It's always a good idea to consider reviews and recommendations from experienced users before purchasing GMRS equipment. These insights can be highly valuable in assessing performance, durability, and ease of use.
5. **Comply with Regulations**: Make sure your GMRS equipment meets all FCC regulations. It is crucial to have the appropriate licensing and be knowledgeable about the allowed power levels and channel usage to prevent any violations.

Understanding why radio programming cable does not work

The process of radio programming requires a high level of coordination between technology and user expertise. The complexity of General Mobile Radio Service (GMRS) is further intensified by regulatory restrictions, diverse equipment standards, and distinct operational environments. Radio programming cables are crucial tools for configuring and customizing radio devices. Users can easily connect radios to computers, making it possible to program channels, frequencies, and other operational parameters. This capability is essential for customizing radio systems to fulfill specific requirements, whether it involves creating a network for family communication or establishing a connection for emergency services. Although radio programming cables are highly useful, they encounter various challenges when used with GMRS equipment. Now, let's delve into the main factors contributing to these challenges.

Diverse Equipment Standards

Numerous companies produce GMRS radios, each with its unique design and technical specifications. Compatibility issues can arise when programming radios with cables due to the wide range of diversity. Manufacturers use various connector types, communication protocols, and firmware configurations. It is important to note that a cable specifically designed for one brand may not be compatible with another, even if both radios are GMRS. Furthermore, certain manufacturers use their exclusive software for radio programming, which adds an extra layer of complexity to compatibility. Users must possess a thorough comprehension of their particular radio model and suitable programming tools to navigate this situation. Having this knowledge is crucial to minimize the chances of running into problems with programming cables.

Regulatory Compliance

The FCC has strict regulations regarding GMRS. The radios utilized in this service are required to adhere to precise technical standards, encompassing factors such as frequency stability, power output, and bandwidth. The programming process is significantly affected by these regulations, as any deviation from the approved parameters can result in non-compliance. Radio programming cables may not always conform to these regulatory requirements. Using a cable that enables users to program frequencies or settings beyond the legal limits may result in unintentional violations of FCC rules. Some manufacturers are hesitant to provide open access to programming capabilities, which limits users' ability to customize their radios.

Limitations of Software and Firmware

GMRS radios can be programmed using software that is compatible with the radio and communicates through a programming cable. Unfortunately, this software is not consistently accessible or user-friendly. Documentation provided by manufacturers is often lacking, which can make it difficult for users to fully grasp the programming process. In addition, the firmware on GMRS radios can differ, which can impact the way the radio interacts with the programming software. If the firmware version on the radio does not match the software version, there is a possibility that the programming cable will be unable to establish a connection. Many programming failures in GMRS radios can be attributed to this common mismatch.

Challenges Arising from Human Error and Technical Issues

The success or failure of radio programming is heavily influenced by human intervention. Having a solid grasp of radio technology is essential for users, encompassing frequency allocation, modulation, and other technical aspects. Having this knowledge is crucial to avoiding mistakes, preventing programming errors, and protecting the radio from potential damage. Technical challenges often arise due to issues such as incorrect cable connections, improper software installation, and misconfigurations. These issues may result in the programming cable being unable to establish communication with the radio or causing programming errors. Addressing and resolving these challenges often relies on human intervention, which can be demanding due to the expertise it requires.

Effective Solutions and Recommended Practices

Although there are challenges involved, users can implement certain measures to enhance the success rate of programming GMRS radios with cables.

Implementing the following best practices can greatly minimize compatibility issues and significantly decrease the chances of programming failures:

1. **Ensure Compatibility**: Before purchasing a programming cable, make sure it is compatible with the specific make and model of the GMRS radio. Make sure to visit the manufacturer's website to find the cables and software they recommend.
2. **Follow Manufacturer Guidelines**: It is crucial to follow the manufacturer's instructions. It is important to ensure that the correct software version is used, that the recommended connection procedures are followed and that unauthorized modifications are avoided.
3. **Get Professional Help**: If you're uncertain about the programming process, it's a good idea to reach out to experienced radio operators or professional technicians for assistance. They have the expertise to assist you in navigating the process and ensuring accurate programming.
4. **Stay mindful of regulatory compliance**: It's important to always be aware of FCC regulations when programming GMRS radios. Make sure that any adjustments you make to the radio's settings comply with legal regulations.
5. **Regularly Update Firmware and Software:** It is important to regularly update firmware and software. Manufacturers frequently release updates to enhance compatibility and functionality. Maintaining these components regularly can help minimize programming problems.
6. **Document your Configuration**: Make sure to document your radio's programming configuration, which should include frequencies, channels, and other important settings. This documentation is extremely helpful for troubleshooting and future programming.

Troubleshooting common programming issues

There are a few common issues that can arise when programming a GMRS radio. Now, let's carefully analyze them and propose some possible solutions.

1. **Frequency Entry Error**

Incorrectly inputting the frequency can result in communication issues. Make sure to review the frequency chart before programming. Ensure the radio is reprogrammed if necessary.

2. **Incorrect CTCSS/DCS Codes**

CTCSS and DCS codes are used to effectively eliminate any undesired signals from other users who may be operating on the same frequency. If you're facing any issues with interference or communication, it would be helpful to review the CTCSS/DCS settings. Make sure they align with those of your group or intended repeater. Consider reprogramming if needed.

3. **Repeater Settings**

GMRS repeaters enhance signal range by amplifying and retransmitting the signal. If you're experiencing difficulties connecting to a repeater, make sure to check the following:

- **Offset Frequency**: The offset frequency refers to the discrepancy between the input and output frequencies. Make sure it's set correctly, typically at 5 MHz for GMRS.
- **PL/DPL Codes:** These sub-audible tones are used to access the repeater. Make sure the programmed codes are accurate.

If you continue to experience problems with repeater access, it would be advisable to reach out to the owner of the repeater and inquire about any potential additional requirements or restrictions that may be in place.

4. **Transmission Power**

GMRS radios offer a range of power settings. Make sure to adjust the power level accordingly if you're having trouble with communication. For close-range communication, low power might be sufficient, but when it comes to longer distances, high power is necessary. Make sure to review your radio's settings and adjust the power level as needed.

Troubleshooting Interference and Signal Range Issues

Interference and limited signal range can often pose challenges in GMRS communication. Let's tackle these issues with some practical tips.

1. **Identify Interference Sources**

Interference has the potential to disrupt communication and introduce static or unwanted signals. Typical sources of interference can come from other radio users, electronic devices, and various environmental factors.

To address interference issues:

- **Scan for Active Frequencies**: Use the scan function on your GMRS radio to identify any other frequencies that are currently in use. This can assist in determining if there is any overlap in usage.
- **Change Frequencies**: If interference continues, try using a different GMRS channel.
- **Minimize Proximity to Interference Sources**: Try to stay away from potential sources of interference, such as power lines, large metal structures, or electronic equipment.

2. **Maximize Antenna Placement**

The placement and condition of your antenna are crucial factors that affect the range and clarity of your signal. To enhance antenna performance:

- **Optimal Line of Sight Positioning**: Make sure your antenna has an unobstructed view of other radios or repeaters.
- **Use External Antennas**: Consider using an external antenna to enhance the range. This is particularly beneficial for base stations or radios that are mounted on vehicles.
- **Inspect for any potential damage**: A damaged antenna has the potential to diminish signal quality. Make sure to carefully examine your antenna for any signs of damage or wear.

3. **Signal Range Test**

To address the issue of limited signal range, it is recommended to conduct range tests for the radio under different conditions. This can assist in determining whether the issue is caused by environmental factors or radio settings.

- **Test in Open Areas**: Evaluate the signal range in open environments with minimal obstructions.
- **Test in Urban Areas:** Signal range may be affected in urban environments due to buildings and other obstacles.
- **Test with and without Repeaters**: This allows for an investigation into whether the repeater setup is the root cause of the issue.

Addressing Hardware and Firmware Issues

Occasionally, the root cause of GMRS issues can be traced back to hardware or firmware problems. Here is a guide to help you troubleshoot these issues.

1. **Examine Radio Hardware**

Communication problems can be caused by hardware issues. To verify the hardware of your radio:

- **Inspect the Battery:** Make sure to inspect the battery as it can affect the transmission power if it is weak or faulty. Make sure your battery is fully charged and in good condition.
- **Check for Physical Damage**: Be sure to inspect the radio for any signs of physical damage, such as cracks or loose components.
- **Check the Microphone and Speaker**: Make sure the microphone and speaker are working properly. If there is any distortion, it may be worth considering replacing these components.

2. **Update Firmware**

Firmware updates have the potential to enhance radio performance and address any known issues. Make sure to visit the manufacturer's website to stay up-to-date with the latest firmware updates.

3. **Performing a Factory Reset**

If nothing else works, you may want to try performing a factory reset. Performing a reset will bring the radio back to its original settings, potentially resolving any ongoing problems.

Programming techniques for GMRS Radios

Customizing the settings of GMRS radios allows you to tailor the device to meet your specific requirements. By doing so, you can:

- **Enhance Communication**: Customize the radio's channels and privacy codes to reduce interference and improve clarity.
- **Improve Security**: Incorporate privacy codes to minimize the risk of unintended eavesdropping.
- **Enable Repeater Access**: Configure the radio to communicate with repeaters, thereby extending the range of communication.
- **Standardize Across Multiple Radios**: Ensure all radios in a group have a consistent configuration for reliable communication.

Tools and Software for Programming GMRS Radios

Before delving into programming techniques, it is essential to have the necessary tools and software. Some commonly used tools for GMRS programming are:

- **Programming Cable**: Enables the connection between the radio and a computer for programming purposes. Make sure the cable is suitable for your particular radio model.
- **Programming Software**: Chirp is widely used open-source software that allows programming for a variety of radio models. The interface is designed to be user-friendly, making it easy to customize radio settings.
- **Driver Installation:** Certain programming cables necessitate the installation of specific drivers on your computer. Make sure to install the appropriate drivers to prevent any potential connection problems.

Advanced Programming Techniques

Let's dive into advanced programming techniques to take your GMRS radio experience to the next level, armed with the right tools.
1. **Custom Channel Assignments**
GMRS radios usually come with preset channels, but personalizing them can offer more control over your communication environment. To generate personalized channel assignments:
- **Identify Unused Channels**: Determine which channels in your area have the least amount of usage to minimize interference.
- **Assign Descriptive Names**: Give channels meaningful names to make them easier to identify. This feature is particularly helpful when programming multiple radios in a group.
- **Configure Privacy Codes**: Set custom privacy codes (CTCSS/DCS) to minimize interference from other users on the same channel.
2. **Repeater Configuration**
Repeaters play a crucial role in expanding the coverage of GMRS radios. To set up your radio for repeater access:
- **Find Local Repeaters:** Research repeaters in your vicinity, taking note of their frequencies, tones, and offsets.
- **Program Repeater Settings**: Ensure the accurate configuration of transmit and receive frequencies, as well as any necessary tones (CTCSS/DCS).
- **Adjust the Repeater Offset**: GMRS repeaters commonly utilize a 5 MHz offset. Make sure to properly configure this in your radio.
3. **Scanning and Monitoring**
Scanning enables you to effortlessly monitor multiple channels at the same time. This is a valuable tool for identifying active channels or staying informed about emergency communications. **To set up scanning:**
- **Create Scan Lists**: Establish a collection of channels to scan, specifically omitting those that are heavily affected by interference.

- **Set Scan Delay**: Configure a delay between scans to ensure ample time for detecting transmissions on each channel.
- **Enable Priority Channels**: Designate certain channels as priorities, guaranteeing they receive more frequent checks during scanning.

4. **Backing up and restoring configurations**

Programming GMRS radios can be quite time-consuming, especially when dealing with multiple devices. The backup and restore features enable you to conveniently save and restore your radio's configuration as required. This technique is incredibly valuable when it comes to upgrading radios or efficiently managing large groups of devices.

- **Backup Configurations**: Preserve your radio's current settings by saving them to a file for future use.
- **Restore Configurations:** When programming new radios, it is important to restore a saved configuration to maintain consistency across devices.

5. **Custom Tone Squelch Settings**

Settings like Continuous Tone-Coded Squelch System (CTCSS) and Digital-Coded Squelch (DCS) can effectively filter out unwanted signals. By adjusting these settings, you can minimize interference and improve privacy.

- **Choose Unique Tones**: Opt for tones that are not frequently used in your area to reduce interference.
- **Explore DCS Codes**: DCS codes provide increased flexibility and can be utilized alongside CTCSS for enhanced security.
- **Adjust Squelch Sensitivity**: Modify the squelch threshold to minimize false positives and enhance signal clarity.

CHAPTER TEN
GMRS RADIO COMMUNICATION WAYS

Overview

Chapter ten goes all the way to discussing GMRS Radio communication ways including understanding GMRS encryption, the types of encryptions in GMRS, implementing it, its advantages, and so much more. Get a grip on this chapter by reading the content below.

How to understand GMRS Encryption

Encryption in the world of radio communication involves transforming audio or data into a coded format that is not easily comprehensible without the correct decryption key or method. GMRS uses encryption to bolster the security and confidentiality of communications, effectively preventing unauthorized individuals from easily intercepting and comprehending conversations.

What are the Benefits of Encryption in GMRS?

Numerous factors drive individuals and businesses to opt for encryption in GMRS communication:

- **Privacy**: Encryption is crucial in maintaining the confidentiality of conversations, minimizing the possibility of unauthorized individuals listening in.
- **Security**: Encrypting communications ensures the protection of sensitive information and prevents unauthorized access to radio channels.
- **Compliance**: In certain situations, encrypted communications may be necessary to meet security requirements set by regulations or industry standards.

Types of Encryption in GMRS

GMRS communication commonly uses various encryption methods. Various factors need to be considered when selecting an encryption method, including the desired level of security, the type of radio equipment being used, and adherence to FCC regulations.

Here are some frequently used encryption methods in GMRS:

1. **Analog Scrambling**

Analog scrambling is a fundamental method of encryption that modifies the audio signal to make it challenging to comprehend without the correct descrambling technique. This technique is straightforward and offers a fundamental level of security for GMRS communication.

- **Advantages**: Analog scrambling is a simple process that does not necessitate advanced technology.

- **Downside**: This method may not provide the same level of security as other encryption methods, making it less ideal for highly sensitive communications.

2. **Digital Encryption**

Digital encryption is a highly advanced technique that transforms the audio or data signal into a digital format using encryption algorithms. This method provides a superior level of security when compared to analog scrambling.

- **Advantages**: Digital encryption offers enhanced security and is highly resistant to cracking.
- **Downside**: This method may necessitate the use of compatible radio equipment and could be slightly more intricate to configure.

3. **Proprietary Encryption**

Certain radio manufacturers provide exclusive encryption systems tailored to their equipment. The systems use advanced algorithms to ensure the utmost security in encrypting and decrypting communications.

- **Advantage**: Proprietary encryption is known for its strong security features and robustness.
- **Downside**: This method may only work with certain radio models and may not be compatible with other equipment.

How to Implement GMRS Encryption

Implementing encryption in GMRS necessitates meticulous planning and a comprehensive grasp of the chosen encryption method.

These are the essential steps to establish encrypted communication in GMRS:

Step 1: Obtain a GMRS License

Before implementing encryption in GMRS, it is crucial to possess a valid GMRS license issued by the FCC. Obtaining this license is necessary to ensure the legal operation of GMRS radios and includes coverage for the immediate family members of the licensee.

Step 2: Selecting the Appropriate Equipment

Choose radio equipment that is compatible with the encryption method you need. Take into account factors like the level of security, compatibility with other radios, and ease of use. Some radios have built-in encryption features, while others might need extra hardware or software for encryption.

Step 3: Set Up Encryption Settings

Configuring the appropriate settings on your GMRS radios will be necessary, depending on the encryption method you choose. There are several steps involved in this process, such as choosing the encryption type, establishing encryption keys, and configuring additional security features.

Step 4: Evaluate Communication

After configuring the encryption settings, it is important to test the communication between radios to verify that encryption and decryption are functioning correctly. Ensure that encrypted communications remain incomprehensible to unauthorized listeners.

Step 5: Educate Users

It is important to make sure that all users are familiar with the operation of the encrypted GMRS radios. Offer comprehensive training on encryption settings, best practices for usage, and effective troubleshooting techniques for common issues. It is important to educate users to prevent accidental disclosure of sensitive information and to ensure secure communication.

Best Practices for GMRS Encryption

For optimal use of GMRS encryption and to guarantee secure communication, it is advisable to adhere to the following recommended guidelines:

1. **Regularly change encryption keys**

For improved security, it is advisable to periodically update the encryption keys utilized in GMRS communication. This practice minimizes the chances of unauthorized access and ensures the preservation of privacy.

2. **Use Robust Encryption Algorithms**

Select encryption algorithms that provide a strong level of security and are resilient against common attacks. It is important to steer clear of weak or outdated encryption methods that can be easily compromised.

3. **Ensure Compatibility**

It is important to make sure that all radios and communication devices are compatible with the chosen encryption method when implementing GMRS encryption. The compatibility of our system ensures smooth communication within your group or organization.

4. **Adhere to FCC Regulations**

Ensure compliance with FCC regulations and guidelines for GMRS operation and encryption. Make sure your encryption setup complies with legal requirements to avoid any potential penalties or legal complications.

5. **Implement Access Control**

Ensure the implementation of robust access control measures to effectively safeguard encrypted GMRS radios and channels against unauthorized access. Various measures can be implemented to ensure that only authorized users have access, such as password protection and physical security.

6. **Maintain Confidentiality**

Inform users about the significance of maintaining confidentiality and ensuring secure communication. Highlight the importance of refraining from disclosing sensitive information or encryption keys to unauthorized individuals.

Understanding the benefits of GMRS Encryption

Encryption is a crucial component of modern communication systems. The process entails transforming data into a cipher to safeguard against unauthorized entry. Encryption in GMRS ensures that only authorized individuals can comprehend the transmitted messages, providing an added layer of security. This holds particular significance in situations where the exchange of sensitive information or the preservation of privacy is at stake. Although GMRS is a versatile communication tool, it is important to note that it is inherently open and accessible to anyone with the appropriate equipment. Privacy and security risks can arise in crowded or high-traffic areas due to this level of openness. Adding a layer of security to GMRS communications, encryption effectively mitigates these risks.

How GMRS Encryption Works

GMRS encryption uses a range of algorithms to encode messages, rendering them incomprehensible to individuals lacking the appropriate decryption key. When a message is transmitted, it undergoes encryption using a specific algorithm, which can range from a straightforward to a more intricate mathematical process. The encrypted message is transmitted through the airwaves and can be received by any GMRS device that is compatible. Only individuals in possession of the appropriate decryption key can transform the encrypted message back to its original state. The transmission is designed to be secure, making it difficult for anyone to decipher its contents without the proper key. The process of encryption and decryption occurs with remarkable speed, ensuring smooth communication without compromising security.

Benefits of GMRS Encryption

1. **Improved Security and Privacy**

GMRS encryption offers a notable benefit in terms of improved security and privacy. Encryption allows users to securely communicate sensitive information, ensuring that it remains private and protected from unauthorized interception. This is of utmost importance in a wide range of situations, including emergency operations, private family discussions, and business communications where maintaining confidentiality is essential.

2. **Ensuring Privacy from Eavesdropping**

Concerns about eavesdropping are frequently raised in open communication systems such as GMRS. It is important to note that conversations can potentially be listened in on by anyone with a GMRS receiver, which can raise privacy concerns. Encryption provides a reliable solution to eliminate the risk of intercepted messages being deciphered without the correct decryption key. Users can rest assured knowing that their communications will remain private.

3. **Reliable Emergency Communication**

During emergencies, it is crucial to have effective and reliable communication. GMRS is commonly utilized by emergency responders, search and rescue teams, and community organizations in times of disaster or critical events. Encryption provides a crucial layer of security for emergency communications, safeguarding them against unauthorized access and minimizing the potential for misinformation or interference. This is crucial for effectively coordinating rescue efforts and prioritizing public safety.

4. **Minimized Chance of Unauthorized Usage**

Encryption is an effective measure in preventing unauthorized use of GMRS frequencies. Requiring a decryption key to understand transmitted messages adds an extra layer of security, making it more difficult for unauthorized users to disrupt legitimate communications. This is especially beneficial in busy locations or during gatherings where numerous GMRS users are present.

5. **Enhanced Dependability and Confidence**

When users have the assurance that their communications are secure, it instills a sense of trust and confidence in the system. GMRS encryption is instrumental in establishing trust as it ensures a dependable and protected communication platform. This is particularly crucial for families and small groups that depend on GMRS for organizing outdoor activities or other group events.

Implementing GMRS Encryption

You need to make sure that their devices have the necessary encryption features to implement GMRS encryption. It is important to choose GMRS radios that have built-in encryption capabilities, as not all models come with this feature. After obtaining an encrypted GMRS radio, users can customize the encryption settings. This usually includes choosing an encryption algorithm and generating a decryption key. Users need to adhere to best practices when setting up encryption to achieve optimal security. It is important to consider various factors when it comes to encryption, such as selecting a robust encryption algorithm, safeguarding decryption keys, and regularly updating encryption settings to ensure security against unauthorized access. In addition, users need to familiarize themselves with the legal obligations regarding GMRS encryption in their respective regions. Certain areas may impose restrictions or provide specific guidelines for encrypted communication.

Challenges and Considerations

Although GMRS encryption has its benefits, it is important to be aware of the challenges and factors that need to be taken into account. Compatibility poses a significant challenge. Some GMRS radios may not offer encryption, while others that do may utilize various encryption algorithms. There may be compatibility issues when trying to communicate with other GMRS users. Another factor to consider is the increased level of complexity that comes with encryption. Although GMRS is generally user-friendly, the use of encryption may bring about some additional technical requirements. Users must have a clear understanding of how to properly configure and utilize encryption settings to prevent any potential communication issues. It is important to acknowledge that encryption is not infallible. While no encryption system is completely impervious to breaches or attacks, it does offer a robust layer of security. Users need to stay alert and adhere to best practices to ensure the security and reliability of their GMRS communications.

How to become an expert in GMRS Encryption

The use of encryption in GMRS ensures that conversations remain confidential and unauthorized listeners are unable to access them, providing a high level of security and privacy. It is worth mentioning that encryption is generally not permitted under FCC rules for GMRS. However, users frequently use privacy tones or codes, like Continuous Tone-Coded Squelch System (CTCSS) or Digital-Coded Squelch (DCS), to decrease interference and limit undesired communications. If you want to become an expert in GMRS encryption, it's crucial to have a radio that can support advanced features such as CTCSS, DCS, and other enhancements that prioritize privacy and security.

When choosing a GMRS radio, it's important to keep the following factors in mind:

- **Frequency Channels**: GMRS operates on a total of 22 primary channels. Make sure your radio is capable of covering these channels and supporting both simplex and repeater communication.
- **Power Output:** GMRS radios have a power output that can vary from 1 to 50 watts. Increased power output offers a greater range, making it particularly advantageous in rural or mountainous regions.
- **Privacy Features:** Consider radios with CTCSS/DCS functionality, as they can enhance communication privacy.
- **Additional Features:** Take into account radios that offer extra functionality such as weather alerts, dual-channel monitoring, and programmable scan functions to enhance their versatility.

Optimizing GMRS Range and Clarity

To make the most of GMRS with encryption and other privacy measures, it's important to prioritize optimizing your communication range and clarity.

Here are a few suggestions to improve your GMRS performance:

- **Antenna Selection**: Opt for a top-notch antenna that aligns with your communication requirements. Longer antennas typically offer improved range, although they may be less convenient to carry around. Take into account the type of communication device (handheld, mobile, or base station) when choosing an antenna.
- **Location and Terrain**: The range of GMRS can be influenced by factors such as geography and obstructions. Consider using a base station situated on higher ground or a mobile unit equipped with an external antenna to enhance range, as elevation tends to have a positive impact on signal strength.
- **Minimizing Interference**: Use CTCSS/DCS to reduce the impact of other radio users on your communication. In addition, it is important to be mindful of electronic devices that may generate interference on the frequency and try to avoid transmitting near them.

Proper Licensing and Regulations

GMRS operates under FCC regulations, so it's important to adhere to the rules when using these radios. To use GMRS legally, it is necessary to obtain a license from the FCC. This license is valid for 10 years and provides coverage for your entire family. While an exam is not necessary, there is a fee that needs to be paid. It is important to adhere to FCC regulations regarding frequency use, power limits, and antenna height. While encryption is not permitted on GMRS, there are alternative methods like CTCSS and DCS that can be used to improve communication privacy within the boundaries of regulations.

Effective Strategies for GMRS Communication

Mastering GMRS encryption goes beyond the basics of radio setup and privacy codes. It requires honing effective communication skills. **Here are some tips to help you effectively communicate and maintain security:**

- **Use Simple Language:** When communicating on GMRS, it's best to avoid using complicated codes or jargon that might confuse the people listening. Stick to language that is clear and concise.
- **Identify Yourself**: To adhere to FCC regulations, please remember to identify yourself at the beginning and end of your transmission. This practice also helps prevent any potential confusion with other radio users.
- **Respect Channel Use**: Be considerate of other users when utilizing shared GMRS channels and refrain from dominating the frequency. Remember to pause during your conversation to give others a chance to speak if necessary.
- **Emergency Preparedness**: It's important to have a list of GMRS frequencies for emergency communication. This can prove to be invaluable in times of natural disasters or other emergencies.

Decoding the mysteries of GMRS Encryption

Exploring the intricacies of GMRS encryption requires a deep dive into the realm of wireless communication and safeguarding data. This topic can be quite intricate and may demand expertise, but it can be comprehended by considering both its technical aspects and real-world implications. GMRS, also known as General Mobile Radio Service, is a radio service specifically designed for short-range, two-way communication. What is the meaning behind the term "**GMRS encryption**" when encryption is not allowed in GMRS? Typically, this term is commonly used to refer to the use of privacy codes or sub-audible tones to minimize interference caused by other users sharing the same channel. These privacy codes are commonly referred to as CTCSS (Continuous Tone-Coded Squelch System) or DCS (Digital-Coded Squelch). CTCSS and DCS do not encrypt the signal; rather, they incorporate a distinct tone or digital code into the transmission. Some radios are programmed to detect and respond to a specific tone or code, causing them to un-mute and allow the signal to be heard. Meanwhile, other radios will stay silent. This system effectively minimizes interference from other users on the same frequency, although it does not provide a guarantee of secure communication that is impervious to interception or comprehension.

GMRS and Data Encryption

If encryption is not permitted on GMRS channels, how can one guarantee the confidentiality of communication? When it comes to applications that demand top-notch security, alternative radio services or communication methods are necessary. For instance, various services such as business radio services, public safety communications, and other licensed frequencies may offer encryption as an additional security measure. These services usually involve more advanced equipment and licensing, but they provide a higher degree of control over communication access. Consider using digital radios or software-based communication systems that offer encryption as an alternative. DMR, for example, is a widely used standard for digital radio communication that supports encryption.

Legal and Ethical Considerations

It is important to have a comprehensive understanding of the legal and ethical implications when discussing encryption and secure communication. Radio communication is regulated by the FCC, and it's important to be aware that using encryption on GMRS channels can result in fines or other penalties. This restriction is in place to maintain the accessibility and openness of GMRS as a communication platform for general use, including emergencies. From an ethical standpoint, encryption can be viewed as having both positive and negative implications. Although it offers privacy and security, it may hinder emergency responders or other authorized personnel from accessing crucial information in times of crisis. Encryption is typically prohibited on public radio services such as GMRS.

Alternatives to GMRS Encryption

If you require a method of communication that prioritizes security but cannot utilize encryption, there are alternative approaches that you may want to explore:

1. **Use Private Channels**: Certain radios provide the option to establish private channels through the use of designated frequencies, tones, or codes. This solution does not offer encryption, but it effectively minimizes interference and prevents unauthorized listeners.
2. **Implement Access Control**: In a group setting, manage and regulate the access to specific radios or communication channels. Limiting unauthorized access to your communication network is crucial.
3. **Use Digital Radios:** Although they are not officially part of GMRS, digital radios often provide advanced features such as encryption, without being subject to the same restrictions. If you require enhanced security in your communication, please consider these options.
4. **Implement Secure Communication Practices:** By implementing secure communication practices, you can effectively safeguard sensitive information, even without encryption. This involves employing language that is both clear and tactful, restricting the disclosure of personal details, and ensuring that only authorized individuals operate radios.

CHAPTER ELEVEN
GMRS RADIO SETTINGS

Overview

Understanding GMRS Radio settings is as important as setting and using the radio. Here, you will learn how to adjust squelch and volume levels, how to adjust the volume, how to integrate a radio system, and others.

How to adjust squelch and volume levels

The squelch feature is specifically designed to minimize any static noise that may occur on a radio channel. This is achieved by effectively eliminating weak signals or interference, guaranteeing that only crystal-clear transmissions are received. If the squelch adjustment is not set correctly, you can encounter persistent static noise or miss crucial transmissions as a result of excessive interference.

How Squelch Works

1. **Threshold Setting:** The operation of squelch involves the adjustment of a threshold. When the signal strength surpasses this threshold, the audio is permitted to pass through; otherwise, the radio remains silent.
2. **Elimination of Unwanted Noise:** Adjusting the squelch allows you to control the amount of signal required for the radio to produce sound, effectively eliminating unwanted noise. This adjustment ensures the elimination of any unwanted noise and prioritizes clear transmissions.

What does Volume Control mean?

The volume control is easy to understand as it controls the level of audio output from the radio. Properly adjusting the volume allows for clear reception without inconveniencing those around you or causing any discomfort from overly high levels of sound.

The Significance of Volume Control

1. **Comfort and Clarity:** The volume adjustment feature ensures that you can listen to transmissions with optimal clarity, striking the perfect balance between being too loud and too soft.
2. **Situational Awareness**: Maintaining situational awareness is crucial, as it allows you to stay alert to your surroundings and not miss any important communications.

Adjusting Squelch on GMRS Radios

Here are the steps to adjust the squelch on a GMRS radio:

1. **Locate the Squelch Control:** The squelch control can be found in different forms, such as a knob, button, or menu option, depending on the model.
2. **Disable the Squelch:** Begin by deactivating the squelch or adjusting it to its minimum level. This step enables you to listen to all signals, including any background noise and static.
3. **Increase the Squelch Level**: Gradually raise the squelch level while actively listening for any signs of noise. Keep making adjustments until the background noise is eliminated and you can hear only clear transmissions.
4. **Adjust for Clarity**: Once you've found a suitable squelch level, make small adjustments to ensure you don't overlook any faint yet significant signals. The optimal squelch level is slightly higher than the threshold at which noise becomes inaudible.
5. **Confirming Squelch Setting:** To ensure the accuracy of your squelch setting, it is recommended to test it with a known signal, such as another GMRS radio transmitting close. If the signal is clear and free from background noise, then your squelch adjustment is complete.

How to Adjust Volume on GMRS Radios

Adjusting the volume on GMRS radios is usually a simple process. Here is a step-by-step guide:

1. **Find the Volume Control:** The volume control is typically a knob or button on the radio. Make sure to identify it before making any adjustments.
2. **Begin with a low volume**: Start by setting the volume to its lowest level to prevent any abrupt loud sounds.
3. **Boost the Volume over time**: Gradually raise the volume while listening to a familiar signal. Keep making adjustments until the audio reaches a level that feels comfortable.
4. **Experiment in Different Environments**: To guarantee that the volume is suitable for a range of settings, try testing it in indoor, outdoor, and noisy environments. Make appropriate adjustments to ensure effective communication without being overly loud.
5. **Discovering the Perfect Volume**: It's important to find a volume level that strikes the right balance - clear enough to hear transmissions without causing any discomfort or being too faint.

Troubleshooting Common Issues

Despite making proper squelch and volume adjustments, you may still come across some common issues. **Here's a guide on how to address them:**

1. **Dealing with Background Noise**: To minimize the impact of background noise, consider adjusting the squelch level. If this doesn't assist, consider examining for potential interference caused by other devices or environmental factors.
2. **Missed Transmissions**: To ensure you don't miss any transmissions, try adjusting the squelch level to allow weaker signals to come through. Additionally, make sure to adjust the volume to a level that is audible to you.
3. **Addressing Inconsistent Audio Levels**: To resolve any issues with inconsistent volume, it is recommended to check for loose connections or potential interference. Make any necessary adjustments to the squelch and volume settings.
4. **No Signal Reception**: Make sure to check if you are tuned in to the correct frequency and that your radio is in good working condition if you are not receiving any signals. Additionally, please ensure that the antenna is thoroughly inspected for any signs of damage or incorrect installation.

Tips for Optimal Squelch and Volume Adjustment

- **Use a Recognizable Signal for Testing**: When fine-tuning squelch and volume settings, it is advisable to employ a familiar signal from either another GMRS radio or a transmission originating from a specific location. This method greatly enhances your ability to pinpoint the optimal settings with precision.
- **Environmental Considerations**: Signal quality can be influenced by various environmental factors such as weather conditions, terrain, and obstacles. Make sure to adjust the squelch and volume settings to match your specific location and the environment around you.
- **Keep up with regular maintenance**: Make sure to regularly check your GMRS radio for any signs of wear and tear. Ensure to clean the contacts, check the battery, and ensure the antenna is securely attached. Regular maintenance is crucial to avoid any potential problems that might impact the squelch and volume levels.
- **Know the Legal Requirements**: Note that GMRS radios must have an FCC license to operate, so it's important to be aware of the legal requirements. Make sure to adhere to all regulations and have a clear understanding of the frequencies permitted for use.

How to integrate and interface a Radio System

GMRS has the following features:

- **License Requirement:** GMRS operation requires a license from the Federal Communications Commission (FCC), unlike the Family Radio Service (FRS). One GMRS license provides coverage for the licensee and their immediate family, enabling more extensive usage.

- **Power Output**: GMRS enables a higher power output compared to FRS, resulting in an extended communication range. Mobile and base stations have a higher transmission power of up to 50 watts, whereas handheld radios usually have a lower limit of 5 watts.
- **Channel Sharing:** GMRS and FRS share certain channels, allowing licensed and unlicensed users to communicate on specific frequencies.
- **Repeater Capability**: GMRS radios can utilize repeaters, which allows for an extended communication range that is not accessible to FRS users.

When it comes to integrating and interfacing a radio system in GMRS, there are several important considerations to keep in mind. Now, we can delve into the necessary steps to establish a GMRS system and connect it with other communication systems.

Step 1: Determine the Purpose and Scope

Before establishing a GMRS system, it is crucial to identify the main objective and extent of the system. Take a moment to reflect on the following questions:

- What is the purpose of the GMRS system? What is the purpose of this? Is it for personal communication, family coordination, or emergency preparedness?
- What is the estimated number of users and the geographical scope of the system?
- Will the system be used alongside other communication systems like FRS, CB, or amateur radio?

These questions are crucial in determining the next steps for setting up and connecting your GMRS system.

Step 2: Acquire a GMRS License

To operate a GMRS system within the bounds of the law, it is necessary to obtain a license from the FCC. The license remains valid for ten years, providing comprehensive coverage for the licensee as well as their immediate family.

Here are the steps to apply for a GMRS license:

- Make sure to visit the FCC's Universal Licensing System (ULS) website and create an account if you haven't done so already.
- Fill out the application form for a GMRS license, ensuring that all the required information is provided.
- Ensure that the application fee is paid following the FCC's requirements.
- After receiving approval, the FCC will provide you with a GMRS call sign. This call sign is essential for identifying your system when communicating.

Step 3: Choose GMRS Radios and Equipment

Choosing the appropriate GMRS radios and equipment is essential for ensuring efficient communication. Here are some different types of GMRS radios to consider:

- **Handheld Radios**: Handheld GMRS radios are perfect for personal use, family outings, and recreational activities due to their portability and convenience. They usually have a modest power output, but they are quite versatile.
- **Mobile Radios**: Perfect for vehicle installation, mobile GMRS radios provide a higher power output, making them a great choice for off-roading, caravans, and emergency response.
- **Base Stations:** These fixed radios are used at a home or office to provide a stable communication point with a broader range.

Furthermore, it would be beneficial to explore the option of incorporating repeaters into your GMRS system to enhance its communication range. Repeaters play a crucial role in extending communication range by receiving and retransmitting signals.

Step 4: Setting Up and Customizing Your GMRS System

Once you have obtained your GMRS license and equipment, you are ready to proceed with the installation and configuration of your GMRS system.

Here are some important factors to keep in mind during the installation process:

- **Location and Antennas**: Select suitable locations for base stations and repeaters. Make sure to mount antennas at the most effective heights to achieve the best signal range.
- **Programming Frequencies**: It is essential to program GMRS radios with accurate frequencies. Make sure to set the input and output frequencies correctly when using repeaters.
- **Repeater Setup**: Make sure to properly configure repeaters with the appropriate tones and offsets. The communication between radios and repeaters is seamless.
- **Emergency Channels:** It may be helpful to designate specific channels for emergency communication to ensure quick access during critical situations.

Step 5: Connect with Other Communication Systems

For optimal use of your GMRS system, it's worth exploring the possibility of integrating it with other communication systems. Here are some frequently used integration:

- **Family Radio Service (FRS):** GMRS shares some channels with FRS, enabling communication between licensed GMRS users and unlicensed FRS users. This integration is beneficial for groups or events that have diverse communication requirements.

- **CB Radio**: Although CB operates on different frequencies; some users prefer to combine GMRS with CB for expanded communication capabilities. One way to accomplish this is by using a dual-radio setup or by using a cross-band repeater.
- **Amateur Radio**: If there are members in your group who have amateur radio licenses, it is possible to connect GMRS with amateur radio through the use of specialized equipment and repeaters.
- **Intercom Systems**: GMRS can be seamlessly integrated with intercom systems, allowing for efficient in-building communication and coordination across multiple sites.

Step 6: Set Up Communication Protocols

Clear and concise communication in a GMRS system depends on established protocols. It is important to establish clear guidelines for using the system to prevent interference and ensure smooth communication. **Take into account the following aspects:**

- **Channel Allocation**: Establishing the appropriate channels for various purposes, including general communication, emergency response, and event coordination.
- **Call Signs and Identifiers**: All users need to use correct call signs and identifiers to maintain accountability and avoid any confusion during communication.
- **Etiquette and Procedures:** Establish guidelines for effective communication, including appropriate radio usage, transmission procedures, and protocols for emergency response.

Step 7: Keep it up to date Your GMRS System

It is crucial to regularly maintain and update your GMRS system to ensure its ongoing reliability. Here are some factors to take into account:

- **Equipment Inspection**: It is important to regularly inspect radios, repeaters, antennas, and other equipment for any signs of wear or damage.
- **Updates for the software**: Make sure to keep your GMRS radios' programmable software up to date for the best performance.
- **License Renewal**: It is important to stay on top of your GMRS license expiration date and make sure to renew it promptly to prevent any interruptions in communication.

Tips and tricks on using GMRS Radio effectively

After setting up and testing your GMRS radio, it's important to shift your attention towards adopting best practices for optimal use. These tips will assist you in effectively and efficiently communicating, regardless of whether you find yourself in the great outdoors or attending a social gathering.

Establishing a Communication Protocol

To ensure effective communication using GMRS radios, it is crucial to establish a clear and concise protocol.

Here are a few important factors to keep in mind:

- **Call Signs**: Assign unique call signs to individuals or teams. This practice helps prevent misunderstandings and improves the efficiency of communication.
- **Message Clarity:** Ensure that you speak slowly and clearly. Use clear and straightforward language to ensure your message is easily understood.
- **Confirmation**: It is important to acknowledge receipt of a message by responding with a simple **"copy"** or **"received."**
- **Priority Communication:** Implement a system to ensure urgent messages are given precedence over routine communication.

Using GMRS Radios in Different Environments

GMRS radios are highly adaptable and can be used in a variety of settings, although their performance may vary depending on the surrounding conditions.

Here's a guide to help you make the most of their effectiveness in different situations:

- **Urban Areas**: Radio signals can be affected by the presence of buildings and other structures in cities. Consider using higher power settings and potentially incorporating a repeater to effectively extend the range.
- **Rural Areas:** GMRS radios perform exceptionally well in open environments. Take advantage of elevated positions to maximize your range and be mindful of the weather, as it can affect signal strength.
- **Forested Areas:** The presence of trees and foliage can limit the range. Optimize your channel selection to minimize interference and enhance signal strength by using an external antenna.
- **Mountains and Hills:** The elevation of the terrain can have both positive and negative effects on GMRS communication. Ensure that you have unobstructed views and utilize repeaters whenever feasible to uphold effective communication.

GMRS Radios for Emergency Preparedness

GMRS radios are highly dependable and have an extensive range, making them perfect for emergencies. **For optimal using of your GMRS radio during emergencies, keep the following tips in mind:**

- **Emergency Channels:** Establish dedicated channels for emergency communication within your group. This ensures that everyone is aware of where to turn for assistance when it is needed.
- **Weather Alerts:** Stay informed about severe weather conditions by using GMRS radios with NOAA weather alert capability.
- **Redundancy**: Ensure continuous communication during extended emergencies by having backup radios and batteries for redundancy.
- **Coordination**: It is important to establish a communication plan with your group or community to ensure a well-coordinated response in emergencies.

CHAPTER TWELVE
CARING FOR YOUR GMRS RADIO

Overview

Chapter twelve talks about how to properly care for your GMRS Radio including checking regularly and inspecting your GMRS Radio, maintaining the radio, and troubleshooting some issues.

How to regularly check and inspect your GMRS Radio

A GMRS radio usually consists of multiple components that need to be inspected regularly.

Here are the components:

- **Antenna**: The antenna is responsible for transmitting and receiving signals.
- **Microphone**: The microphone converts voice into electrical signals.
- **Speaker**: Transforms electrical signals into sound.
- **Battery**: Supplies power to the radio.
- **Controls and Displays**: Consists of a user-friendly interface with buttons, knobs, and digital displays for easy operation of the radio.
- **Housing**: The protective outer shell for internal components.

Regular Inspection

It is important to regularly inspect GMRS radios to proactively identify any potential issues that may arise.
Here are a few crucial steps to keep in mind:
1. **Visual Inspection**
Begin by visually examining the exterior of the radio. Inspect the item for any visible signs of physical damage, such as cracks, scratches, or loose components. It is important to give careful consideration to the antenna and housing, as these components are frequently exposed to damage over time. If any damage is observed, it may be worth considering repairing or replacing the affected parts.
2. **Check the Antenna**
The antenna plays a crucial role in the functionality of the GMRS radio. Examine it closely for any signs of bends, breaks, or other indications of damage. The quality and range of your signal can be greatly impacted by a damaged antenna. Make sure the antenna is firmly connected to the radio and does not move around. Ensure to inspect the connection point for any signs of corrosion or debris if the antenna is removable.

3. **Test the microphone and speaker**

Clear communication relies on the microphone and speaker. Ensure the microphone is functioning properly by speaking into it and checking the output. If there are any issues with distortion or low volume, it could be due to the need for cleaning or replacement. Assess the speaker's performance by playing a sample transmission at various volumes. Make sure to check for any obstructions or damage if you're experiencing static or low output.

4. **Battery Inspection**

The GMRS radio relies heavily on its battery for power. Make sure to carefully examine the battery for any indications of swelling, corrosion, or leakage. Replacing a damaged battery is crucial due to the potential hazards it can pose. Inspect the battery contacts for any signs of corrosion and, if needed, gently clean them using a soft cloth or alcohol. Make sure the battery is securely placed in its compartment if it can be removed.

5. **Testing Controls and Displays**

The controls and displays are designed to facilitate the easy operation of the GMRS radio. Make sure to test every button and knob to ensure they are functioning correctly. The digital display should be easily readable and easy to understand. If the display appears dim or difficult to read, it is recommended to check the backlight or consider replacing the display module.

6. **Check for Firmware Updates**

Most modern GMRS radios are equipped with firmware that governs their operation. Make sure to visit the manufacturer's website and see if there are any firmware updates. If there are, go ahead and install them. Firmware updates have the potential to enhance performance and address any existing bugs.

Testing Radio Functionality

Once the physical components have been thoroughly inspected, it is important to test the functionality of the radio to ensure that it is operating as expected.

Here is a suggested course of action:

1. **Testing Transmission and Reception**

For a thorough evaluation of the radio's transmission and reception capabilities, it is recommended to engage in communication with another GMRS radio at different distances. This will assist you in assessing the radio's efficiency in transmitting and receiving signals. If the signal quality is not up to par or if there is an abundance of static, it could suggest a problem with the antenna, microphone, or other components.

2. **Experiment with various channels**

GMRS radios can be used on a variety of channels. Make sure to test every channel to ensure proper functionality. This will assist you in determining whether there are any problems with certain frequencies or if the radio is being affected by interference.

3. **Testing Privacy Codes and Tones**

GMRS radios commonly feature privacy codes and tones to minimize interference. Please test these features to ensure they are functioning correctly. Make sure to verify the radio's settings and reset them if needed, in case they are not functioning properly.

GMRS Radio Maintenance

Performing regular maintenance on your GMRS radio is crucial for maximizing its lifespan and ensuring it operates at its best.

Here are a few maintenance suggestions:

1. **Maintain a Clean Radio**

The radio's performance can be affected by the accumulation of dust and debris on its exterior. Regularly clean the radio with a soft, damp cloth to maintain its cleanliness. It is advisable to refrain from using harsh chemicals, as they have the potential to cause harm to the housing or internal components.

2. **Keep it in a secure place**

It is important to store the GMRS radio in a secure and dry place when it is not being used. It is important to protect the radio from extreme temperatures, moisture, or direct sunlight. Storing the radio correctly is crucial for avoiding any harm and ensuring its longevity.

3. **Ensure Proper Battery Charging**

It is important to adhere to the manufacturer's instructions when charging the battery. It is important to be cautious when it comes to charging your device. Using an incorrect charger or overcharging can potentially harm the battery. For optimal battery performance, it's a good idea to rotate the use of your spare batteries to promote even wear and tear.

4. **Review FCC Regulations**

The FCC regulates GMRS radios. Make sure to obtain a valid FCC license for GMRS use and strictly adhere to all regulations about frequencies, power output, and operating guidelines. Adhering to FCC regulations is crucial for avoiding penalties and maintaining a safe operating environment.

5. **Schedule Regular Inspections**

Regular inspections and testing are essential for maintaining the optimal condition of your GMRS radio. The frequency of the billing cycle can vary, depending on your radio usage. Regular inspections are crucial in detecting potential issues at an early stage, thereby preventing more serious problems in the future.

Troubleshooting common GMRS Radio issues

Despite being well maintained and cared for, GMRS radios can still encounter technical issues. **Here is some of the most common issues users' encounter, along with steps to troubleshoot and resolve them:**

1. **Reception Issues or Lack of Signal**

Signs:
- Struggling to hear other users.
- There seems to be a frequent occurrence of static or noise on the line.
- The signal was lost completely.

Troubleshooting Steps:

- **Verify the Antenna**: Make sure the antenna is securely connected and in excellent condition. The quality of reception can be greatly affected by a damaged or loose antenna.
- **Check the Battery**: A weak battery can cause a decrease in transmission power, which can impact reception. Make sure the battery is fully charged or replace it if necessary.
- **Adjusting the Squelch**: The Squelch feature allows you to control the level of noise required for the radio to activate the audio channel. Setting it too high could potentially hinder your ability to detect faint signals. Adjust it slightly to enhance reception.
- **Confirm the Frequency and Tone:** Ensure that you are tuned to the appropriate frequency and using the correct CTCSS or DCS tone, if necessary. Communication issues can arise from a mismatch.

2. **Interference and Noise**

Signs and symptoms:

- Consistent or sporadic static noise.
- Unwanted signals or cross-talk from other users can be quite frustrating.

Troubleshooting Steps:

- **Switch the Channel**: Interference can occur when there are other GMRS or FRS users nearby. Perhaps trying a different channel could help resolve the issue.
- **Move to a Different Location**: Consider relocating to a different area if you find yourself in a location with a lot of radio traffic. This change in scenery could potentially help minimize any interference you may be experiencing.
- **Check for Nearby Electronics**: Be mindful of any nearby devices such as microwaves, wireless routers, and other electronics that may cause interference. It is advisable to keep your radio away from such devices.

3. **Inadequate Battery Life**

Signs:

- Battery life depletes quickly.
- Has trouble maintaining battery life.

Troubleshooting Steps:

- **Replacing the Battery**: As time goes on, batteries naturally lose their ability to retain a charge. If your battery is showing signs of wear or is often drained, it may be time to consider getting a replacement.
- **Verify the Functionality of the Charging Equipment:** Make sure the charger is operating properly. Consider trying a different charger or charging cable to see if that resolves the issue.
- **Prevent Overcharging**: Excessive charging can harm the battery's lifespan. It is important to adhere to the manufacturer's guidelines regarding charging times.
- **Use Battery-Saving Features**: Numerous GMRS radios come equipped with power-saving modes that effectively prolong battery life. If these features are available, please enable them.

4. **Audio Output Issue**

Signs:

- Not able to hear any sound coming from the radio.
- The speaker or earpiece is not providing any response.

Troubleshooting Steps:

- **Verify the Volume**: Although it may seem like a basic step, make sure the volume is turned up. Improper adjustments may result in radios that do not produce sound.
- **Check the Speaker:** Examine the speaker for any signs of damage or obstructions that could affect its performance. Handle it with care, using a gentle touch and a soft cloth or compressed air.
- **Test with Headphones or an External Speaker**: Consider using headphones or an external speaker if your radio has an audio output jack. If the audio is functioning properly with these, there may be an issue with the internal speaker.
- **Perform a Factory Reset**: If the issue continues, you may want to reset the radio to its original factory settings. This can effectively address software-related issues that may be causing audio problems.

5. **Transmission Problems**

Signs:

- When transmitting, it seems that others are unable to hear you.
- Your voice sounds faint or distorted.

Troubleshooting Steps:

- **Inspect the Microphone:** Make sure the microphone is not obstructed or in a damaged condition. Handle it with care if necessary.
- **Confirm the Frequency and Tone:** Just like with reception problems, make sure you are tuned to the correct frequency and use the appropriate CTCSS or DCS tone.
- **Inspect the Antenna**: Make sure to inspect the antenna as it can have an impact on transmission if it is damaged or not properly attached. If necessary, replace or reattach it.
- **Test with a Different Radio:** Consider trying a different GMRS radio for transmission, if available. If the problem continues, it could be a potential issue with the transmitter of your original radio.

6. **Malfunctioning Controls and Display**

Signs:

- Buttons or controls are unresponsive.
- The display appears to be blank or distorted.

Troubleshooting Steps:

- **Try restarting the Radio**: Occasionally, powering off and then on the radio can help resolve control issues.
- **Check the Buttons**: Ensure there is no dirt or debris around the buttons. Use a gentle cloth or compressed air to clean them.

- **Make sure to check the display connections**. In case the display appears blank or distorted, the internal connections may be loose. Professional repair is usually necessary for this.
- **Perform a Factory Reset**: If other troubleshooting steps prove ineffective, consider resetting the radio to its original factory settings.

How to know basic spectrum analyzer operation

A spectrum analyzer is a crucial tool for individuals who work with radio frequencies (RF), including General Mobile Radio Service (GMRS) users. This tool allows you to effectively visualize and analyze the frequency spectrum, ensuring that operations are carried out correctly and in compliance with regulations. A spectrum analyzer is a device that accurately measures the magnitude of an input signal across its entire frequency range. This tool is commonly used to display the frequency components of a signal, which is extremely useful for tasks such as signal identification, bandwidth measurement, and interference detection. There are two main types of spectrum analyzers: swept-tuned and Fast Fourier Transform (FFT) analyzers. Each type has its unique advantages.

Spectrum Analyzers with Swept-Tuning

The spectrum analyzers with swept-tuned technology are capable of scanning through a designated frequency range, allowing for the immediate visualization of signals. The devices operate by adjusting across a range of frequencies using a filter that focuses on a specific bandwidth while assessing the strength of the signal at each frequency point. These analyzers are versatile and can be used in many different applications. They have a high dynamic range, which makes them perfect for analyzing a wide range of frequencies.

FFT Spectrum Analyzers

FFT spectrum analyzers use the Fast Fourier Transform algorithm to convert time-domain signals into frequency-domain data. This method enables quicker analysis of a broad frequency range, although its dynamic range is often restricted compared to swept-tuned analyzers. FFT analyzers are highly effective for capturing transient signals or monitoring frequency changes over time.

Important Features of Spectrum Analyzers

Before diving into the applications of spectrum analyzers in GMRS, it's important to familiarize yourself with some essential features that will help you make the most of these devices.
- **Frequency Range**

A spectrum analyzer's ability to analyze signals is determined by its frequency range. A spectrum analyzer for GMRS applications should cover the frequency range of 462-467 MHz, as this is the operating range for GMRS. There are analyzers with broader ranges that allow for the examination of a wider spectrum, while others are specifically optimized for certain bands.

- **Resolution Bandwidth (RBW)**

The resolution bandwidth is a measure of the frequency bandwidth that the spectrum analyzer is capable of measuring. The smaller RBW provides a higher level of frequency resolution, allowing you to differentiate signals that are closely spaced. On the other hand, opting for a narrower RBW will result in slower scanning speeds. Consider selecting an RBW that aligns with your specific requirements. For GMRS, a typical RBW range is between 10 kHz to 100 kHz.

- **Video Bandwidth (VBW)**

The video bandwidth is the filter that is applied to the signal after detection to eliminate noise and enhance the clarity of the display. A wider VBW can result in a smoother trace, although it may also decrease the sensitivity to faint signals. Optimal results can be achieved by carefully balancing RBW and VBW.

Sweep Time and Span

The sweep time is the duration required for the spectrum analyzer to cover the entire frequency range. Increasing the sweep time enhances the chances of detecting weaker signals, whereas shorter sweep times are beneficial for observing rapid changes. The span refers to the frequency range that is displayed on the screen. Setting the span to cover the entire band (462-467 MHz) is a recommended starting point for GMRS.

Reference Level

The reference level determines the highest signal level that is shown on the spectrum analyzer screen. Understanding how to adjust the reference level allows for better visualization of signals with varying amplitudes. Setting the reference level too high may cause weaker signals to go unnoticed. On the other hand, if the display is set too low, it might saturate and make it difficult to see signal details.

Using Spectrum Analyzers for GMRS

Now that you have a good grasp of how spectrum analyzers work, let's delve into their practical use in GMRS.

Here are some typical situations where a spectrum analyzer can come in handy:

- **Signal Analysis**

If you're dealing with GMRS radios, it's important to analyze the signal to ensure it complies with regulations and functions properly. The spectrum analyzer allows you to visually analyze the frequency components of the signal, ensuring that it falls within the authorized GMRS band and does not generate any undesired emissions or harmonics.

- **Interference Detection**

Interference has the potential to cause disruptions in communication and negatively impact the quality of the signal. Using a spectrum analyzer allows you to easily detect and pinpoint the origin of any disruptive signals. Through careful analysis of the frequency spectrum, one can identify any unauthorized transmissions or spurious emissions that may have an impact on GMRS operations.

- **Antenna Tuning**

The effectiveness of GMRS radios is impacted by the antenna system's quality. A spectrum analyzer is a useful tool for tuning antennas as it can display the return loss or Voltage Standing Wave Ratio (VSWR). Optimizing these parameters can enhance signal strength and extend transmission range.

- **Power Measurements**

Power output regulations must be followed when using GMRS radios. With a spectrum analyzer, you can effectively gauge the output power of your radio and make sure it complies with the required standards. This ensures that you won't face any penalties for non-compliance and guarantees a safe operation.

- **Signal-to-noise ratio (SNR)**

SNR plays a crucial role in determining the quality of communication. Using a spectrum analyzer, you can accurately measure the SNR and pinpoint any potential sources of noise and interference. Enhancing SNR can significantly improve the clarity and reliability of communication.

- **Harmonic and Spurious Emissions**

Spectrum analyzers are capable of detecting harmonics and spurious emissions, providing valuable insights into potential issues with your GMRS equipment. Addressing and resolving these concerns is crucial for meeting regulatory requirements and preventing any disruptions for other users.

Using Spectrum Analyzer in GMRS

For optimal use of a spectrum analyzer in GMRS, it is important to adhere to the following steps:

1. **Setup and Calibration**: Connect the spectrum analyzer to a suitable power source and make sure it is correctly calibrated. Calibration is essential for achieving precise measurements and minimizing errors in measurements.
2. **Connect the GMRS Radio**: Connect the radio's antenna output to the spectrum analyzer's input using a coaxial cable. Ensure that the connections are properly secured to prevent any potential signal loss.
3. **Set Frequency Range and Span:** Configure the spectrum analyzer's frequency range to cover the GMRS band (462-467 MHz). Ensure that the span is adjusted to encompass the full range to effectively visualize all potential signals.
4. **Adjust RBW and VBW:** Choose appropriate RBW and VBW settings to ensure optimal resolution while minimizing noise. A typical RBW for GMRS analysis is around 10 kHz to 100 kHz.
5. **Set Sweep Time**: Adjust the sweep time to best suit the expected signal strength and level of detail you desire. It is important to consider the sweep time when detecting signals. Longer sweep times are ideal for detecting weak signals, while shorter times are more suitable for quick scans.
6. **Adjust the Reference Level:** Ensure that the reference level is properly set so that all signals are visible on the display without any saturation. Make any necessary adjustments depending on the strength of the signal.

7. **Examine the Spectrum**: Once the setup is finished, begin the sweep and carefully observe the spectrum. Be sure to carefully scan the GMRS band for any signs of abnormal peaks or interference.
8. **Identify Interference**: If signals are detected outside the expected frequency range, it is important to investigate their source. Identify whether the source of the problem lies with external radio services or internal equipment malfunctions.
9. **Conduct Power Measurements**: Ensure compliance with regulations by measuring the output power of your GMRS radio. Examine the results concerning the manufacturer's specifications and regulatory limits.
10. **Check for Harmonics and Spurious Emissions**: Ensure the presence of harmonics and spurious emissions by carefully analyzing the spectrum. If you come across any, thoroughly examine the possible causes and promptly address them.
11. **Document your Findings:** Make sure to maintain a detailed log of your spectrum analyzer settings, measurements, and any problems you come across. This documentation is valuable for troubleshooting and showcasing compliance during inspections.

Tips to Maintain Your GMRS Radio

They include the following:

1. **Read the Manual:** Make sure to consult the user manual for your GMRS radio, as it contains important details on how to operate and take care of the device. It is important to have a clear understanding of the specific requirements of your model.
2. **Handle with Care**: Be cautious when handling the radio to prevent any accidental drops or impacts. Proper care is essential to maintain the integrity of internal components and ensure optimal performance.
3. **Maintain Cleanliness**: Dust and dirt tend to build up over some time. Remember to use a soft, dry cloth when cleaning your radio. It is advisable to refrain from using harsh chemicals or abrasive materials, as they have the potential to cause harm to the casing.
4. **Use the Appropriate Channels and Frequencies**: It is crucial to use the correct GMRS channels and frequencies to prevent any interference or potential legal complications.

Maintaining Your Battery

The battery of your GMRS radio plays a crucial role and taking good care of it can significantly prolong its lifespan.
1. **Ensure Proper Charging**: It is important to always use the charger specifically designed for your radio's battery. It's important to be cautious when charging your battery to avoid any potential damage.
2. **Be mindful of temperature**: Extreme heat or cold can have an impact on the battery's lifespan and how well it functions. It is important to protect the radio and battery from extreme temperatures and direct sunlight.

3. **Proper Storage**: To ensure the longevity of your radio, it is recommended to remove the battery when storing it for a long period. This will prevent any potential leakage and damage to the radio.
4. **Check for Corrosion:** Inspect the battery contacts for any signs of corrosion to ensure they are in good condition. If you come across any, use a gentle cloth and a small quantity of isopropyl alcohol to clean them.

Antenna Care

The antenna plays a crucial role in the functionality of your GMRS radio. Here are some tips for keeping it in good condition:
1. **Proper Installation is Key:** It is crucial to ensure that the antenna is securely attached to the radio. Strong connections are essential for optimal signal quality.
2. **Inspect for Damage:** Ensure there are no cracks or any indications of damage. It is crucial to promptly replace a damaged antenna to prevent any negative impact on radio performance.
3. **Avoid Bending or Twisting**: It is important to refrain from bending or twisting the antenna as this can weaken its structure. Maintain its natural shape for optimal performance.

Microphone and Speaker Maintenance

Effective communication is crucial when using GMRS radios, making it vital to maintain the microphone and speaker in optimal condition.
1. **Ensure the Microphone and Speaker are Clean**: Use a gentle cloth to wipe down these crucial components. It is important to refrain from blowing into the microphone, as this can lead to moisture buildup and potential damage.
2. **Verify Connections**: Make sure the microphone and speaker connections are properly secured. Having loose connections can result in subpar audio quality.
3. **Regularly Test Audio**: It is important to periodically test the microphone and speaker to make sure they are functioning correctly. If any distortion or other issues are noticed, it is important to promptly investigate and address them.

Regular Maintenance and Testing

Regular maintenance and testing are crucial for detecting potential issues before they escalate into significant problems.
1. **Conduct Functionality Tests**: Regularly test all functions of your GMRS radio. One important aspect to consider is the evaluation of signal strength, audio quality, and range.
2. **Check for Signs of Wear and Tear:** Examine the radio's casing, controls, and other components for any indications of damage or deterioration. Take immediate action to address any issues you come across to avoid any further damage.

3. **Protect Your Radio**: It's a good idea to use a protective case to keep your radio safe from any potential damage. This is particularly beneficial if you often use your radio outside.
4. **Update Firmware and Software**: GMRS radios may have the option to update their firmware or software. Make sure to visit the manufacturer's website for any updates and carefully follow their installation instructions.

Properly Storing Your GMRS Radio

Ensuring proper storage is essential for preserving the longevity of your GMRS radio.
1. **Keep in a Dry Location**: Excessive moisture can cause harm to electronic parts. It is important to ensure that your radio is kept in a dry environment. You may also want to consider using desiccants to help absorb any excess moisture.
2. **Avoid Direct Sunlight**: It is important to protect the radio from direct sunlight as it can cause damage to both the casing and internal components due to UV rays and heat. It's important to keep your radio in a cool and shaded area.
3. **Consider Using Storage Containers**: If you plan on storing your radio for a long time, it's a good idea to use a storage container to shield it from dust and debris.
4. **Label and Organize**: To ensure easy identification, it's helpful to label your multiple radios or accessories. Keeping your equipment organized is crucial for avoiding confusion.

Troubleshooting Common Issues

Although you may have put in a lot of effort, problems can still occur with your GMRS radio. Here are some typical issues and their solutions:
1. **Signal Quality Issue**: Ensure the antenna is not damaged and all connections are secure. Consider testing in various locations to eliminate any potential interference if the issue continues.
2. **Battery Drain**: Make sure the battery is properly charged and not overheating. If the battery is old or damaged, it should be replaced.
3. **Audio Distortion**: Ensure proper maintenance of the microphone and speaker. If you're still experiencing distortion, try using a different microphone or speaker to help identify the problem.
4. **Display Problems:** In case of any issues with the display, it is recommended to inspect for any signs of moisture or physical damage. If needed, reset the radio by carefully following the instructions provided by the manufacturer.

CHAPTER THIRTEEN
GMRS RADIO INTEGRATION WITH ADDITIONAL RADIO SYSTEMS

Overview

Chapter thirteen discusses GMRS Radio integration with additional radio systems like the compatibility with DRS radio, how to use GMRS and FPS radios, etc.

What is the compatibility with FRS Radios?

FRS and GMRS operate on the same frequency bands, but there are differences in the rules and permissions for each service. FRS is a radio service that is specifically designed for family and personal use, with a focus on low power. Operating it doesn't require a license, which is why it's a popular choice among casual users. On the other hand, GMRS permits higher power output and offers extra capabilities, although obtaining a license from the FCC is necessary. FRS radios function on 22 channels spanning the 462-467 MHz frequency range, with a maximum power output of 2 watts. The purpose of this limitation is to maintain FRS as a low-power communication service. On the other hand, GMRS shares channels with FRS but allows for higher power levels, reaching up to 50 watts on certain channels. This enables a wider coverage area and stronger communication capabilities.

Compatibility between GMRS and FRS Radios

GMRS and FRS can be compatible under certain conditions since they share the same frequency bands. Nevertheless, it is important to take into account certain limitations and regulatory aspects.

Shared Channels

FRS radios function on channels 1-22, with channels 1-14 being specifically allocated for FRS use. Channels 15-22 are shared with GMRS, with FRS radios limited to a maximum output of 2 watts. GMRS radios can utilize the same channels, but with a higher power output, resulting in an extended range and improved ability to penetrate obstacles.

Comparing FRS and GMRS

FRS and GMRS radios can communicate on the same channels (15-22), as long as the FRS radio stays within its power limits. This compatibility proves to be quite convenient for families or groups with a mix of FRS and GMRS radio users. GMRS users need to adhere to the legal power output limit for FRS to avoid any potential violations of FCC regulations.

Licensing Requirements

FRS does not require a license, whereas GMRS does require one. The licensing requirement is a crucial factor that impacts compatibility. Obtaining an FCC license for GMRS usage requires users to go through a fee-based application process. The license remains valid for ten years, granting the holder the privilege to operate GMRS radios at elevated power levels and with supplementary functionalities, including the use of repeaters. FRS users can communicate with GMRS users on shared channels, but they need to follow the power restrictions. Users of GMRS can utilize these channels without a license as long as they adhere to the FRS limits. However, a license is required for higher power levels or exclusive GMRS features.

GMRS-Specific Features

GMRS radios provide a range of additional features that are not typically found in FRS radios, making them more versatile for various applications such as business and emergency communications.

Here are some of the features:

- **Increased Power Output:** GMRS radios can operate at power levels of up to 50 watts on certain channels, resulting in an extended communication range.
- **Repeater Functionality**: GMRS radios can utilize repeaters, which allows for an extended communication range. This is a feature that FRS users do not have access to.
- **Improved Signal Transmission and Reception**: GMRS radios are equipped with external antennas, which enhance the quality of signal transmission and reception.

These extra features are advantageous for users who require more advanced communication options, but they do necessitate an FCC license. The significance of following regulations when using GMRS radios with FRS compatibility is highlighted by this distinction.

Practical Applications

The practical applications of the compatibility between GMRS and FRS radios are beneficial for families, businesses, and outdoor enthusiasts. **Here are a few situations where this compatibility proves to be valuable:**
- **Family Communication**: FRS radios can be used by families during outings or emergencies for basic communication. In case of longer-range communication or emergency scenarios, a GMRS user can be designated.

- **Business Operations**: Companies can use GMRS radios for wider communication across their outdoor areas, while employees can rely on FRS radios for more localized communication. This setup enables smooth interaction while complying with FCC regulations.
- **Outdoor Activities**: Groups on camping trips or hiking excursions can use FRS radios for short-range communication and designate a GMRS radio for a broader range, ensuring everyone remains connected.

Compliance and Best Practices

For optimal compliance with FCC regulations and to maximize the compatibility between GMRS and FRS radios, it is recommended that users adhere to the following best practices:

- **Be aware of Licensing Requirements**: GMRS users need to obtain a license to operate legally. Make sure to obtain the appropriate license before using GMRS radios with higher power levels or additional features.
- **Ensure Proper Power Levels**: When using GMRS radios alongside FRS users, it is important to make sure that the power output remains within the FRS limit on shared channels (15-22). This practice helps prevent any disruption to other users and ensures that everyone follows the rules.
- **Considerate Frequency Use**: GMRS users should make an effort to avoid causing interference with FRS users and adhere to the designated frequency allocations. Utilize GMRS-only features and higher power levels sparingly and judiciously.
- **Adhere to Local Regulations**: It is important to familiarize yourself with the laws and regulations that pertain to radio communication in your area. Having this knowledge can prevent any penalties or disruptions in communication services.

How to use FRS and GMRS Radios for local disaster

Effective communication during a local disaster can mean the difference between survival and tragedy. Reliable communication methods are crucial for families, emergency response teams, and community members, especially when traditional systems fail. FRS and GMRS radios are two popular options for short-range communication. These radios provide a simple and affordable solution for staying connected during emergencies, particularly when cell towers are unavailable or internet connections are interrupted.

FRS and GMRS radios are two types of two-way radios that operate on specific frequency bands **regulated by the Federal Communications Commission (FCC) in the United States. Each type of communication device is designed for short-range use and has its distinct characteristics:**

- **FRS Radios**: These radios operate on low power and can be used without a license. They are perfect for families and small groups, with a range that is usually limited to a few miles, depending on the terrain and obstacles.
- **GMRS Radios**: GMRS radios provide increased power and therefore have a greater range. Operating requires an FCC license, which conveniently covers an entire family. GMRS radios are commonly used by amateur radio enthusiasts and emergency response teams due to their extensive range and versatility.

Why choose FRS and GMRS for Local Disaster Communication?

FRS and GMRS radios are incredibly useful during local disasters for a variety of reasons:

- **Dependability**: In contrast to cell phones, which are dependent on towers and infrastructure that can be vulnerable in times of disaster, FRS and GMRS radios function autonomously without relying on external networks.
- **Ease of Use**: These radios are incredibly user-friendly, ensuring that anyone, regardless of their age or technical expertise, can operate them with ease.
- **Affordable**: FRS radios are budget-friendly, and although a license is needed for GMRS radios, the expenses are relatively low compared to alternative communication systems.
- **Range and Flexibility**: FRS radios are ideal for communicating over short distances within a neighborhood or community, while GMRS radios offer a broader coverage area, enabling more extensive coordination.

Getting Ready for Emergencies with FRS and GMRS Radios

Effective disaster communication requires thorough preparation. Here's a guide on preparing your FRS or GMRS radios for use during a local disaster:

1. **Select the Appropriate Radios**
- **Identify Your Requirements**: Take into account the range you require. FRS radios are ideal for short-distance communication, while GMRS radios provide a greater coverage area. FRS radios are typically adequate for families and small groups. GMRS radios are a better choice for facilitating coordination within the community.
- **Choose Trusted Brands:** Opt for reputable brands that have received positive reviews to ensure dependable performance and long-lasting quality.
2. **Master the Art of Operating Radios**

- **Make sure to read the manual**: Take the time to become familiar with the various functions of your radio, such as channel selection, volume adjustment, and the activation of additional features like privacy codes.
- **Practice with Your Group**: It's important to conduct drills with family members or your community group to make sure everyone is familiar with operating the radios and communicating effectively.

3. **Set up Communication Protocols**

- **Define Channels and Privacy Codes:** Channels and privacy codes can be defined as important elements to consider in communication. Allocate distinct channels for various groups or objectives. Use privacy codes to minimize interference caused by other radio users.
- **Establish a Communication Plan**: Identify the individuals accountable for communication, define the necessary information to be shared, and establish a regular check-in schedule during a disaster.

4. **Keep your Radios Ready**

- **Maintain Batteries**: Remember to keep your radios powered up by regularly checking and replacing the batteries or making sure they are fully charged. Make sure to have spare batteries or a charging station readily available.
- **Proper Storage of Radios:** Make sure to keep radios in a convenient and easily reachable spot in case of an emergency. It's a good idea to store them in a waterproof bag to safeguard against any potential water damage.

Using FRS and GMRS Radios When faced with a disaster

For effective communication with your FRS and GMRS radios during a local disaster, it is important to follow these steps:

1. **Stay Calm and Communicate Clearly**
- **Ensure clear and deliberate speech**: During a crisis, individuals often experience feelings of anxiety and stress. It is important to speak slowly and enunciate your words for effective communication.
- **Use Clear and Concise Language:** Use simple language and avoid technical terms. Communicate important information using clear and straightforward language.
2. **Stick to Your Communication Plan**
- **Maintain Regular Check-Ins**: Ensure consistent communication by adhering to your established check-in schedule. It is important to ensure that everyone is accounted for and informed about the situation.
- **Use Assigned Channels**: Stick to the assigned channels to prevent any confusion or interference from other radio users.
3. **Provide Crucial Details**
- **Location and Status:** Share your whereabouts and let others know if you are safe. Provide information regarding any injuries or immediate hazards.

- **Requests for Assistance**: If you require assistance, ensure that your communication is clear and includes specific details about your location and the type of help you need.
- **Situation Updates:** Provide timely information on the disaster, including updates on weather conditions, road closures, and other pertinent details.
4. **Ensuring Safety and Privacy**
- **Be Mindful of Sensitive Information:** FRS and GMRS radios operate on public airwaves, which means that anyone with a radio can potentially listen in. It is important to refrain from sharing personal information or any details that may jeopardize your safety.
- **Exercise caution when using privacy codes:** Although privacy codes can help minimize interference, they do not offer comprehensive security. It's important to keep in mind that your communication may still be audible to others.

Working in collaboration with Emergency Response Teams

During a local disaster, emergency response teams often rely on FRS or GMRS radios for communication. Here are some effective ways to coordinate with them:

1. **Get in touch with emergency services**
- **Identify Common Channels:** Find out the channels that local emergency services utilize and make sure you do not disrupt their communication.

Receiving Channel	Receiving Frequency	Transmitting Channel	Transmitting Frequency	GMRS power
15R	462.5500 MHz	23	467.5500 MHz	50 W
16R	462.5750 MHz	24	467.5750 MHz	50 W
17R	462.6000 MHz	25	467.6000 MHz	50 W
18R	462.6250 MHz	26	467.6250 MHz	50 W
19R	462.6500 MHz	27	467.6500 MHz	50 W
20R	462.6750 MHz	28	467.6750 MHz	50 W
21R	462.7000 MHz	29	467.7000 MHz	50 W
22R	462.7250 MHz	30	467.7250 MHz	50 W

- **Provide Clear Information:** Ensure that the information provided is clear and easy to understand. It is important to provide clear and concise information when reaching out to emergency services. Make sure to include your exact location, a detailed description of the emergency, and any urgent requirements you may have.
2. **Collaborate with Community Groups**

- **Use Designated Channels**: It is important to assign specific channels for communication with emergency response teams and community groups to prevent any interference.

- **Effective Information Sharing**: Collaborate with other community groups to ensure seamless communication and alignment.
3. **Adhere to Safety Guidelines**
- **Pay close attention to emergency instructions**: Emergency services often rely on radios to communicate important instructions or updates. Make sure to keep an eye on the specified channels for this information.
- **Minimize unnecessary communication**: It is important to maintain concise and focused communication, particularly during times when emergency response teams are in action.

How to connect to GMRS Repeaters in your vicinity

Locating GMRS Repeaters in Your Area

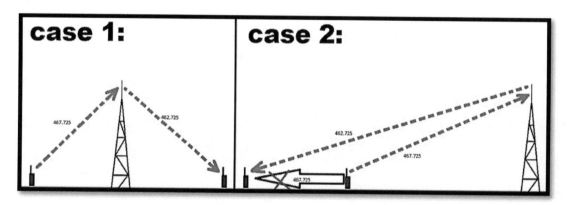

To connect to GMRS repeaters in your area, the first thing you need to do is find them. Here are a few different approaches:

- **Repeater Directories**: Websites such as RepeaterBook and MyGMRS provide easily searchable directories of GMRS repeaters throughout the United States. To find repeaters in your area, you have the option to search by location, frequency, or call sign.
- **Local Radio Clubs**: Numerous communities have radio clubs that oversee GMRS repeaters. These clubs are a valuable resource for connecting with other GMRS users, as they often have information about repeaters in the area.
- **Social Media and Forums**: Online communities and social media groups focused on GMRS and other radio services can offer valuable insights on repeaters in your vicinity. Users can ask questions, share experiences, and receive recommendations from other users.

Connecting to the GMRS Repeater

After programming your GMRS radio, you'll be able to easily connect to the repeater. Here is a step-by-step guide:

1. **Identify Yourself**: It is important to remember to identify yourself with your call sign when transmitting on a repeater for the first time. It is important to note that this step is crucial for several reasons. Firstly, it allows other users to easily identify who is currently on the channel. Additionally, it ensures that the channel complies with FCC regulations.
2. **Check for activity**: Before transmitting, it is important to listen to the repeater and ensure that no one else is currently using it. It is important to follow proper repeater etiquette, which involves waiting for a pause in communication before transmitting.
3. **Press the Push-to-Talk (PTT) Button:** When you're prepared to transmit, simply press the PTT button and speak into the microphone. Ensure that your message is succinct and unambiguous, and remember to conclude with your call sign.
4. **Release the PTT Button**: Once you have finished transmitting, simply let go of the PTT button and wait for a response. Feel free to keep the conversation going if someone responds. If not, give it another shot after a brief pause.
5. **Follow Repeater Etiquette:** Remember to follow proper etiquette when using a repeater. It is important to adhere to common etiquette practices when using a repeater. It is important to avoid monopolizing the channel, keep your transmissions brief, and always allow others to use the repeater.

Resolving Connection Problems

If you're having trouble connecting to a GMRS repeater, here are some common troubleshooting steps:

1. **Review Your Settings:** Ensure that you double-check the frequency, offset, and CTCSS or DCS tones for accuracy. Even the slightest mistake in these settings can hinder your ability to access the repeater.
2. **Ensure a Strong Signal:** If you're experiencing a weak signal, consider relocating or adjusting the antenna on your radio. Signal strength can be influenced by various factors such as buildings or terrain.
3. **Ensure the Repeater is Active**: Occasionally, repeaters may be offline due to maintenance or other factors. Make sure to reach out to local radio clubs or refer to repeater directories to verify the repeater's current status.
4. **Adjust the Offset and Tone**: Try adjusting the offset and tone if you're still facing difficulties. Experiment with different settings to find the right combination. Certain repeaters may have distinct configurations that necessitate particular adjustments.
5. **Reach out to local radio clubs**: If you encounter any difficulties, consider contacting local radio clubs or GMRS groups for help. They are available to provide guidance and assist with troubleshooting any connection issues you may encounter.

CHAPTER FOURTEEN
GMRS RADIO SAFETY GUIDELINES

Overview

In this chapter, you will learn the several GMRS Radio safety guidelines and the environmental considerations for GMRS.

What is the list of safety guidelines for GMRS users

Presented below are some safety guidelines to consider when utilizing GMRS:

1. **Get the Right License**

Before using a GMRS radio, individuals must obtain the required FCC license. Operating without a license is against the law and may lead to financial penalties. The application process is quite simple, just submit FCC Form 605 along with the required fee. The license remains valid for 10 years and provides coverage for the licensee as well as their immediate family members.

2. **Use the proper channels and frequencies**

GMRS operates on designated channels and frequencies. Using these designated frequencies is crucial to prevent any interference with other radio services. The GMRS system consists of a total of 22 channels. Out of these, 8 channels are specifically designated for simplex communication, while the remaining 7 channels are commonly utilized for repeater communication. It is important to use the designated channels for GMRS to comply with FCC regulations.

3. **Adhere to Power Limitations**

The power output of GMRS radios can vary depending on the channel. Repeater-capable channels allow for a maximum power output of 50 watts, while other channels may have lower power limits. Understanding the power limits for your specific channels and adjusting your radio's power output accordingly is crucial. Violating power limits can result in interference and a breach of FCC regulations.

4. **Minimize Unnecessary Transmission**

GMRS users need to engage in responsible communication. Refrain from making unnecessary transmissions, keeping the microphone button pressed for extended periods, or triggering repeaters without any intended communication. These practices may result in interference and disruption of other users' communications.

5. **Respect Other Users**

It is crucial to show respect for others' communications when using GMRS channels, as they are shared among multiple users. It is important to respect ongoing conversations and adhere to proper call signs or identifiers when using a radio. Following established radio etiquette includes waiting for a break in communication before transmitting if a channel is already in use.

6. **Follow the Appropriate Radio Protocol**

Having proper radio etiquette is crucial for effective communication and preventing conflicts with other users. Ensure that your speech is clear and delivered at a moderate pace. Remember to use call signs or identifiers when communicating and always signal the end of your transmission. It is important to refrain from using slang or offensive language and to always be respectful towards other users.

7. Familiarize Yourself with Repeater Etiquette

Repeaters are commonly employed to increase the coverage area of GMRS communications. It is important to adhere to proper etiquette when using repeaters. It is important to always identify yourself with a call sign or identifier when accessing a repeater. Additionally, it is crucial to be aware of and follow the repeater's rules, including any time limits or usage restrictions that may be in place. It is important to be considerate of other users and not hog the repeater so that everyone has a chance to communicate when necessary.

8. Ensure Radio Equipment is in Good Condition

Make sure to regularly inspect your GMRS radio equipment for any signs of wear or damage. We thoroughly examine antennas, microphones, batteries, and other accessories. Ensuring equipment is well-maintained is crucial for minimizing malfunctions and safety hazards during operation.

9. Use Authorized Accessories

Make sure to only use accessories that are approved for GMRS radios. Using unauthorized accessories or making modifications can lead to interference, decreased performance, or potential safety hazards. It is important to always buy from trusted sources and make sure that the accessories you choose are compatible with your particular GMRS radio model.

10. Stay mindful of Electromagnetic Interference (EMI)

GMRS radios, like all electronic devices, have the potential to generate electromagnetic interference. It is important to exercise caution when using radios in the vicinity of sensitive electronic equipment, such as medical devices or aircraft navigation systems. It is important to adhere to local regulations and safety guidelines to minimize the potential for causing interference.

11. Ensure Safety in Hazardous Environments

It is important to adhere to safety precautions when utilizing GMRS radios in hazardous environments like construction sites or industrial settings to prevent accidents. It is important to wear the necessary protective gear and securely fasten radios to avoid any potential accidents or harm. It is important to stay alert and focused on your surroundings to prevent any potential accidents.

12. Respect Privacy and Confidentiality

GMRS radios lack secure communication capabilities, making it possible for other users to intercept transmissions. Refrain from sharing any sensitive or confidential information over GMRS channels. If you're looking for a more secure way to communicate, it might be worth exploring alternative methods like encrypted radios or other secure communication platforms.

13. Prepare for Emergencies

GMRS radios are incredibly useful in emergencies. Make sure your radio is fully charged and functioning properly. It's important to have spare batteries or a charging system available, especially when you're in a remote location or participating in extended outdoor activities. It is important to become familiar with emergency frequencies and protocols, as well as to participate in emergency preparedness exercises to practice your communication skills.

14. **Use GMRS for Authorized Purposes**

GMRS is designed for personal and family communication, as well as business-related communications within certain limitations. This should not be used for broadcasting, commercial activities, or any other unauthorized purposes. It is important to adhere to FCC regulations when using GMRS to avoid any potential penalties or fines.

Environmental Considerations for GMRS

Regulatory Framework and Environmental Impact

The FCC establishes regulations for GMRS to guarantee that its usage does not disrupt other communication systems and adheres to safety standards. The regulations effectively strike a balance between functionality and minimizing environmental impact. Power output limits are an important regulatory aspect to consider. GMRS radios have limited transmission power to ensure minimal interference with other services and to prioritize environmental safety. High-power transmissions can result in higher energy consumption and potential interference with wildlife and other communication systems. Obtaining a license is a requirement set by the FCC for GMRS users to operate on these frequencies. The licensing process acts as a necessary regulatory measure to ensure that users are well-informed about the rules and that their use of GMRS does not have any negative impact on the environment or other users.

Energy Consumption and Environmental Impact

Considering the environmental impact, it is important to take into account the energy consumption of GMRS devices. The widespread use of individual radios can have a substantial cumulative effect on power consumption. Battery usage is a significant concern due to the negative impact of disposable batteries on the environment and the problem of electronic waste. Rechargeable batteries are frequently touted as a greener option due to their reusability and longer lifespan compared to disposable ones. On the other hand, the production and charging of rechargeable batteries have a significant environmental impact due to the materials used and the energy consumption involved. Another factor to take into account is the complete lifespan of GMRS devices. The environmental impact is influenced by manufacturing, transportation, and disposal processes. One way manufacturers can minimize their environmental impact is by incorporating recycled materials, creating products that can be easily disassembled and recycled, and establishing programs to collect and recycle end-of-life products. Another important consideration is the potential impact of electromagnetic interference on wildlife.

Electromagnetic Interference and Wildlife

EMI is a common concern that arises with radio-based technology. Although GMRS operates at lower power levels, there is still a potential for interference with wildlife and other natural systems. Birds and insects, especially, demonstrate sensitivity to electromagnetic fields, which can have an impact on their behavior and migration patterns. Ongoing research is being conducted on the environmental effects of EMI, indicating potential impacts on plant growth, animal navigation, and soil health. Although GMRS's influence in this region may be relatively small compared to larger communication networks, it is crucial to take these effects into account during any environmental evaluation.

Sustainable Practices in GMRS

Users and manufacturers can adopt sustainable practices to minimize the environmental impact of GMRS. Here are some examples:

- **Energy-efficient design**: Manufacturers can create GMRS devices that consume less energy by incorporating power-saving modes and efficient charging systems.
- **Battery recycling programs**: Encouraging the recycling of batteries is crucial in minimizing electronic waste and reducing the environmental impact of GMRS devices.
- **Green manufacturing processes**: Manufacturers can use sustainable materials and processes to minimize waste and decrease the energy needed for producing GMRS devices.
- **Environmental education:** Educating GMRS users about the environmental impact of their devices can promote responsible use and proper disposal.

Future Trends and Environmental Considerations

With the advancement of technology, the environmental considerations linked to GMRS also progress. The development of new communication protocols and the integration of GMRS with other technologies, such as smartphones, present exciting possibilities and potential hurdles. There is a noticeable rise in the use of digital technology in GMRS devices. While digital communication has its advantages, such as improved energy efficiency and additional features, it also brings up concerns regarding data privacy and security. The environmental impact could be influenced by these advancements, given that digital devices typically involve intricate manufacturing processes and materials. Another notable trend is the growing use of GMRS in various applications, including emergency response and disaster recovery. Although there are benefits to public safety, the increased use of devices may harm the environment. It is crucial to find a balance between the benefits of GMRS and its impact on the environment.

CHAPTER FIFTEEN
RESOURCES AND GLOSSARY TERMS

Overview

In this chapter, you will learn the resources and glossary terms in GMRS Radios, the role of GMRS organizations, the key terms and definitions in GMRS, and the numerous acronyms and abbreviations used in GMRS Radios.

GMRS Organizations and Communities

The Role of GMRS Organizations

GMRS organizations are valuable centers for enthusiasts, emergency responders, and community members who are interested in utilizing two-way radio communication. They frequently offer training, support, and resources to assist members in obtaining licenses and operating their GMRS equipment with proficiency. These organizations can also contribute significantly to building a strong sense of community among users, connecting individuals who have shared interests in radio communication. GMRS organizations have a crucial role in promoting education and ensuring compliance with FCC regulations. They frequently organize workshops and training sessions to assist members in navigating the licensing process and gaining a comprehensive understanding of the regulations governing GMRS use. These organizations provide valuable guidance to help prevent unintentional violations and ensure that GMRS users comply with the law. GMRS organizations not only focus on education but also play a crucial role in establishing communication networks that go beyond individual families or groups. Repeater devices were used to enhance the communication range, enabling members to connect over larger distances. This infrastructure is extremely valuable in emergencies, offering a dependable method of communication when other systems become unreliable.

Building Communities through GMRS

GMRS communities are centered on the concept of fostering connections among individuals through radio communication. Communities can vary in scope, ranging from local to national, where members come together to exchange knowledge, share experiences, and discuss best practices. Forming connections within these communities allows GMRS users to find support and encouragement as they navigate the world of two-way radio communication. Local GMRS communities frequently coordinate events and activities to foster a sense of unity among members. Participants have the opportunity to set up temporary radio stations in outdoor locations during field days. This allows them to test equipment and practice their communication skills. Such events offer a chance for members to connect, exchange stories, and gain insights from each other. GMRS communities frequently work together with other radio services, like

Amateur Radio (ham radio), to promote a stronger sense of camaraderie among radio enthusiasts. These collaborations can result in the sharing of resources, expanded networking opportunities, and collective efforts in emergency response and disaster preparedness.

GMRS and Emergency Response

GMRS organizations and communities play a crucial role in emergency response, making their contributions highly significant. During times of crisis, when traditional communication networks may be compromised, GMRS can serve as a dependable alternative. GMRS organizations frequently collaborate with emergency services, including fire departments, police, and emergency medical teams, to establish communication networks that can be activated in times of crisis. These networks are specifically designed to enable the seamless flow of critical information between responders and affected communities, thereby promoting a highly coordinated response. GMRS communities can also set up neighborhood watch programs, allowing members to use GMRS radios to monitor their neighborhoods and promptly report any suspicious activity or emergencies to local authorities. This approach promotes safety and security within the community through collaboration. GMRS can also be valuable in disaster preparedness. Drills and simulations are frequently carried out by organizations and communities to enhance their emergency response capabilities. These exercises provide an opportunity for participants to improve their communication skills and evaluate the efficiency of their equipment. Engaging in these activities allows GMRS users to enhance their preparedness for emergencies, ensuring that communication remains reliable during critical times.

The Future of GMRS Organizations and Communities

With the ever-changing landscape of technology, GMRS organizations and communities must stay ahead of the curve and embrace new trends and challenges. The growing accessibility of affordable GMRS equipment has made it more convenient for individuals to participate, resulting in a significant increase in interest. The growth in this area provides GMRS organizations with the chance to broaden their reach and provide additional resources to their members. Nevertheless, this expansion also presents its fair share of difficulties. As the popularity of GMRS increases, the potential for frequency congestion and interference also grows. GMRS organizations must collaborate to promote responsible use of the airwaves and educate users about the significance of adhering to communication protocols. Another obstacle to consider is the seamless integration of GMRS with other communication technologies. In an increasingly interconnected world driven by digital platforms, GMRS organizations must stay relevant and provide distinctive advantages to their members. One possibility to consider is the exploration of new applications for GMRS, such as its integration with smartphone apps or other digital communication tools.

Key Terms and Definitions in GMRS Radio

GMRS is a land mobile radio service specifically created for short-distance communication. GMRS is primarily used for personal and family activities and operates under the regulations set by the Federal Communications Commission (FCC) in the United States.

1. **What exactly is GMRS?**

GMRS is a licensed radio service that offers communication for personal or family use. It is commonly used for activities like hiking, camping, or general outdoor communication. The GMRS differs from the FRS in that it necessitates an FCC license, although its frequencies do overlap with those of the FRS, enabling some level of compatibility.

2. **Frequency Bands**

GMRS operates within the ultra-high frequency (UHF) band, specifically ranging from 462 MHz to 467 MHz. The band is divided into channels, each with 30 frequencies specifically designated for GMRS use. These channels serve different purposes, including direct communication between two radios or using repeaters to increase the range.

3. **Licensing Requirements**

To use GMRS legally, individuals are required to obtain a license from the FCC. The license extends to the licensee and their immediate family, granting them the ability to operate on GMRS frequencies without the need for additional individual licensing. The license remains valid for 10 years and does not necessitate the completion of an examination. To acquire the license, applicants are required to complete FCC Form 605 and submit the necessary fee.

4. **Repeaters**

Repeaters function by receiving a signal on one frequency and then transmitting it on a different frequency. They are commonly utilized in GMRS to enhance communication range, enabling users to effectively communicate over larger distances. GMRS repeaters are typically installed in elevated areas or carefully chosen spots to ensure optimal coverage.

5. **Simplex and Duplex Communication**

- **Simplex Communication**: This refers to direct communication between two or more radios on the same frequency. GMRS is widely used for various activities such as family outings or event coordination, making it a popular form of communication.
- **Duplex Communication:** This mode utilizes separate frequencies for transmitting and receiving. When using repeaters to extend communication range, duplex communication is usually employed.

6. **Channels and Sub-channels**

There are a total of 30 channels in GMRS, with 16 primary channels and 14 interstitial channels. The primary channels are typically utilized for simplex and repeater communication, whereas the interstitial channels are generally designated for lower-power transmissions. Sub-channels also referred to as privacy codes or Continuous Tone-Coded Squelch System (CTCSS), can be utilized to enhance privacy and minimize interference. The codes effectively filter out any undesired transmissions, ensuring that only signals with corresponding codes are received.

7. **Power Levels**

GMRS radios are specifically designed to operate at various power levels, which are determined by the frequency and type of communication. Typically, GMRS radios have a maximum power limit of 50 watts. However, handheld devices usually operate at lower power levels, typically ranging from 1 to 5 watts. The communication range and battery life of the radios are influenced by power levels.

8. **Antennas**

The choice of antenna for GMRS radios plays a crucial role in determining the range and quality of communication. Fixed-base antennas are commonly installed on towers or rooftops to optimize their range, especially when used with repeaters. Mobile antennas are specifically designed to be used with vehicles, while handheld antennas are intended for use with portable radios. Choosing the right antenna and positioning it correctly can significantly improve the performance of GMRS communication.

9. **Emergency Communication**

GMRS is a popular choice for emergency communication because of its dependable performance and user-friendly nature. It is a widely used tool for families and groups to coordinate during emergencies or natural disasters. The GMRS users are diligent in their efforts to establish communication plans and protocols for emergencies, guaranteeing that all individuals are well-informed about the appropriate channels to utilize and the proper radio operation procedures.

10. **Applications of GMRS**

GMRS is incredibly versatile and finds use in a wide array of applications, spanning from family outings and outdoor activities to emergency response and community events. It is also used by volunteer organizations, search and rescue teams, and neighborhood watch groups. Many people prefer this option for short-distance communication due to its flexibility and user-friendly interface.

11. **FRS Compatibility**

GMRS and FRS frequencies can be shared, making them compatible for communication. Nevertheless, there are notable distinctions, including variations in power levels and licensing requirements. GMRS permits the use of higher power levels and necessitates obtaining a license, whereas FRS is limited to lower power levels and does not mandate licensing. It's crucial to have a clear understanding of the differences between GMRS radios and FRS radios when using them to communicate, to comply with FCC regulations.

12. **Tips for Effective GMRS Communication**

For optimal results with GMRS, users should adhere to recommended communication practices. It is important to have a clear understanding of the regulations, acquire the required license, and become proficient in operating the radios. Effective communication protocols, such as using call signs and ensuring clear and concise communication, enhance the overall experience.

Acronyms and Abbreviations Used in GMRS Radio

Having a good grasp of the acronyms and abbreviations used in the GMRS domain is essential for effective navigation.

Presented below is an extensive compilation of frequently used terms, accompanied by their respective definitions:

- **FCC**: The Federal Communications Commission is responsible for regulating GMRS in the United States. The text outlines rules and guidelines that are essential for the safe and legal operation of radio equipment.
- **UHF**: UHF, or Ultra High Frequency, pertains to radio frequencies that fall within the range of 300 MHz to 3 GHz. GMRS operates within a specific spectrum, usually between 462 and 467 MHz.
- **FRS**: Family Radio Service is comparable to GMRS, with lower power limits and no need for a license. There are some shared frequencies between GMRS and the mentioned system, but GMRS users have the advantage of operating at higher power levels and using repeaters.
- **PL**: Private Line, or CTCSS (Continuous Tone-Coded Squelch System), is a system that effectively reduces interference by using sub-audible tones to regulate the signals received by a radio.
- **DCS**: Digital-Coded Squelch is an alternative approach to dealing with interference by using digital codes rather than analog tones.
- **PTT**: Push-to-Talk is a commonly used feature in GMRS radios where users need to press a button to transmit their voice.
- **NOAA**: The National Oceanic and Atmospheric Administration offers weather alerts and information through dedicated weather channels, which are often accessible on GMRS radios.
- **CTCSS**: Continuous Tone-Coded Squelch System, also referred to as Private Line (PL), enables users to effectively eliminate undesired transmissions by configuring specific sub-audible tones. When radios have matching tones, they can communicate more effectively, which helps to minimize interference.
- **REPEATER**: A repeater is a device that receives a signal and retransmits it, effectively extending the communication range of GMRS radios. Repeaters play a crucial role in GMRS, enabling communication across greater distances by utilizing signal bouncing between radios.
- **OFFSET**: The use of offset is often paired with repeaters. The frequency difference between the input and output frequencies of a repeater is what it refers to. The ability of a repeater to both receive and transmit at the same time allows for smooth and uninterrupted communication.
- **HT**: The HT: Handheld Transceiver is a compact and convenient GMRS radio that you can easily carry with you. These devices are highly favored by GMRS users due to their portability and adaptability.
- **BASE STATION**: A base station refers to a stationary GMRS radio setup equipped with a stronger antenna to enhance range and reliability.

- **MOBILE UNIT:** A mobile unit refers to GMRS radios installed in vehicles, allowing for communication while on the move. These units generally offer greater power compared to handheld transceivers.
- **FREQUENCY:** The frequency of a radio wave is measured in hertz (Hz) and refers to the rate at which it oscillates. GMRS operates on specific frequencies and has designated channels for communication.
- **CHANNEL:** GMRS radios communicate on specific frequencies or frequency ranges. GMRS radios come with a predetermined number of channels that allow users to easily connect.
- **SQUELCH:** The squelch feature is designed to eliminate background noise by muting the radio until a signal with the correct parameters is received. Communication becomes clearer and interference is reduced.
- **SCAN:** The scan function enables a GMRS radio to swiftly search through its channels to locate any ongoing transmissions. This feature is valuable for discovering other users or keeping track of different channels.
- **TX:** Transmitting involves the act of sending a radio signal. When a GMRS user activates the Push-to-Talk (PTT) button, their voice is transmitted.
- **RX:** Receive pertains to the capability of a GMRS radio to detect and receive incoming signals. The radio is in receiving mode when it is not transmitting, and it listens for signals on the selected channel.
- **BATTERY LIFE:** The duration of operation for a GMRS radio on a single charge or set of batteries. It's a crucial factor to keep in mind when it comes to portable and handheld radios.
- **POWER OUTPUT:** The power output of a GMRS radio is measured in watts and represents the energy used to transmit a signal. Having a higher power output enables longer communication ranges, although it may necessitate obtaining a license.

CHAPTER SIXTEEN
FREQUENTLY ASKED QUESTIONS AND THE FUTURE OF GMRS

Overview

We have come to the end of this guide; however, there are still some things to learn. This chapter is dedicated to learning the frequently asked questions about GMRS Radios and the common questions asked concerning GMRS Radios.

Common Questions about GMRS Radios

What is GMRS?

GMRS is a radio service in the United States that is regulated by the Federal Communications Commission (FCC). Operating on UHF (Ultra High Frequency) bands, it provides a broader communication range in comparison to FRS. GMRS is perfect for outdoor adventures, essential for emergencies, and great for keeping families connected.

Is a License Required for GMRS?

Indeed, to operate GMRS radios legally in the United States, an FCC license is required. Obtaining the license is a straightforward process that does not involve taking an exam. Applying online through the FCC website and paying a fee is all that's required. The validity of a GMRS license is for 10 years, providing coverage for the entire family, including spouses, children, and other relatives residing in the same household.

What are the frequencies used by GMRS?

GMRS radios operate within the UHF range, specifically between 462 MHz and 467 MHz. There are a total of 22 channels in this frequency range, some of which are shared with FRS. On the other hand, GMRS permits a higher power output of up to 50 watts and the utilization of repeaters, greatly expanding the communication range.

What is the Range of GMRS Radios?

Various factors can affect the communication range of GMRS radios, such as terrain, power output, antenna type, and the use of repeaters. Under optimal circumstances, with ample power and unobstructed visibility, GMRS radios can transmit signals across several miles. Nevertheless, in urban areas with obstacles, the range may be restricted to just a few blocks.

What is a GMRS Repeater?

A GMRS repeater functions as a radio system that effectively boosts the power level of incoming signals before retransmitting them. Repeaters are commonly situated on high structures such as towers or buildings, enabling them to expand the communication range of GMRS radios. Repeaters are valuable in regions with challenging terrain or dense urban development, where direct communication can be difficult.

Can GMRS Radios be used for Emergency Communication?

Indeed, GMRS radios are highly regarded for their dependability and versatility when it comes to emergency communication. During a disaster or emergency, they play a crucial role in communication when traditional networks are unavailable. GMRS radios are widely utilized by community emergency response teams, search and rescue groups, and families who prioritize emergency preparedness.

What is the necessary equipment for GMRS?

To begin using GMRS, it is necessary to have at least one GMRS radio. Handheld radios, mobile radios for vehicles, and base stations for fixed locations are all available options. Choosing the right type of radio will depend on your specific needs and how you plan to use it. Additionally, you may want to explore accessories such as antennas, repeaters, and headsets to further enhance your setup.

Do GMRS Radios Work with FRS Radios?

There are certain limitations when it comes to GMRS radios communicating with FRS radios on the shared frequencies. FRS radios operate at lower power levels and cannot support repeaters. If you happen to own a GMRS radio, it is possible to communicate with FRS users, although it is important to note that the range may be restricted to the capabilities of the FRS.

What advantages does GMRS offer compared to other radio services?

There are several advantages to choosing GMRS over other radio services. GMRS offers a higher power output, a greater range, and the added advantage of using repeaters, making it a favorable choice when compared to FRS. GMRS is highly suitable for outdoor enthusiasts, emergency responders, and families who require dependable communication. GMRS radios offer a greater range of options for equipment and customization.

Is it possible to use GMRS radios internationally?

GMRS is a radio service based in the United States and is regulated by the FCC. It is important to note that using GMRS radios in other countries may be against the law or necessitate obtaining additional licenses. Before you embark on your journey with GMRS radios, it's advisable to thoroughly review the local regulations to ensure compliance and prevent any potential legal complications.

How can I properly maintain my GMRS radios?

For optimal performance of your GMRS radios, it is important to adhere to these maintenance tips:

- **Regular Cleaning**: Ensure that the radios and accessories are kept clean to avoid the accumulation of dirt and grime. It is recommended to use a gentle cloth and refrain from using strong chemicals.
- **Battery Care:** Ensure the longevity of your batteries by following proper charging and storage practices. It is important to avoid overcharging and exposing the device to extreme temperatures.
- **Antenna Inspection**: Inspect the antenna thoroughly to identify any signs of damage or wear. If any issues are found, make sure to replace the antenna promptly. The performance can be affected by a damaged antenna.
- **Software Updates**: Certain GMRS radios provide the option for software updates. Make sure to contact the manufacturer to inquire about any updates that could enhance performance or introduce new features.
- **Storage**: For optimal storage, it is recommended to keep radios in a dry and cool place when they are not in use. This effectively prevents any potential damage caused by moisture and extreme temperatures.

Are GMRS Radios Secured?

GMRS radios lack encryption, which compromises their overall security. They also provide privacy codes, such as Continuous Tone-Coded Squelch System (CTCSS) or Digital-Coded Squelch (DCS), to minimize interference from other users. The codes used here do not encrypt the communication, but they enhance the likelihood of receiving only the transmissions intended for you.

What factors should you take into account when purchasing GMRS radios?

Before buying GMRS radios, it's important to take into account the following factors:
- **Power Output:** A higher power output can increase the range of the device, but it may also result in faster battery drainage.

- **Repeater Capability:** Make sure the radio you choose supports the use of repeaters if you plan on using them.
- **Durability**: When considering radios for outdoor use, it's important to look for models that have sturdy construction and are designed to withstand various weather conditions.
- **Battery Life:** Take a look at the battery life and think about getting extra batteries or power options for longer periods of use.
- **Accessories**: Take into account the various accessories that can improve your setup, such as antennas, headsets, and mounts.

CONCLUSION

GMRS is a highly versatile communication tool that has proven to be incredibly useful in a variety of personal, business, and emergencies. The appeal of this product lies in its straightforwardness, dependability, and adaptability. GMRS radio is known for its wide accessibility, making it highly appealing. The process of obtaining a license from the Federal Communications Commission (FCC) in the United States is relatively straightforward. One license is all you need to connect your entire family, enabling seamless communication no matter the distance. The fee is quite reasonable, and the license is valid for a generous ten years, making it an excellent communication solution for families, small businesses, and community groups. The license's straightforwardness promotes responsible usage, and the FCC offers explicit instructions to guarantee adherence. GMRS radios have a wide range of uses, from personal communication to coordinating emergency responses. These radios provide a dependable means of communication for families during outdoor activities such as hiking or camping, even in areas without cell phone service. Off-road vehicle enthusiasts often rely on GMRS radios to stay connected in remote areas where other communication methods may not be reliable.

INDEX

(

(FRS) radios, 1, 92
(GMRS) emerges as a dependable and easily
  accessible choice, 1

4

462 MHz and 467 MHz, 6, 16, 29, 55, 158

A

A GMRS base station typically comes equipped with
  channel scanning capabilities, 22
A GMRS repeater functions as a radio device, 50
A GMRS repeater functions as a radio system that
  effectively boosts, 159
A higher-gain antenna, 75
A spectrum analyzer is a crucial tool for individuals
  who work, 133
ability to deliver reliable communication, 3
ability to deliver reliable results, 1
About GMRS Radio, 2
About Radio wave behavior and interference, 54
Access Control, 76, 114, 119
Access to Repeaters, 90
Accessories, 23, 62, 96, 97, 104, 149, 161
accommodate the increasing popularity of GMRS, 3
Acquire a GMRS License, 123
adaptability, 20, 156, 161
additional features, 4, 19, 66, 87, 140, 141, 143, 151
additional power and the option, 1
address interference issues, 108
Addressing Inconsistent Audio Levels, 122
adhere to legal boundaries, 92
Adhere to Power Limitations, 148
Adhere to Privacy and Etiquette, 75
Adhere to Repeater Guidelines, 59
Adhere to Safety Guidelines, 145
Adjust for Clarity, 121
Adjust RBW and VBW, 135
Adjust Squelch Sensitivity, 111

Adjust the Offset and Tone, 147
Adjustable Antenna, 67
Adjusting Squelch, 121
Adjusting the Antenna, 71
Adjusting the Squelch, 131
adjustment of a threshold, 120
advanced features, 66, 82, 87, 117, 119
ADVANCED GMRS FEATURES, 35
Advanced modulation schemes, 52, 54
Advanced Modulation Schemes, 53
advanced noise reduction technology, 18
Advanced Programming Techniques, 110
advancement of GMRS technology, 87
Advantages, 4, 24, 38, 40, 41, 53, 112, 113
Advantages and applications of GMRS, 4
advantages of GMRS for streamlining, 4
Advantages of Integrating GMRS-MURS, 41
Advocating for Inclusivity and Diversity, 92
Affordable, 142
Age Requirement, 26
alert features, 20, 82, 84
allowing individuals and groups to easily connect, 1
Alternatives to GMRS Encryption, 119
Amateur Radio, 8, 33, 40, 94, 125, 153
Amateur Radio (Ham Radio), 8
Amateur radio (ham radio) is a versatile radio service,
  40
amateur radio clubs and organizations, 94
amateur radio enthusiasts, 93, 142
amateur radio licenses, 27, 29, 125
amateur radio operators, 94, 104
Amidst the ever-changing landscape of
  communication technology, 1
ample power and unobstructed visibility, 158
An antenna system, 45
Analog Scrambling, 112
Antenna Analyzer, 67
Antenna Design and Height, 22
Antenna Gain, 102
Antenna Height, 75, 102
Antenna Inspection, 160
Antenna Mismatch, 70
Antenna Options, 20, 103
Antenna Placement, 71, 73, 108

Antenna Position, 47
Antenna Quality, 73
Antenna Restrictions, 28
Antenna Selection, 117
Antenna System, 45
antenna type, 16, 158
Antenna Type, 75
Antennae, 104
Antennas, 96, 98, 102, 124, 155
Antennas are essential for optimizing the range and
    performance of GMRS radios, 96
Antennas play a crucial role, 98
antennas, headsets, and mounts., 161
any interference, 10, 28, 33, 37, 46, 47, 50, 78, 80,
    131, 136, 145, 148
Applicants are required to complete FCC Form 605
    online, 29
application process and a one-time fee, 19
Applications of GMRS, 5, 11, 52, 85, 155
Applying online through the FCC website, 158
approach promotes a more thorough and efficient
    neighborhood watch, 93
Appropriate Antenna Placement, 56
approval of your application, 13, 60
Are GMRS Radios Secured?, 160
around 465 MHz, 68
Assess Your Budget, 105
Assign Descriptive Names, 110
Assigning patrol duties, 93
Audio Distortion, 138
Audio Output Issue, 131
Audio Quality and Clarity, 18
Authorized Frequencies, 29, 32
available options, 15, 80, 159
available to both GMRS and FRS users, 10
Avoid Bending or Twisting, 137
Avoid Direct Sunlight, 138
avoid overcharging and exposing the device, 160
avoid using unauthorized frequencies, 32
Avoiding Obstructions, 74
Await Approval, 28

B

background noise, 22, 39, 76, 121, 122, 157
Backing up and restoring configurations, 111
Backup Channel, 49
Backup Communication for Critical Services, 90

Backup Configurations, 111
Backup Power Maintenance, 48
balancing RBW and VBW., 134
Baofeng, 49
BASE STATION, 156
Base Station Mounts, 97
Base station mounts are essential for securely
    installing GMRS radios in fixed locations, 97
Base Stations, 103, 124
base stations for fixed locations, 159
Base/mobile GMRS radios, 17, 18
Base/Mobile GMRS Radios, 17
Base/mobile GMRS radios are larger units, 17
base/mobile units, 16, 17
Batteries and Chargers, 97, 104
Battery Care, 160
Battery Life, 21, 25, 103, 131, 161
BATTERY LIFE, 157
Battery Maintenance, 74
Battery Packs, 97
Battery packs provide extended battery life, 97
Battery Saver Modes and Battery Monitoring, 82
battery-operated, 16
Battery-Powered, 17
battery's charge level through battery monitoring
    features, 82
Be Mindful of Sensitive Information, 144
Be mindful of temperature, 136
begin using GMRS,, 159
Begin with a low volume, 121
Benefits of GMRS Encryption, 115
Benefits of GMRS for Neighborhood Watch, 91
Benefits of Using a GMRS Repeater, 51
Best Practices for GMRS Encryption, 114
Best Practices for GMRS in Neighborhood Watch, 92
Best Practices for GMRS in Neighborhood Watch and
    Community Safety, 92
Best Practices for Managing Batteries, 64
between buildings in urban settings., 5
Bone Conduction Headsets, 97
Boost the Volume over time, 121
both personal and recreational communication,, 1
Bringing Along Extra Batteries, 65
Broadcasting or Transmission of Music, 32
broader range in comparison, 12
bug fixes, 67
Building Communities through GMRS, 152
Business and Commercial Use, 11

Business and Industry, 52
business and professional purposes, 1
Business and Professional Use, 6
Business and Worksite Communication, 85
business needs, 11, 20
Business Operations, 40, 88, 141
Business Radio Service or the Industrial/Business
    Pool., 32
business, and emergencies, 161
Businesses and Organizations, 26
Buttons or controls are unresponsive., 132
buying GMRS radios, 160

C

Cabling and Connectors, 46
call sign during radio communication., 49
Call Signs, 10, 30, 49, 57, 125, 126
Call Signs and Identification, 10
Can GMRS Radios be used for Emergency
    Communication?, 159
capabilities of both systems, 94
CARING FOR YOUR GMRS RADIO, 128
Carrying Cases and Holsters, 97, 104
catering to personal use, 11
CB has a power limit of 4 watts, 9
CB Radio, 7, 125
CB radio has a long-standing history, 7
CB radio operates in the 27 MHz band, 7
CB radios are commonly used for road trips and
    outdoor activities, 9
cell phone service, 161
Certain antennas may necessitate more intricate
    installation processes, 103
Certain GMRS radios offer the option, 73
Certain GMRS radios provide the option for software
    updates, 160
certain instances, 33
certain limitations when it comes to GMRS radios,
    159
Certain radio manufacturers provide exclusive
    encryption systems, 113
Challenges and Considerations, 54, 91, 116
Challenges and Limitations, 40, 41
Challenges Arising from Human Error and Technical
    Issues, 106
challenging terrain or dense urban development, 159
changes to GMRS rules, 31

CHANNEL, 157
channel according to your communication
    requirements, 14
Channel Scanning, 22, 37, 81
Channel Scanning and Privacy Codes, 22
Channel scanning is perfect for users, 81
Channel Selection, 44, 74
Channel Sharing, 85, 123
Channel Sharing and Selective Calling, 85
Channel Use, 10, 118
Channels 15-22, 10, 43, 44, 139
Channels 1-7, 10, 43
Channels 8-14, 10, 43
Channels and Frequency Compatibility, 13
Channels and Privacy Codes, 18, 19, 73, 83, 143
Chapter one introduces us to GMRS Radios as a
    whole, 2
Charge and Test Radios, 62
Charging Stations, 97
Charging Your Device Correctly, 64
Check Connections, 47, 71
Check for activity, 146
Check for Corrosion, 137
Check for Harmonics and Spurious Emissions, 136
Check for Nearby Electronics, 131
Check for Physical Damage, 109
Check for Signs of Wear and Tear, 137
Check the Buttons, 132
Check the Coaxial Cable, 71
Check the Microphone and Speaker, 109
choice for families, 4, 57, 85
Choose a Channel, 36
Choose a frequency to test, 71
Choose a Privacy Code or Tone, 36
Choose the option "**Apply for a New License.**", 28
Choose Trusted Brands, 142
Choose Unique Tones, 111
choose your payment method, 28
choosing a Privacy Code or Tone, 36
Choosing the Appropriate Equipment, 61
Choosing the Perfect Spot for Your Repeater, 46
Choosing the right type of radio will depend on your
    specific needs, 159
Citizens Band, 7, 9
Citizens Band Radio (CB Radio), 7
Citizenship Requirement, 27
Cleaning, 74
clear communication protocol, 77

clearer communication even in loud surroundings., 98

Coaxial Cable and Connectors, 67

codes are quite effective in minimizing interference and ensuring privacy, 81

Collaborate with Community Groups, 144

Collaborate with Your Group, 37

Comfort and Clarity, 120

commercial activity, 32

Commercial Use, 32

Common Legal Issues and Pitfalls to Avoid, 31

Common Questions about GMRS Radios, 158

common questions asked concerning GMRS Radios, 158

commonly utilized by emergency, 3, 18, 115

communicate with FRS users, 159

communicate without depending on cellular networks, 11

communicating with FRS radios on the shared frequencies, 159

communication activity, 81

communication and coordination within teams, 4

communication infrastructure, 6, 93

communication networks, 4, 5, 6, 42, 52, 88, 93, 94, 105, 151, 152, 153

communication over longer distances and through obstacles like buildings is necessary., 6

communication over longer distances., 9

Communication Protocol, 77, 126

communication roles, 93

communication settings, 66

communication system, 23, 51, 53, 54, 90, 95

communication takes place directly between radios, 3

Communication with Affected Populations, 90

communication with EOCs enables the transmission, 94

communications during disasters or critical events., 30

communities for a range of applications, 2

Community and Social Groups, 52

community and teamwork, 92

Community Coordination, 48

Community Events, 40, 80

community groups, 5, 11, 24, 93, 145, 161

Community-Based Networks, 6

Companies and organizations that use GMRS, 26

Comparing FRS and GMRS, 139

Comparing GMRS to Other Radio Services, 6

Comparing GMRS to Other Radio Services (e.g., FRS, CB, Ham Radio), 6

comparison to Family Radio Service, 1

Compatibility between GMRS and FRS Radios, 139

compatibility with FRS channels, 5

Compatibility with Other Radios, 25

Complete the Application, 60

Complete the application process for a GMRS License, 28

Compliance, 12, 21, 29, 112, 141

comprehensive grasp of the chosen encryption method., 113

comprehensive overview of the GMRS channel spectrum, 10

CONCLUSION, 161

Conduct Functionality Tests, 137

conduction technology, 97

Confirmation, 126

Confirming Squelch Setting, 121

connect external antennas, 73

Connect the Radio, 15

Connect the SWR Meter, 68, 71

Connect with GMRS Communities, 16

Connect with Other Communication Systems, 124

Connecting GMRS and amateur radio operators, 94

Connecting GMRS to Other Emergency Services, 93

Connecting to the GMRS Repeater, 146

Consider accessibility, 46

Consider Reviews and Recommendations, 105

Consider the channels you want to program, 14

Consider the Length and Gain, 73

considering GMRS, 8

considering radios for outdoor use, 161

considering the adoption of GMRS-like services, 4

Considering the environmental impact, 150

Consistent Maintenance and Updates, 62

Consistent or sporadic static noise., 131

consistently seek feedback on communication protocols, 93

contact details., 27, 29

Continuous Monitoring, 37

Controls and Displays, 128, 129

conveniently installed in strategic locations, 98

conventional communication systems, 6, 89

coordinate practice sessions, 95

Coordinated Operations, 38

coordinating emergency responses, 161

Coordination, 51, 76, 80, 91, 104, 127

Coordination and Efficiency, 51

coordination during events, 1, 104

Coordination with Other Communication Systems, 91

correct decryption key or method, 112

Coverage and Range, 4

Create Scan Lists, 110

Creating a Communication Plan, 48

Criminal Charges, 33

critical applications, 6

crucial role in disaster response, 4

crucial role in disaster response and recovery efforts, 4

Custom Channel Assignments, 110

Custom Tone Squelch Settings, 111

Customizable Settings and Programmable Channels, 82

D

Damaged Coaxial Cable, 70

Data Cables and Programming, 98

Data Cables and Programming Software, 98

Dealing with Background Noise, 122

Deciding on the Appropriate GMRS Equipment, 105

Deciding on the Perfect GMRS Radio, 13, 19, 72

Decoding the mysteries of GMRS Encryption, 118

deliberate disruption of emergency communications, 33

delving into programming techniques, 110

delving into the programming process, 12

dependability, 48, 51, 159, 161

Dependability, 51, 116, 142

Dependable Communication, 92

Designated Frequencies, 30

Determine the main purpose for your GMRS equipment, 105

Determine the Objective of Your Communication Plan, 48

Determine the Purpose and Scope, 123

device status, 42

Different Environments, 126

different levels, 8, 53, 97

Diffraction, 55

Digital Displays and User-Friendly Interfaces, 87

Digital Encryption, 113

Dipole Antennas, 100

direct communication can be difficult., 159

Disable the Squelch, 121

disaster or emergency, 39, 159

disaster preparedness groups, 26

Disaster Response and Public Safety, 6

disasters and emergencies., 90

Discovering Active Conversations, 38

Discovering the Perfect Volume, 121

Display Problems, 138

Disposable Batteries, 63

distinct characteristics and practical uses, 16

Diverse Equipment Standards, 105

Do GMRS Radios Work with FRS Radios?, 159

Document your Configuration, 107

Document your Findings, 136

documentation is a valuable resource, 15

Double-check the SWR, 69

Downside, 113

Driver Installation, 110

Dual-Watch and Scanning Functions, 86

Dual-Watch Scanning, 39, 81

Duplex Communication, 154

Duplexer, 45, 46

Durability, 13, 17, 23, 25, 61, 102, 103, 161

during radio communications, 30

E

earthquakes, 93

Ease of Use, 91, 142

Educate Users, 113

Education and community outreach, 95

Education and Community Outreach, 95

Effective Collaboration, 89, 90

Effective communication, 57, 93, 105, 137, 141, 155

effective communication becomes crucial, 6

Effective communication is crucial in emergencies, 93

Effective communication is crucial when using GMRS radios, 137

Effective communication on GMRS channels, 57

Effective Communication within the Community, 85

effective coordination, 24, 52, 85, 87, 94

Effective coordination is crucial to ensure a prompt and well-organized response, 90

Effective Information Sharing, 145

Effective Solutions and Recommended Practices, 107

effectively coordinate activities and exchange crucial information, 6

effectively prevents any potential damage, 160

efficient communication, 1, 19, 54, 77, 84, 86, 124
Efficient communication, 88
Elevation, 46
Elimination of Unwanted Noise, 120
embark on your journey with GMRS radios, 160
embrace diversity, 92
Emergency Alerts, 47
Emergency and Public Safety, 52
Emergency Channel, 49
Emergency Channels, 58, 82, 84, 87, 124, 127
Emergency Communication, 24, 40, 51, 115, 155, 159
Emergency Features, 18, 23
emergency medical services, 90, 94
Emergency Response, 65, 83, 85, 89, 90, 144, 153
emergency response or business operations., 54
emergency response tasks, 93
Emergency Services and Preparedness Groups, 26
Emergency Situations, 38, 39, 93
Enable Repeater Access, 109
enables hands-free operation, 82
enabling all members of your household to utilize, 13
enabling individuals with a license to tune in, 9
enabling neighborhood watch, 92
enabling seamless communication, 50, 51, 161
encoding information, 52
encounter various challenges, 105
Encouraging Feedback and Improvement, 93
encryption in GMRS, 112, 113, 116
Encryption in the world of radio communication, 112
Encryption is crucial in maintaining the confidentiality
    of conversations, 112
endure rough handling, 98
Energy Consumption and Environmental Impact, 150
Energy-efficient design, 151
Enforcement and Penalties, 30
Enhance Communication, 109
enhance public safety and emergency management,
    93
enhance the communication experience, 8
enhance the effective radiated power of GMRS
    radios, 96
enhance the likelihood of receiving only the
    transmissions intended for you., 160
Enhance Your Radio Communication Practices, 77
Enhanced Coordination, 36
Enhanced Data Rates, 54
Enhanced Dependability and Confidence, 116
enhanced flexibility, 73, 79

Enhanced Privacy, 36
Enhanced Scanning Capabilities, 38
Enhanced Signal Clarity, 51, 54
enhanced versatility, 3
**Enhancing Community and Neighborhood
    Communication**, 83
Enhancing Voice Modulation and Clarity, 22
Ensure a Clear Line of Sight, 77
Ensure a Strong Signal, 147
Ensure clear and deliberate speech, 143
Ensure Compatibility, 67, 107, 114
ensure compliance and prevent any potential legal
    complications., 160
Ensure Equipment Authorization, 31
Ensure optimal communication, 77
Ensure Proper Channel Usage, 37
Ensure Proper Charging, 136
Ensure Proper Power Levels, 141
Ensure Radio Equipment is in Good Condition, 149
ensure reliable communication in hard-to-reach
    areas., 3
Ensure Safety in Hazardous Environments, 149
Ensure Signal Strength, 58
Ensure Software is Up to Date, 67
Ensure that the radios and accessories are kept clean
    to avoid the accumulation of dirt and grime, 160
Ensure that the tone of each channel aligns with the
    communication group., 14
Ensure the Antenna is Secure, 69
ensure the effectiveness of a neighborhood watch
    program, 93
Ensure the longevity of your batteries, 160
Ensure the Repeater is Active, 147
ensure the smooth coordination of rescue operations,
    93
Ensure Your Group's Understanding, 37
ensuring a more secure communication experience, 9
Ensuring Regulatory Adherence, 28
**Ensuring Regulatory Compliance and Prioritizing
    Safety Features**, 21
ensuring stability during emergency response and
    recovery operations., 90
Environmental Considerations, 122, 150, 151
Environmental education, 151
Environmental Factors, 102
Environmental Plan, 77
Environmental Resistance, 23
Equipment Checks, 50

Equipment Compatibility, 54
Equipment Confiscation, 33
Equipment Inspection, 125
Equipment Maintenance, 59
Equipment Required for a GMRS Repeater, 44
Establish a Communication Plan, 143
Establish Communication Channels, 49
Establish Effective Communication Etiquette, 61
Establishing Base Stations, 62
Establishing Clear Roles, 93
Establishing Clear Roles and Responsibilities, 93
Evaluate Communication, 113
Event Coordination, 39, 83, 88
event management companies, 6
event organizers, 1, 11, 20, 39, 40, 88
Examine Radio Hardware, 109
Examine the Spectrum, 136
Examining GMRS in Comparison to Other Radio
     Services, 8
exceptional performance, 64
Exciting Off-Road Adventures and Thrilling Trail
     Rides, 87
Exercise caution when using privacy codes, 144
expand communication capabilities, 41
expand the communication range of GMRS radios,
     159
expand the coverage area, 3, 22
expanding the communication range, 20, 158
expanding the reach of communication, 82, 86
Experiment in Different Environments, 121
Experiment with various channels, 129
Exploring the GMRS Channel Spectrum, 9
Exploring the Great Outdoors and Traveling, 52
Exploring the intricacies of GMRS encryption, 118
Exploring the Potential of GMRS with GPS, 65
extend the range of communication, 3
Extended Communication Range, 40
extensive radio service, 8
External Antennas, 73, 96, 108
external GPS modules, 66, 67
External GPS Modules, 66
External Speakers, 98
External speakers significantly improve the audio
     quality of GMRS radios, 98
Extra Features, 5
extra sub-channels, 9
extremely advantageous, 5, 42

F

facilitating communication between various locations,
     26
Factors to Consider When Choosing a GMRS Antenna,
     102
Factors to Keep in Mind, 81
Failure to comply with GMRS regulations can result in
     penalties imposed by the FCC, 30
Failure to Obtain a License, 31
Familiarize Yourself with Repeater Etiquette, 149
families who prioritize emergency preparedness., 159
families who require dependable communication, 159
families, and businesses, 3
Family and Neighborhood Communication, 6
Family Communication, 11, 24, 66, 83, 85, 140
Family Outings and Group Camping, 87
Family Radio Service, 1, 3, 7, 9, 12, 21, 24, 29, 32, 83,
     92, 122, 124, 156
Family Safety, 48
Family Trips and Camping, 39
family, business, and emergency use., 2
faster battery drainage., 160
fast-paced environments,, 87
Faulty Connections, 70
FCC license is required, 158
FCC's website, 48
Features and Components, 19
FFT Spectrum Analyzers, 133
Fill Out Form 605, 13
Fill out the application form, 28, 60, 123
Find the Volume Control, 121
Fine-tune the Antenna, 69
Firmware Updates, 48, 129
Fixed Antennas, 18
flexibility and versatility, 4
Follow Manufacturer Guidelines, 107
Follow Repeater Etiquette, 146
Follow the Appropriate Radio Protocol, 148
Forested Areas, 126
Frequencies, 23, 44, 47, 50, 69, 71, 76, 108, 124, 136
Frequencies and Channels, 23
FREQUENCY, 157
Frequency Allocation, 29, 56
frequency band, 7, 41
Frequency Bands, 21, 41, 154
Frequency Modulation, 53
Frequency Range, 19, 133, 135

frequency ranges, 157

FREQUENTLY ASKED QUESTIONS AND THE FUTURE OF GMRS, 158

friendly nature, 17, 24, 26, 91, 99, 155

FRS and amateur radio, 4

FRS and CB are perfect for casual users, 9

FRS and CB have restrictions, 9

FRS and GMRS operate on the same frequency bands, 139

FRS and GMRS radios, 139, 141, 142, 143, 144

FRS and GMRS radios are incredibly useful during local disasters for a variety of reasons, 142

FRS and GMRS radios can communicate, 139

FRS has a power limit of 2 watts, 9

FRS is a widely used radio service in the U.S.,, 40

FRS modes, 4

FRS Radios, 139, 142, 159

FRS radios are great for family and casual communication., 9

FRS radios function on channels 1-22, 139

FRS radios limited to a maximum output of 2 watts, 139

FRS radios operate at lower power levels, 159

FRS, CB, Ham Radio, 6

fulfill specific requirements, 105

functionalities, 140

funding of FCC operations, 34

G

Gain Antennas, 96

Get a GMRS License, 31, 48

Get Professional Help, 107

Get the Right License, 148

Getting a GMRS License, 57, 60

Getting Ready for Emergencies with FRS and GMRS, 142

GMRS ACCESSORIES AND PROGRAMMING, 96

GMRS ADVANCED FUNCTIONS, 78

GMRS also offers repeater channels, 10

GMRS also plays a vital role in emergency response, 90

GMRS and Data Encryption, 119

GMRS and FRS can be compatible under certain conditions, 139

GMRS base stations need to be highly durable, 23

GMRS base stations often include external connectivity options, 23

GMRS can be seamlessly integrated with intercom systems, 125

GMRS can serve as a reliable backup method of communication, 90

GMRS Channels, 9, 57

GMRS channels have a diverse range of applications, 11

GMRS channels or just a few selected ones, 38

GMRS Communication, 55, 56, 87, 118, 155

GMRS communities are centered on the concept of fostering connections, 152

GMRS enables communication on 22 designated channels, 9

GMRS enables effective group communication, 92

GMRS equipment, 9, 31, 32, 33, 34, 59, 61, 96, 103, 105, 135, 152, 153

GMRS falls under the umbrella of "**personal radio services**,", 9

GMRS FOR EMERGENCIES AND PREPAREDNESS, 89

GMRS for Neighborhood Watch and Community Safety, 91

GMRS group call features can be a valuable asset, 85

GMRS has a wide range of applications, 5

GMRS has adapted over time to keep up with the evolving needs of users and advancements in technology, 3

GMRS has already demonstrated its value in disaster response scenarios, 4

GMRS has gained popularity worldwide, 4

GMRS has seen a significant increase in adoption, 4

GMRS in Disaster Preparedness and Emergency, 89

GMRS in Practical Scenarios, 87

GMRS in terms of the frequency band and communication range, 7

GMRS is a great option for localized communication, 39

GMRS is a great tool for creating communication networks within communities, 6

GMRS is a highly versatile communication tool, 161

GMRS is a licensed radio service, 19, 154

GMRS is a popular choice for various recreational activities like hiking, 5

GMRS is a radio service based in the United States, 160

GMRS is a radio service based in the United States and is regulated by the FCC, 160

GMRS is a radio service in the United States, 158

GMRS is a valuable backup communication, 90

GMRS is a valuable tool for maintaining contact in settings, 6

GMRS is commonly used by families,, 2

GMRS is commonly used for personal and business communication, 9

GMRS is commonly used in a range of business and professional environments, 6

GMRS is commonly utilized by neighborhood watch, 6

GMRS is highly favored by a wide range of individuals and groups, 1

GMRS is highly favored by radio enthusiasts and families, 31

GMRS is highly suitable for outdoor enthusiasts, 159

GMRS is known for its ability to deliver reliable communication over short to moderate distances, 3

GMRS is known for its impressive ability to facilitate communication, 85

GMRS is not only effective for local communication, 94

GMRS is often used for communication among families and neighbors, 6

GMRS Key Features, 3

GMRS license is a breeze, 19

GMRS License Renewal, 34

GMRS offers a dependable and trustworthy alternative, 6

GMRS offers a notable advantage over FRS with its impressive range, 4

GMRS offers a wide range of applications, 1

GMRS offers several key advantages that can be grouped into a few main areas, 4

GMRS operates within the UHF, 10, 19

GMRS operates within the ultra-high frequency (UHF) band, 3, 83, 154

GMRS operations, 33, 134

GMRS operators, 10, 30, 94

GMRS Organizations and Communities, 152, 153

GMRS organizations are valuable centers for enthusiasts, 152

GMRS permits a higher power output of up to 50 watts, 158

GMRS Protocols for Efficient Communication, 58

GMRS provides a variety of communication options, 3

GMRS provides enhanced privacy features, 9

GMRS RADIO BASICS, 12

GMRS RADIO COMMUNICATION WAYS, 112

GMRS RADIO INTEGRATION WITH ADDITIONAL RADIO SYSTEMS, 139

GMRS radio is a highly versatile communication tool, 2

GMRS radio is a licensed radio service in the United States that operates on specific frequencies, 1

GMRS radio is a versatile and easy-to-use platform, 1

GMRS radio is known for its wide accessibility, 161

GMRS RADIO SAFETY GUIDELINES, 148

GMRS RADIO SETTINGS, 120

GMRS RADIO WORKSPACE SETUP, 60

GMRS Radios, 2, 12, 26, 35, 36, 43, 49, 80, 89, 109, 110, 121, 124, 126, 141, 142, 143, 152, 158, 159, 160

GMRS radios also offer emergency channels, 87

GMRS radios are highly adaptable and can be used in a variety of settings, 126

GMRS radios are highly dependable and have an extensive range, 126

GMRS radios are highly regarded for their dependability and versatility, 159

GMRS radios are now incorporating digital features, 4

GMRS radios are perfect, 16, 124

GMRS radios are specifically designed to facilitate communication, 16

GMRS radios are widely utilized by community emergency response teams, 159

GMRS radios can be programmed using software, 106

GMRS radios can be used in two modes, 3

GMRS radios can transmit at higher power levels than FRS radios, 10

GMRS radios can transmit signals across several miles., 158

GMRS radios evolved to include new features like digital data transmission, 3

GMRS radios frequently include a range of features, 5

GMRS radios generally operate on UHF frequencies, 1

GMRS radios greatly benefit from being user-friendly, 20

GMRS radios have a decent range, 5

GMRS radios have a wide range of uses, 161

GMRS radios have seen significant advancements, 38

GMRS radios have the advantage of higher power outputs, 12

GMRS radios have the advantage of operating at higher power levels, 5

GMRS radios in their early days were simple devices with few features,, 3

GMRS radios is influenced by various factors, 61

GMRS radios lack encryption, 160

GMRS radios must be licensed, 18

GMRS radios must meet specific technical standards, 29

GMRS radios offer a dependable solution, 92

GMRS radios offer a greater range of options for equipment and customization, 159

GMRS radios offer more than just basic communication capabilities, 82

GMRS radios often include programming software, 14

GMRS radios often rely on disposable batteries, 63

GMRS radios operate within the UHF range, 158

GMRS radios serve a practical purpose in facilitating communication, 92

GMRS radios typically have a range of 1-5 miles, 49

GMRS radios usually come with preset channels,, 110

GMRS radios usually provide a variety of channels for communication, 18

GMRS radios utilize a variety of power sources, 62

GMRS radios with GPS, 65, 67

GMRS radios without requiring separate licenses, 13

GMRS radios without the requirement of individual licenses, 29

GMRS Repeater Maintenance, 48

GMRS signals and amateur radio, 94

GMRS stands out, 1, 3, 7, 31

GMRS stands out from other unlicensed services, 1

GMRS users can expand their coverage and access a wider emergency response network., 94

GMRS users can look forward to enjoying wider coverage, 4

GMRS users have the opportunity to create community-based groups, 95

GMRS users need to adhere to specific operational rules, 30

GMRS with broader emergency response networks, 93

GMRS, also known as General Mobile Radio Service, 2, 6, 54, 118

GMRS, short for **"General Mobile Radio Service,"**, 1

GMRS's multi-user, 87

GPS and Data Transmission Capabilities, 42

GPS Functionality, 66

GPS integration with GMRS requires both hardware and software components, 66

greater range, 9, 19, 24, 117, 142, 159

greater range of options for equipment, 159

Green manufacturing processes, 151

Ground Plane Antennas, 99

Ground plane antennas are commonly used for stationary GMRS base stations, 99

Group Calls, 83, 84

Group Communication, 86, 92

Group Communication and Repeater Systems, 86

Group Communication in GMRS, 86

groups, and businesses, 4

Guidelines for Ensuring GMRS Compliance, 31

H

Ham Radio communication is typically open, 9

ham radio enthusiasts, 101

Ham Radio is capable of operating at higher power levels, 9

Ham Radio is primarily designed for non-commercial purposes, 8

Ham Radio is primarily intended for non-commercial use, 9

Ham Radio offers a wide range of advantages, 8

Ham Radio offers a wide range of communication options, 8

handheld devices, 16, 20, 22, 99, 100, 155

Handheld GMRS radios, 16, 17, 21, 22, 24, 25, 63, 89, 124

Handheld GMRS Radios, 16, 24

Handheld GMRS radios are compact devices, 16

Handheld radios, 13, 49, 61, 103, 159

Handheld Radios, 103, 124

Handle with Care, 136

Hard Cases, 98

Hardware Integration, 66

hardware or firmware problems, 109

Harmonic and Spurious Emissions, 135

having privacy codes, 37

Head over to the FCC's Universal, 13

Headsets, 97, 104

Headsets offer a convenient way to communicate without the need for hands with GMRS radios., 97

headsets to further enhance your setup, 159

helpful tips for effective communication, 77

high population density, 92

higher elevation, 22, 71

High-gain antennas can greatly enhance signal strength and extend the range of coverage., 75 highly beneficial for users, 81, 96

highly effective at penetrating obstacles, 3

highly flexible, 8

history and future, 2

History and Future of GMRS, 2

Holsters, 98

housing or internal components., 130

Housing or Shelter, 46

How can I properly maintain my GMRS radios?, 160

How GMRS Encryption Works, 115

How Scanning Works, 38

How Squelch Works, 120

How to adjust squelch and volume levels, 120

How to become an expert in GMRS Encryption, 116

How to Get a GMRS License, 26

How to go about GMRS Radio programming, 12

How to Implement GMRS Encryption, 113

How to integrate and interface a Radio System, 122

How to integrate GPS and location services, 65

How to know basic spectrum analyzer operation, 133

How to properly tune a GMRS Antenna, 67

How to set up a GMRS Repeater, 44

How to understand GMRS Encryption, 112

HT, 156

hurricanes, 93

I

ideal for use in urban and suburban environments, 3

identify any signs of damage, 71, 160

Identify your Channels, 14

Identify Your Use Case, 105

Identify Yourself, 57, 118, 146

If you happen to own a GMRS radio, 159

impedance of the antenna, 70

Implement Secure Communication Practices, 119

Implementing encryption in GMRS necessitates meticulous planning, 113

Implementing GMRS Encryption, 116

importance of effective communication, 93

important communications., 120

Important operational regulations for GMRS users, 30

important to choose models, 73

improper software installation, 106

Improve Security, 109

improve the safety and cohesion of the community, 93

improved ability to penetrate obstacles., 139

Improved Bandwidth Use, 54

Improved Clarity, 36

Improved Dependability and Backup Systems, 51

Improved Resistance, 54

improved security, 114, 115

Improved Signal Transmission and Reception, 140

including battery levels, 42

including cellular networks,, 93

including families, 1

including spouses, 158

increase the range of the device, 160

Increase the Squelch Level, 121

Increased Channels, 73

increasingly acknowledge, 4

incredibly valuable, 22, 84, 94, 111

indicating very little reflected power, 68

Individuals and Families, 26

individuals may face criminal charges that could result in imprisonment., 33

individuals or organizations, 33

industrial inspections, 42

industrial or agricultural settings, 42

In-Ear Headsets, 97

initiate the tuning process., 68

Input Repeater Frequencies, 14

inquire about any updates that could enhance performance or introduce new features., 160

Inspect for any potential damage, 108

Inspect for Damage, 137

Inspect the antenna thoroughly to identify any signs of damage or wear, 160

Inspect the Battery, 109

Install Mobile Radios, 62

Install the Antenna, 46

Installation Complexity, 102

integrated GPS functionality, 3

Integrating GMRS, 40, 41, 94

Integrating GMRS with Other Emergency Services, 94

Integrating GPS with GMRS, 65, 66

Integrating GPS with GMRS offers numerous practical applications, 65

Integration with Emergency Operations Centers (EOCs), 94

Integration with FRS, 40

Integration with MURS, 41

Integration with Other Radio Services, 39

integrity of the GMRS frequency band, 18

Intercom Systems, 125
interference can be minimized, 9
interference from other users, 8, 83, 86, 118
Interoperability, 4
interoperability and foster collaboration, 4
interstitial channels, 10, 154
INTRODUCTION, 1
Intuitive and easy-to-use interface, 20
Intuitive Interface and Easy-to-Use Controls, 23
Is a License Required for GMRS?, 158
Is it possible to use GMRS radios internationally?, 160
issues such as incorrect cable connections, 106
It became popular in the 1960s as a solution, 2
it is important to adhere to these maintenance tips,
    160
It is important to avoid overcharging and exposing the
    device to extreme temperatures., 160
it is important to note that the range may be
    restricted to the capabilities of the FRS., 159
It is important to note that using GMRS radios, 160
it is necessary to have at least one GMRS radio, 159
its applications,, 2
it's important to look for models that have sturdy
    construction, 161
it's important to take into account the following
    factors, 160

J

joint training exercises and emergency drills, 94
J-Pole Antennas, 101

K

Keep it in a secure place, 130
Keep it up to date Your GMRS System, 125
keep radios in a dry and cool place, 160
Keep Transmissions Short, 57
Keep up with regular maintenance, 122
Keep your Radios Ready, 143
keeping the microphone, 148
Key Considerations, 43
key focus of modernization efforts, 4
knowledge necessary for Ham Radio can be
    intimidating for certain users, 8

L

Label and Organize, 138
land-mobile FM UHF radio service, 2
Launch the Software, 15
leading to potential permanent damage, 70
learning the frequently asked questions about GMRS
    Radios, 158
Legal and Ethical Considerations, 119
Legal Compliance, 75
Lengthen or Shorten the Antenna, 69
License Fee Payment, 60
License Renewal, 29, 125
License Requirement, 122
License Revocation, 33
licensed radio service specifically for personal and
    business communication, 2
Li-ion batteries are highly advanced rechargeable
    batteries, 64
Limitations of Software and Firmware, 106
Limited Direct Integration, 41
Limited Number of Codes, 81
Limited Range, 42
Line-of-Sight, 55
List of GMRS Antennas, 98
lithium-ion, 63
Lithium-Ion (Li-ion) Batteries, 64
local disaster, 141, 142, 143, 144
local EOCs and participate in training sessions, 94
Local Radio Clubs, 145
Locating a Repeater, 73
Location, 76, 104, 117, 124, 131, 138, 143
location sharing, 66
Looking ahead to the future of GMRS, 4
lower environmental impact, 63
lower resonant frequency, 69

M

Maintain a Clean Radio, 130
maintain accountability, 30, 125
Maintain Batteries, 143
Maintain Cleanliness, 136
maintain communication with one another, 92
Maintain Confidentiality, 114
Maintain Records, 31
Maintain Regular Check-Ins, 143

maintain the repeater's efficiency., 76

maintaining a constant connection, 90

maintaining communication, 11

maintaining community safety during emergencies., 92

Maintaining Compliance, 34

maintaining signal integrity, 69

maintaining signal integrity and optimal performance, 69

make adjustments and implement changes, 93

Make small adjustments to prevent over-tuning., 69

Make sure to check the display connections, 133

Make sure to contact the manufacturer, 160

Make sure to read the manual, 143

make sure to replace the antenna promptly, 160

Make the Right Hardware Choice, 66

making communication more efficient, 87

making it an excellent communication, 161

making them ideal for users who require longer operating times, 97

Malfunctioning Controls and Display, 132

Manual Programming, 14

Manufacturer Software, 66

Many GMRS radios provide the option to adjust the power settings., 76

Master the Art of Operating Radios, 142

Mastering the art of proper channel etiquette and protocols, 57

matter the distance, 161

maximize power and range, 74

Maximize Radio Settings, 76

maximum power of 5 watts, 10

measure SWR, 71

Measure SWR, 71

Measure the SWR, 68

Measuring SWR, 71

members of the community, 92

Message Clarity, 126

Microphone, 109, 128, 132, 137

Microphones, 96, 97, 104

Midland, 49, 72

miles under ideal conditions, 17, 24

minimize interference and maintain clear communication, 14

minimize interference from other users, 110, 160

Minimize Nearby Electronic Noise, 77

minimize the environmental impact of GMRS. Here are some examples, 151

Minimize unnecessary communication, 145

Minimize Unnecessary Transmission, 148

Minimized Chance of Unauthorized Usage, 115

minimizes the chances of interference., 73

minimizing processing time, 34

minimizing the possibility of unauthorized individuals listening in, 112

misconfigurations, 106

Missed Transmissions, 122

Misuse of GMRS Frequencies, 32

Mobile antennas, 102, 155

Mobile Antennas, 102

Mobile Radios, 103, 124

mobile radios for vehicles, 159

Mobile Repeaters, 98

MOBILE UNIT, 157

moderate gain of approximately 2 dBi, 100

moisture and extreme temperatures, 160

monitor the GMRS spectrum for any activity., 81

Monitoring Activity, 38

more adaptable for individuals, 3

more streamlined application procedure, 3

Motorola, 49, 72

Mountains and Hills, 126

Mounting and Installation, 103

Mounting external antennas, 73

multiple channels, 2, 15, 38, 61, 81, 83, 84, 86, 110

multiple conversations, 81

multiple jurisdictions is crucial., 94

Multiple User Support, 51

Multi-Use Radio Service, 9

Multi-user and group communication in GMRS, 85

MURS is an unlicensed radio service in the U.S., 41

N

natural disasters, 5, 48, 89, 93, 118, 155

Neighborhood watch programs should actively encourage inclusivity, 92

NiCd batteries, 63, 64

NiCd batteries can experience a memory effect, 63

nickel-cadmium, 63

Nickel-Cadmium (NiCd) Batteries, 63

Nickel-Metal Hydride (NiMH) Batteries, 63

NiMH batteries, 63, 64, 65

NiMH batteries are a significant upgrade, 63

No Examination, 27

No Signal Reception, 122

NOAA, 18, 20, 23, 82, 87, 127, 156
NOAA Weather Alerts, 20, 87
Not a Security Guarantee, 81
Not Renewing the License, 31
Note Channel Protocol, 58
Numerous companies produce GMRS radios, 105
Numerous factors drive individuals and businesses, 112
Numerous new applications can be explored through data transmission, 42

O

Obtain a GMRS License, 113
Obtain Permission, 50
Obtaining a GMRS License, 12
Obtaining a license, 8, 10, 12, 91, 150
obtaining additional licenses, 160
Obtaining FCC certification, 29
Obtaining the license is a straightforward process, 158
offering a total of 22 channels for communication, 1
offering assistance, 94
off-road enthusiasts, 7, 11, 18, 24, 88
Off-road vehicle enthusiasts, 161
OFFSET, 156
often rely on GMRS radios to stay connected in remote areas, 161
Once your application is submitted, 28
One license is all you need to connect your entire family, 161
ongoing expansion of repeater networks, 4
operate GMRS radios, 10, 28, 48, 140, 158
operate GMRS radios legally in the United States, 158
operate on the same 22 primary channels as FRS radios, 12
Operate with Licensed Equipment, 75
operating GMRS radios, 10, 43, 72
Operating GMRS radios legally requires obtaining a license, 1
operating GMRS requires, 9
operating rules, 3
Operating within the boundaries of the law, 32
opt for encryption in GMRS communication, 112
Opt for Shielded Cables, 77
Optimal Line of Sight Positioning, 108
optimal performance of your GMRS radios, 160
optimal repeater operation, 45

optimal storage, 65, 160
optimal use of GMRS encryption and to guarantee secure communication, 114
Opting for a longer antenna with higher gain can enhance signal strength, 73
Organizations involved in emergency response, 26
organizations that use GMRS for internal communication, 26
organizing neighborhood watch activities, 92
original use for personal purposes, 4
Orthogonal Frequency Division Multiplexing, 53
other communication methods may not be reliable., 183
other communication systems., 21, 70, 123, 124, 150
Other Features and Factors to Consider, 18
Other regions' regulatory bodies, 4
other relatives residing in the same household., 158
Outdoor Activities, 141
outdoor activities such as hiking or camping,, 161
outdoor adventures, 1, 7, 20, 103, 158
Outdoor Adventures, 39, 83
outdoor enthusiasts, 1, 3, 17, 20, 57, 83, 140
Outdoor Recreation, 65
over short to medium distances, 1, 16
overall effectiveness, 93
overall security, 160
overcharging and thermal runaway, 64
Over-Ear Headsets, 97
overlook brief transmissions, 38

P

part of the process, 28, 93
Participants have the convenience of seamless communication, 92
participants to consistently enhance the program, 93
particular communication stream, 38
Pause for a Moment, 58
Pay close attention to emergency instructions, 145
paying a fee is all that's required, 158
Penalties, 30, 33
perfect GMRS Radio, 12
Perform a Factory Reset, 132, 133
perform regular checks on batteries, 92
Performing a Factory Reset, 109
Performing regular maintenance, 130
personal communication, 123, 161
Phase Shift Keying, 53

PL, 108, 156
PL/DPL Codes, 108
play a crucial role in communication, 159
Polarization, 102
popular choice for truckers, 7
popular option among recreational users, 3
Portability, 17, 25, 49
potentially leading to the global expansion of GMRS,
    4
Power and Range, 24
Power Level, 76
Power Levels, 155
Power Limits, 10, 28, 43, 44, 75
Power Measurements, 135, 136
power options for longer periods of use, 161
Power Output, 5, 9, 14, 17, 21, 32, 47, 72, 103, 117,
    123, 140, 160
POWER OUTPUT, 157
Power output regulations must be followed when
    using GMRS radios, 135
Power Source, 46
Power source and battery management, 62
Power Supply, 18, 46, 48, 104
powerful transmitters, 9
Practice with Your Group, 143
Prepare for Emergencies, 149
Press the Push-to-Talk (PTT) Button, 146
Prevent Overcharging, 131
prevent unauthorized use, 76
Preventing Deep Discharges, 64
preventing misunderstandings, 37
Primary Channel, 49
primary channels and interstitial channels, 10
primary GMRS channels, 14
Priority Channels, 39, 111
Priority Communication, 126
Privacy and security, 79, 115
Privacy and Security, 9
Privacy Codes, 24, 35, 36, 82, 110, 129
Privacy Codes and Squelch, 24
privacy codes,, 19, 49, 61, 85
professional technicians for assistance, 107
programmed channels, 15, 81
Programming Cable, 110
programming process, 106, 107
programming radios, 105
Programming Software, 98, 104, 110
Programming techniques, 109

Programming with Software, 14
Programming Your GMRS Radio, 14
Programming Your Radio, 73
Promote inclusivity and engagement, 92
proper charging and storage practices, 160
proper etiquette, 57, 58, 146, 149
Proper Etiquette, 57, 74
Proper Installation is Key, 137
Proper Radio Handling, 77
Properly Position the Antenna, 68
Proprietary Encryption, 113
Protect Your Radio, 138
prove ineffective, 133
provide a dependable means of communication for
    families, 161
provide a significant boost in power, 17
Provide Clear Information, 144
provide clear instructions, 49
Provide Crucial Details, 143
provide greater power and extended range, 1
Provide the necessary information, 27
provides 40 channels, 7
providing coverage for the entire family, 158
providing the flexibility to tailor them to your vehicle
    and the surrounding landscape., 103
providing users with the ability to communicate
    privately, 3
PTT, 97, 104, 146, 156, 157
Public Safety and Emergency Communications, 30
Public-Private Partnerships, 94
Push-to-Talk, 146, 156, 157

Q

Quadrature Amplitude Modulation, 53
quality of communication on GMRS channels, 58

R

Radio Etiquette, 49
radio service in the United States, 1, 2, 19
radio service in the United States that enables
    convenient two-way communication, 1
radio services, 9, 29, 34, 39, 40, 93, 119, 136
radio set to the same frequency, 81
Radio waves can bend around obstacles, 55
Range and Power, 13

range of communication, 5, 8, 18, 21, 40, 41, 51, 62, 73, 88, 94, 109

range of GMRS radios, 72, 76, 103

Range Test, 47, 108

ranging from 462 MHz to 467 MHz, 10, 19, 154

ranging from local to global, 8

Reach out to local radio clubs, 147

Read the Manual, 136

Reasons for High SWR, 70

rebroadcasting signals, 93

Receive your License, 13, 49, 60

Reception Issues or Lack of Signal, 130

Recharge and Replace Batteries, 62

Rechargeable batteries, 25, 62, 63, 150

Recommended GMRS Equipment, 103

Record Your Settings, 15

Recreational Activities, 5, 11, 24

recycling programs, 151

Reducing SWR, 71

reduction in fees, 3

Redundancy, 127

Reference Level, 134, 135

Reflection and Refraction, 55

Regular Cleaning, 160

Regular Communication Drills, 49

Regular Inspection, 128

Regular Inspections, 48, 62, 130

Regular Maintenance, 65, 92, 137

Regular maintenance and testing are essential for ensuring the proper functioning of GMRS radios., 92

Regular maintenance is crucial for ensuring the long-term durability, 48

regular walkie-talkies, 3

Regularly change encryption keys, 114

regularly monitor the priority channel, 81

Regularly Test Audio, 137

Regularly Update Firmware and Software, 107

Regulations, 10, 16, 29, 30, 33, 105, 114, 117, 130, 141

Regulatory Changes and Modernization, 3

Regulatory Compliance, 21, 40, 42, 54, 106

Regulatory Considerations, 52

Regulatory Framework and Environmental Impact, 150

Release the PTT Button, 146

Reliability and Construction, 20

Reliability and Independence, 89

reliable communication, 3, 5, 19, 21, 25, 51, 57, 62, 90, 93, 102, 109, 115

Reminder about Channel Sharing, 58

Remote Control, 42

remote devices, 42

REPEATER, 156

Repeater Capability, 18, 20, 82, 103, 123, 161

repeater capability,, 2

Repeater Channels, 43

Repeater Configuration, 110

Repeater Directories, 145

Repeater Functionality, 140

Repeater Operation, 43

repeater operations, 43, 82

Repeater Operations, 10

Repeater Settings, 107, 110

Repeater Setup, 124

Repeater Station, 44, 46

Repeater Support, 84

Repeater Systems, 98

Repeater systems enhance the coverage of GMRS radios, 98

Repeater Use, 30

Repeaters and Duplex Operations, 22

Repeaters are commonly situated on high structures, 159

Repeaters are commonly used in emergencies, 3

Repeaters are devices that receive a signal on one frequency and retransmit it on another, 84

Repeaters are valuable in regions, 159

reporting any suspicious behavior, 92

Requests for Assistance, 144

require a license, 9, 40, 139, 140

requirement and the option, 9

requiring a high-gain antenna, 45

requiring an online form and a fee, 10

rescue organizations, 3

Resolution Bandwidth (RBW), 134

Resolving Connection Problems, 147

resonant frequency, 69

RESOURCES AND GLOSSARY TERMS, 152

Respect Other Users, 148

Respecting Privacy and Legal Boundaries, 92

responsible behavior, 8

Restore Configurations, 111

resulting in extended communication ranges, 9

retransmitting, 50, 51, 56, 82, 104, 107, 124, 159

Review and Revise, 50

Review Configuration, 47
Review Your Settings, 147
Revise Communication Protocols, 62
role of GMRS organizations, 152
Rural Areas, 126
RX, 157

S

Save your Settings, 14
SCAN, 157
Scan Lockouts, 39
Scanning and Monitoring, 37, 38, 39, 84, 110
scanning functionality, 38
Scanning-capable GMRS radios, 38
seamless coordination of activities, 6
seamless information sharing, 6
Seamless integration with various communication systems, 21
search and rescue groups, 159
Search and Rescue Operations, 90
search for antennas, 73
Secure Data Transmission, 67
Security, 81, 112, 115
security patches, 67
seek feedback from neighborhood, 93
Select "ZA - General Mobile Radio Service", 28
Select the Appropriate Radios, 142
Selecting a Repeater Location, 50
Selecting the Appropriate Equipment, 113
selective signal reception, 36
Send a Signal, 68
sensor readings, 42
serving as supplementary communication hubs, 94
Set Channels, 61
Set Communication Protocols, 49
Set Scan Delay, 111
Set Sweep Time, 135
Set the SWR Meter, 71
set up a GMRS repeater, 44
Set up Communication Protocols, 143
Set Up Communication Protocols, 125
Set Up Encryption Settings, 113
set up scanning, 110
Set up the Channels, 15
Set up the Code or Tone, 36
Set Up the Equipment, 68
setting the radio to a GMRS frequency,, 68

setting up and connecting your GMRS system., 123
Setting Up and Customizing Your GMRS System, 124
Setting up Communication Protocols, 61
SETTING UP GMRS RADIOS, 43
Setting up GMRS Workspace Radio, 60
Setting up the Repeater, 46
settings like camping trips, 36
Setup and Calibration, 135
several advantages to choosing GMRS, 159
Several factors influence the behavior of radio waves, 55
Several GMRS radios, 20
sharing of communication plans, 94
Shielding and Grounding, 56
shorter range, 93
Signal Analysis, 134
Signal Quality Issue, 138
signal strength, 19, 22, 47, 56, 58, 72, 74, 75, 100, 102, 117, 120, 126, 135, 137
Signal-to-noise ratio (SNR), 135
significant impact on various aspects, 53
significant strength, 94
significantly extends the communication range, 1
Signs and symptoms, 131
simplex and repeater, 3, 117, 154
Simplex Communication, 154
simplex mode, 3, 50
single license, 5, 7, 13, 25, 26
Situation Updates, 144
Situational Awareness, 120
small businesses, 11, 57, 80, 83, 85, 161
smooth communication during emergencies, 94
smooth integration of GPS and GMRS, 66
SNR plays a crucial role in determining the quality of communication, 135
Social and Family Connectivity, 51
Social Media and Forums, 145
Soft Cases, 98
software and choosing your radio model, 15
Software Installation, 15
Software Integration, 66
Software Updates, 50, 74, 160
solution for families, 25, 161
some guidelines, 28, 61
some of which are shared with FRS, 103, 158
some typical situations where GMRS is used, 11
spanning only a few miles, 93
sparking interest in various countries, 4

Speaker, 97, 128, 132, 137

speakers are specifically designed to deliver exceptional volume and clarity, 98

specialized equipment, 54, 125

specific communication requirements., 40

specific primary channels., 10

specific requirements. For GMRS, 134

specifically created for convenient and efficient voice communication over short distances, 1

specifically designated for emergency use, 58

specifically designed for short-distance, 2, 6

Spectrum Analyzers, 133, 134

Spectrum analyzers are capable of detecting harmonics, 135

Spectrum Analyzers with Swept-Tuning, 133

SQUELCH, 157

Squelch Control, 76, 121

Stand-Alone Repeaters, 98

Standardize Across Multiple Radios, 109

Standing Wave Ratio, 67, 70, 135

stationary or vehicle-mounted use, 17

Stay Calm and Communicate Clearly, 143

Stay Connected with Family Members, 28

Stay Informed, 16, 31

Stay mindful of regulatory compliance, 107

Steer clear of popular codes, 37

Stick to Your Communication Plan, 143

Storage, 64, 137, 138, 143, 160

straightforward nature, 1

streamlining the procedure, 34

Struggling to hear other users., 130

sub-audible tones, 9, 78, 85, 108, 118, 156

Submit a License Application, 48

Submit the Application and Fee, 13

Submit the form to receive your FRN., 27

substantial increase in communication range, 9

suffer damage or become overwhelmed, 93

Sustainable Practices in GMRS, 151

Sweep Time and Span, 134

Switch off the radio, 71

T

Take a look at the battery life and think about getting extra batteries, 161

Take into account the various accessories, 161

Take into account the various accessories that can improve your setup, 161

Take into account your surroundings, 105

Technical Complexity, 41, 54

Technical Differences, 41

Technical Flexibility, 40

technical knowledge necessary for Ham Radio, 8

Technical Specifications, 23

technology progressed, 3

Telemetry Data, 42

Terrain, 77, 117

Test before Use, 67

Test in Open Areas, 109

Test the microphone and speaker, 128

Test the Repeater, 47, 50

Test with a Different Radio, 132

Test with Headphones, 132

Test with Others, 16

Test Your Radio, 15

Testing and Troubleshooting, 47

Testing Radio Functionality, 129

Testing Transmission and Reception, 129

Text Messaging, 42

the "Transmitter" port on the SWR meter, 68

the 462-467 MHz range, 3

the ability to seamlessly integrate GPS with GMRS., 66

the added advantage, 159

The advent of radio communication has revolutionized human interaction, 54

The antenna is responsible for transmitting and receiving signals, 128

The antenna plays a vital role in the functionality of every radio system, 75

The appeal of this product lies in its straightforwardness, 161

the application is deemed satisfactory, 34

The Application Process, 27

The application process is simple and convenient,, 10

The codes used here do not encrypt the communication, 160

the demand for a communication system, 2

The design of dipole antennas is quite straightforward, 100

The display appears to be blank or distorted., 132

The duplexer is a device that enables the antenna to handle both transmission and reception at the same time, 45

The Evolution of GMRS, 3

the FCC in 2017, 3

the FCC offers explicit instructions to guarantee adherence, 161

The fee is quite reasonable,, 161

the fields of photography, 42

the General Mobile Radio Service, 1

The General Mobile Radio Service, 2

The GMRS frequency range spans from 462 to 467 MHz,, 1

The GMRS regulations outline specific rules for operation, 10

the help of data cables and programming software., 98

The integration of GMRS, 4

the license is valid for a generous ten years, 161

The license's straightforwardness promotes responsible usage, 161

The licensing process for GMRS users, 3

the licensing requirement, 2, 8

The licensing system enables the FCC to effectively regulate the utilization of GMRS frequencies, 3

the mid-20th century, 7

the need for remote monitoring of equipment or environmental conditions arises., 42

The performance can be affected by a damaged antenna, 160

the possibility of interference when selecting GMRS radios., 2

the power level of incoming signals, 159

The primary channels are commonly utilized for general communication, 10

The process of obtaining a license from the Federal Communications Commission, 161

the radios and accessories, 160

the range may be restricted to just a few blocks., 158

The Renewal Process, 34

the repeater capability, 6

The Role of GMRS Organizations, 152

the root cause of GMRS issues, 109

The signal was lost completely., 130

The Significance of Privacy Codes and Tones in GMRS, 36

The significance of SWR, 70

The Significance of Volume Control, 120

the transmission is complete, 37

the types of GMRS Radios, and so son much more., 12

the Ultra High Frequency (UHF) band, 1, 55

the United States has made changes to licensing requirements, 3

the United States is relatively straightforward, 161

the use of repeaters, 7, 10, 28, 83, 91, 140, 158, 161

the user's voice,, 87

the utilization of repeaters, 158

The validity of a GMRS license is for 10 years, 158

The volume control is easy to understand, 120

There are a total of 22 channels in this frequency range, 158

there are still some things to learn, 158

There are two primary types of GMRS radios available, 16

there have been changes in the regulatory landscape surrounding GMRS, 3

They also provide privacy codes, 160

thoroughly review the local regulations, 160

Threshold Setting, 120

through dense forests, 5

Tighten All Connections, 69

times of disaster or crisis, 92

Tips for Optimal Squelch and Volume Adjustment, 122

Tips for Optimizing GMRS Radio Programming, 15

Tips for Seamlessly Combining GPS and GMRS, 66

Tips for Using Privacy Codes and Tones Effectively, 37

Tone Codes for Privacy and Coordination, 86

Tools and Equipment, 67

Tools and Software for Programming, 110

tornadoes, 93

towers or buildings, 159

traditional communication networks, 92, 153

traditional navigation methods, 65

traditional networks are unavailable, 159

Training and Drills, 50

Training and Education, 91

Training and Refresher Courses, 62

training sessions and workshops, 95

Transforms electrical signals into sound, 128

Transmission Power, 19, 108

Transmission Problems, 132

transmit data, 42, 53

transmitter's impedance, 70

transmitters or high-tension power lines, 46

transmitting information, 94

Transmitting involves the act of sending a radio signal, 157

transmitting signals over longer distances, 43, 98

Troubleshooting Common Issues, 121, 138

Troubleshooting common programming issues, 107

Troubleshooting Steps, 131, 132
Try restarting the Radio, 132
Tuning a GMRS Antenna, 67
Turn On the Radio, 68
two conductive elements, 100
two-way communication., 2, 118
TX, 71, 157
Type of Radios, 61
Types of Encryption in GMRS, 112
Types of GMRS Antennas, 99
Types of GMRS Radios, 16

U

ULS by providing your FRN and password, 28
Ultra High Frequency, 1, 10, 16, 19, 44, 55, 156, 158
Unauthorized Equipment, 32
Under optimal circumstances, 158
understand and operate, 20
UNDERSTANDING GMRS RADIOS, 2
Understanding responsibilities and adhering to FCC
    rules, 30
Understanding the benefits of GMRS Encryption, 114
Understanding the objective of your plan, 48
Understanding tone codes, 86
Understanding tone codes is crucial for effective
    GMRS group communication, 86
Understanding what SWR is about and how to set
    GMRS, 70
Understanding why radio programming cable does
    not work, 105
uninterrupted communication, 36, 51, 58, 79, 83, 92,
    95, 156
Unlicensed Accessibility, 41
Unwanted signals or cross-talk from other users can
    be quite frustrating., 131
Update Firmware, 107, 109, 138
Updates for the software, 125
Upgrade to High-Gain Antennas, 75
Upgrading the Antenna, 73
Upgrading the antenna is a highly effective method,
    73
uphold effective communication., 126
uphold order on the airwaves, 3
Urban Areas, 77, 109, 126
urban areas with obstacles, 158
USB Data Cables, 98
Use a Different Antenna, 71

Use a Recognizable Signal for Testing, 122
Use Clear and Concise Language, 143
Use Clear Language, 57
Use Digital Radios, 119
use GMRS equipment within a specific framework., 9
Use GMRS for Authorized Purposes, 150
Use GMRS Frequencies, 28
Use of Repeaters, 9, 56, 58
Use Repeaters, 28, 76
Use Robust Encryption Algorithms, 114
Use Simple Language, 118
user and group communication, 85, 87
User Communication Test, 47
User-Friendly Design, 24
**Users and manufacturers can adopt sustainable
    practices**, 151
Users can conveniently charge multiple GMRS radios,
    97
Users can easily communicate across hills, 5
users to customize settings, 14
Using a Repeater, 73, 74
Using a Repeater System, 73
using emergency channels for non-urgent
    conversations, 58
Using Multi-User and Group Communication, 87
Using Privacy Codes, 37, 61
Using repeater systems, 5
Using Spectrum Analyzer in GMRS, 135
using state-of-the-art equipment., 94
using strong chemicals, 160
Using Your GMRS License, 28
usually designated for more specific purposes, 10
usually ranging from 1 to 5 watts, 20

V

valuable in GMRS applications where data
    communication is crucial, 54
variety of personal, 161
Various factors can affect the communication range
    of GMRS radios, 158
various types available, 96
Vehicle Mounts, 97
verbal communication, 3, 42
Verify Connections, 137
Verify the Functionality of the Charging Equipment,
    131
Verify the Reading, 68

versatile option for personal, 2
Versatility, 18
versatility and flexibility, 8
Video Bandwidth (VBW), 134
videography, 42
voice activation, 20, 87, 88
voice communication and data transmission, 3
volunteer fire departments, 26
volunteer groups rely on GMRS, 6
VOX functionality, 61

W

Walkie-Talkies, 103
weather alerts, 18, 20, 23, 42, 49, 61, 83, 87, 117, 156
Weather Alerts, 42, 82, 127
Weather Conditions, 77
Weather Considerations, 56, 74
Weather Resistance, 73
Weatherproofing, 48
What advantages does GMRS offer compared to
  other radio services?, 159
What are the Benefits of Encryption in GMRS?, 112
What are the frequencies used by GMRS?, 158
What does Volume Control mean?, 120
What factors should you take into account when
  purchasing GMRS radios?, 160
What is a GMRS Repeater?, 159
What is GMRS?, 158
What is the compatibility with FRS Radios?, 139

What is the list of safety guidelines for GMRS users,
  148
What is the necessary equipment for GMRS?, 159
What is the Range of GMRS Radios?, 158
What is the Significance of SWR?, 70
When to Renew, 34
Whip Antennas, 96, 99
Who Needs a GMRS License?, 26
Why choose FRS and GMRS for Local Disaster
  Communication?, 142
Why is it compulsory to use a GMRS repeater, 50
wide range of GMRS antennas available, 99
wide variety of applications, 2, 39
wider range of people., 3
wildfires, 93
withstand various weather conditions, 102, 161
worth mentioning, 13, 52, 116

Y

Yagi Antennas, 100
**You can easily customize GMRS radios and manage
  frequency programming**, 98
you may want to explore accessories such as
  antennas, 159
you will about GMRS Radio basics, 12
you will learn what GMRS Radio is, 2
you will need to provide your contact information, 28
your GMRS repeater, 46, 47, 48
your name,, 27

Made in the USA
Middletown, DE
08 September 2024